PRAISE FOR JEFF ZYCINSKI AND
THE RED LIGHT ZONE

'An entertaining, rambunctious account of his 30 year career which he calls a "laugh 'n' tell".'
Janet Boyle, *Sunday Post*

'Undeniably well-written and entertaining ... a must-read for every student seeking a career in broadcasting.'
Gavin Docherty, 'Doc Showbiz', *Scottish Daily Express*

'A natural story-teller, Jeff shares a lifetime of good stories as well as insights into his own life. The book is packed with funny anecdotes.'
Margaret Chrystall, Seven Days, *Highland News*

'Really well-written. It's not everyone who can write a memoir as interesting and engaging as this.'
Dan O'Day, Danoday.com, Los Angeles

'A tale told by a supreme anecdotalist, an excellent journalist and a very accomplished writer.'
Tom Morton, *Scottish Review*

'Full of humorous anecdotes and a refreshingly honest, self-deprecating take on a career spent in both commercial and BBC radio.'
Mary Picken, liveanddeadly.net

'Brilliant stories. Really enjoyed reading this.'
Bev Lyons, theshowbizlyon.com

'The book's real charm lies in the author's humorous writing style and his ability – like a Scottish Bill Bryson – to find comedy in the tiniest of details.'
Chatterbox Magazine

'A very well written book which gives an excellent insight into the life of a BBC producer and station controller. It deserves to be successful.'
David Harris, *Radio User Magazine*

'I read it on the bus and it made me laugh out loud.'
Cat Gibson, Camglen Radio

'His book describes encounters with politicians, the Royal Family and Hollywood stars as well as some of the more absurd happenings and baffling decisions during his 24 years [at the BBC].'
Grampian Online

'Jeff's frankness is refreshing, he is open about successes and failures over the span of his career, the impacts his career had on his family and indeed shares various anecdotes of family life, all of which endear him to the reader.'
Kate Noble, The Quiet Knitter

'If you remove the radio aspect from this biography, it still works as a description of 25 years of life in Scotland. I like the sound of Jeff's wife. And their children. But I would rather that the dog had lived …'
Bookwitch

'Want to know what REALLY happens in radio? Read this book!'
Pete Gavin, North Highland Radio

'A boss with a brain, a heart and a funny bone too.'
Kaye Adams, BBC Radio Scotland

'As well as laugh-out-loud moments, he also writes of the impact a high-pressure job can have on family life. Now that Zycinski has one book under his belt, you get the feeling he has plenty more to tell.'
Stuart McHugh, Scotsman.com

TRAVELS FROM my TWILIGHT ZONE

morphine, memories and make-believe

JEFF ZYCINSKI

THE LUNICORN PRESS

THE LUNICORN PRESS LTD

Scotland

First published 2020 by The Lunicorn Press Ltd.

1

Printed by Martins the Printers, Berwick-upon-Tweed

Cover design and book typeset by Heather Macpherson at Raspberry Creative Type

Cover artwork © Laura Jackson 2020

Author photograph © Emma McGregor 2019

Set in Sabon Lt Std

British Library Cataloguing in Publication Data

A CIP catalogue record for this book is available from the British Library

ISBN: 978-0-9929624-8-9

This is for my wife, Anne, a scientist, who only worries about small stuff like forgetting to put the chain on the front door, but stays calm in the face of global pandemics. It's also for all the frontline workers who got us through 2020. That includes NHS heroes like our daughter, Sarah, a radiographer at Glasgow Royal Infirmary, and our son, Alan, a reporter with Global Radio who kept telling us the news whether we liked it or not.

FOREWORD

Forewords tend to be written as favours. Payback for a career opportunity afforded or a friendly review, or in lieu of an unpaid loan from twenty years ago. I am pleased to confirm that none of the above applies in this case, unless I've forgotten about an emergency tenner borrowed in a bar some Saturday night. Jeff Zycinski and I have crossed paths but we have never worked together. I have, though, watched his career with a certain fascination from the time he took over as Head of BBC Radio Scotland.

I pitched up at Queen Margaret Drive, Glasgow, a year and a half before Radio Scotland launched; at that time, the BBC's radio output in Scotland was based on Radio 4, with opt-outs for Scottish news bulletins, arts programmes with frequent bouts of Scottish dance music and occasional symphony concerts. In 1978 the 'new national station for Scotland' was born and immediately ran into a blizzard of complaints from the press, the most memorable of whose criticisms was the stinging phrase 'pop, pap and prattle'. (Although I was an announcer at that time and delivering deadpan news bulletins, I was also presenting some music programmes and therefore may have been partially responsible for some or all of the three 'p's.) The main fault of the new offering was inevitably caused by the very reason it had been introduced: in trying to provide a wide-ranging station to appeal to all tastes and communities across the nation, it risked appealing to none and annoying all.

I headed south to join Radio 2 in 1985 with the BBC still chopping and changing Radio Scotland and no clear unified purpose to its output. It was, as far as I and many others believed, an impossible task. And then, from afar, I became aware of Jeff Zycinski, who had come into a position of influence back at the old homestead and was quietly and slowly creating some sort of order from chaos.

The fact that he survived twenty-five years at the BBC and twelve of those in front of a station which each person in Scotland expects to reflect his or her own interests speaks for itself. A job that had been regarded in the BBC as a poisoned chalice, or the equivalent of being sent to the colonies in disgrace, became under his stewardship an important, respected and ultimately successful position. No one else has ever remained in that post for as long, and I daresay no one will again. Surviving the labyrinthine machinations of BBC management for a quarter of a century may be even more of an achievement.

Now Jeff has survived an altogether more challenging and personal crisis. And it is the measure of the man that his trademark ability to find humour in the most difficult of situations remains undimmed. His writing skills, for too long not fully used thanks to the demands of running a radio station, are on full display again, and the honest depiction of his illness and recovery, the vibrant memories of a Glasgow childhood and his irrepressible desire to entertain enliven every page.

Now, about that tenner ...

Ken Bruce, BBC Radio 2

June 2020

ACKNOWLEDGEMENTS

My thanks, once again, to Lyn and Laura at the Lunicorn Press for their encouragement and advice ... and for not batting any eyelids when I told them I wanted to write 'a sort of drug-induced travel book of my subconscious memories'. Not much of a pitch, but they went for it. Thanks also to my editor, Merle Read, and to the online staff at Glasgow City Archives, who kindly tracked down some memory-jogging facts. A transatlantic Zoom call with fellow St Leonard's pupils – Paul Curran, Clare Murray and Dawn McKie – helped me remember the names of our former teachers and classmates. Hopefully some of the stories in this book will bring back memories for them too. Although I have no qualms about revealing the idiotic antics of my own childhood, I realise that others may not feel the same about my memories of them. In one or two cases, therefore, I have altered the names of some schoolfriends. The fictional stories are just that, and any resemblance to persons other than myself is entirely coincidental.

A few of the stories and characters in this book have previously appeared in a different version or with different titles. Nelson S. Pipsqueak first appeared in a series of stories broadcast on Radio Clyde in 1981. 'Room for One More on Top' was published in *The Renfrew Line* magazine in 1982. 'Just Right' was published as 'Goldilocks: The Truth at Last' in the student newspaper *The Globe* in 1986. 'Teacake Tales' featuring Hector Auld and Wee Jessie was a regular feature on *Tom Morton's Morning Show* on BBC Radio Scotland in 1995. Johnny Sellotape featured in the radio play *Stuck!* broadcast on BBC Radio

Scotland in 1999. The story of Frank Zycinski's welding examination was told as 'Thirteen Pipes' and performed at the Storytelling Centre in Edinburgh in 2013. 'Take Me to the Orphanage' was originally told as 'Horror in the Night' and performed at an event organised by the Far from the Madding Crowd bookshop in Linlithgow in 2019. 'The Wrong Flag' was previewed at the Portsoy Book Festival in 2020. A sample collection of stories from this book, plus additional content, is available in audio form on the *Writes and Speaks* SoundCloud page. The author gratefully acknowledges the kind support of all publications, platforms and broadcasters.

CONTENTS

Introduction: Morphine   1

PART ONE: MEMORIES   5

See You on the Other Side   7

The Square   20

Jumping Forward   29

The Wrong Flag   39

The Shock of the Bunny   48

Take Me to the Orphanage   54

Enter Captain Hoopla!   62

Where Seagulls Dare   71

Roll Over, Beethoven   80

Believe It or Not   88

The Summer Hut   99

Boy about Town   113

You're in the Book, Mum   128

When I Grow Up   138

The Day I Didn't Die   146

PART TWO: MAKE-BELIEVE   157

The Tartan Traveller   159

Negotiating Positions   181

Just Right   187

The Day of the Dog   193

Room for One More on Top   197

Teacake Tales with Hector Auld   205

I Saw Mommy Killing Santa Claus   214

Johnny Sellotape: An Obituary   223

The Back Room   230

Epilogue   241

Jeff's Twilight Guide to Scotland   249

twilight zone

noun

A situation or conceptual area that is characterized by being undefined, intermediate, or mysterious:

'the twilight zone between the middle and working classes'

An urban area in a state of dilapidation or economic decline.

The lowest level of the ocean to which light can penetrate.

Oxford English Dictionary

INTRODUCTION: MORPHINE

I'd been in hospital for almost a fortnight when two nurses came by my bedside, one of them holding a clipboard. This was a follow-up interview, they said, and they asked me to describe what I recalled from the time I had spent in the intensive care unit. This was going to be difficult. I had no memory of my first twenty-four hours because, of course, I had been unconscious. I did remember waking up on the second day. I was face down on the bed and someone was squeezing my hand and asking me to return the squeeze if I could hear them. They were telling me they were about to extract a tube from my throat. They were warning me that it was *very important* that I shouldn't cough. I understood, I squeezed. They turned my head to the side, pulled out the tube and congratulated me on staying calm. I acknowledged this with a modest grunt. I was then turned face up and my pillows were raised so that I could see what was going on around me.

There were beds either side of mine and six more beyond those. It was early evening in late January and, as far as I could tell, I was the only patient awake. Nurses – one for each bed – sat on chairs taking notes, and there was a central bank of desks where medics in green scrubs stared at computer monitors. Seeing that I was now fully conscious, the nurse assigned to my

1

individual care asked if I would like to watch some television. Unable to speak, I nodded, and a set was wheeled forward on a trolley and tuned to BBC One. The quiz show *Pointless* was on the screen and this was followed by the *News at Six*. The top story concerned a deadly virus that had originated in China for which, the newsreader told us, there was no cure, treatment or vaccine. Best we could do was wash our hands for twenty seconds and sing 'Happy Birthday' to mark the time. As it happens, it *was* my birthday that day. I've had better ones, as you might imagine, but on the plus side, I didn't have that virus.

'The News was awful,' I told the nurse with the clipboard, 'But easier to watch than *Pointless*.'

She gave a polite laugh and I was grateful for that. At least she could understand what I was saying. I told her what I remembered, she asked a few more questions and then, with noticeable hesitation, posed one final query.

'Do you remember having any vivid dreams or hallucinations?'

I thought about this.

'Not sure if they were hallucinations as such,' I said, 'but mixed-up memories. Most of those have come to me while I've been dozing here in the general ward. I've been remembering moments from my childhood, times spent with my parents before they died … laughs with my big sister. That kind of thing.'

'And dreams?'

I was embarrassed to tell her about the dreams, because cameo appearances from dead relatives had merged, somehow, with fictional characters from stories and sketches that I had once written for various magazines and radio shows. There was the luckless stand-up comedian and the smart-ass private investigator. There was a jumping frog and a talking elephant. God had also popped up, offering me useful advice on taxation. These crazy visions had come to me in a swirl of purple-patterned mist, reminiscent of the 1970s wallpaper we had in the living room of our council flat in Easterhouse. I learned later that such confused thoughts and images, emerging in that twilight zone before falling asleep, are known as hypnagogic hallucinations. We all have them from time to time.

'That will be the drugs you were on,' said one of the nurses, scribbling a few final notes on her clipboard. 'Patients often have strange dreams when they are given morphine for the first time. It's quite common.'

I nodded, but I had the feeling that my 'quite common' experiences had disappointed my interviewers. Maybe they were looking for something juicier from my nine hours under general anaesthetic: a spot of astral travelling, perhaps, or an out-of-body shopping trip. Frankly, I was happy enough to have survived the surgery. Supernatural experiences had not been on my list of desired outcomes. All I wanted now was to get out of hospital and get back to normality. As the nurses thanked me and left, I thought about that quote that's often attributed to John Lennon but has been coined by others.

'Life is what happens when you are busy making other plans.'

So it was with me and this book. I had always intended to write about growing up in a part of Glasgow which too became something of a twilight zone as it transitioned from modernity to decay. There was also that zone between childhood and adolescence, and another between the influences of a Scottish mother and a Polish father, influences that at various times in my life have made me feel like an outsider, an observer and, let's say it out loud, a bit of a freak. In the back rooms of my subconscious there were also the happy memories of summers spent around Dundee – Carnoustie, Monifieth and Broughty Ferry – of long journeys in a clapped-out Dormobile and of school trips to run-down zoos and seaside towns, of optical illusions and sneaky peeks into an American president's bedroom. There was my eccentric Auntie Jean and Uncle Jimmy, who believed demons caused backache and who taught me more about Scottish history than I ever learned at school. There was another uncle, the one from Poland, whose arrival in Glasgow became the source of such teenage unhappiness that I turned my back on school and wandered the city streets for six weeks.

I had intended a trip to Krakow, a research jolly, to reconnect with my Polish roots. That was thwarted by the shutdown of air travel. Social distancing then put paid to plans for a stage show, of sorts, with the fictional stories from this book performed by the actor Karen Bartke and with visuals created by the artist Laura Jackson, who has provided the book's cover illustrations. Still, the memories remain and here they are in these pages, as are the make-believe tales and some of those strange characters who had crowded into my dreams during my morphine-laced sleep. Between make-believe and memory, I'll disgorge my thoughts about family life, about identity and prejudice, about love and friendship and my fear of priests, escalators and death. But how should I explain the unexpected turn of events that led me to that hospital bed and to the realisation that, though glad to be alive, I was now that bit closer to the twilight of my own life?

Whoa! That sounds a bit too melodramatic, but I suppose that's where I should begin.

PART ONE
MEMORIES

SEE YOU ON THE OTHER SIDE

When my children, Sarah and Alan, were very young, but too old for Goldilocks, I began making up my own bedtime stories about evil wizards, zombie dads and a needy bear called Bobo. This bear, which I portrayed with wide, sad eyes and a trembling mouth, seemed to have something of a death-wish because he was forever getting himself into scrapes on railway lines, busy roads and cliff edges. When we reached that bit in the story where the hapless bear encountered obvious danger, Sarah and Alan would call out, 'No, Bobo, come back! Don't do it!'

At that point I considered my parental duties well and truly discharged, having instilled in my offspring a self-preserving fear of trains, traffic and heights. Then came the day, as it always must, when the children were leery of such tales, and so when Bobo found himself trapped on a causeway with the tide coming in, it was Alan who sealed his fate.

'Let him drown,' he said. 'That stupid bear has had enough chances.'

It was around that time, therefore, that I started sharing true stories about my own childhood. One night I was telling them how the kids on our street used to play extreme games of hide-and-seek. I was describing how Jimmy Palmer would take things too far by concealing himself under parked cars and, on one occasion, he clung to the back end of an ice cream van while it was moving. I was just getting to the excitement about the police chase when Anne, my wife, interrupted me.

'How come all your childhood stories involve sweets, chocolate or ice cream?'

It was a fair point. No matter the story I was telling, some kind of sweet treat would get a mention. It was even true to say that some of my stories were actually no more than a nostalgic list of my favourite confectionery: toffee logs, mint cracknel, flying saucers, sherbet dib dabs and so on.

'No wonder you've had so much trouble with your teeth,' Anne said. 'All that sugar.'

This was *not* a fair point because the problems with my teeth had started long before I had even heard of sticky Drumstick lollipops, mouth-watering Opal Fruits or creamy Milkybars. They said I had been born with a calcium deficiency which caused half of my baby teeth to grow in black, loose or not at all. By the time my adult teeth came along, they had plenty of room for manoeuvre and looked like they had been placed randomly around my mouth like the standing stones of a mythical land called Myopia. There then followed many years of emergency appointments, visits to the Dental Hospital in Glasgow and various lash-up treatments designed to rid me of immediate pain. I learned, the hard way, that there was no cavity filling that could withstand the adhesive pressure of a Cadbury Eclair toffee. I risked the wrath of womankind by declaring that the agony of an abscess was obviously much more painful than the pangs of childbirth. In photographs I always wore a nervous closed-mouth smile, for fear that anyone would glimpse the scene of carnage beyond my lips.

'Actually, I've seen worse,' said my new dentist, when, at the age of fifty-five, I finally decided to get things sorted. I had just taken a redundancy package from my job running BBC Radio Scotland and had time on my hands. A private clinic in Inverness, where we now lived, was offering a good deal on their 'Six Month Smile' treatment. If they got cracking in October, I reasoned, it would be all over by April and I would be gambolling through springtime fields, laughing and grinning. Why, I could even eat with my mouth open if I wanted to, just to show off.

'This might take a bit longer than six months,' said Jennifer, the dentist assigned by the clinic to handle my case. 'You have a lot of gaps. You'll need implants and crowns and some brace-work. Are you prepared to stick it for the long haul?'

I could only gurgle my assent because she was still prodding about in my open mouth with her shiny picks and mirrors. She warned me that I wouldn't be smiling by April, so I asked her if it might be all over by Christmas. She thought that was just about possible but didn't say which Christmas she had in mind. As it turned out, it was to be a full year before she even got started on the implant surgery, having spent the first twelve months straightening my lower teeth and then trying to tease out an upper canine that had never quite emerged from my gums. 'Tease' is too gentle a word to describe the process. She hacked away at my palate until she had unearthed enough of the secreted tooth to work on. Thin wires and rubber bands were deployed to provide leverage, but progress was slow. Months passed, seasons came and went, and then there was more delay when Jennifer, a competitive cyclist, took a tumble during a race and had to take time off work. For a few weeks, her father took charge of my treatment. (I checked he was also a qualified dentist and not just some helpful parent offering to help out his daughter with a bit of dental dabbling.)

Almost two years after starting treatment, Jennifer and I decided between us that the submerged tooth was a lost cause. It was surfacing at such a slow pace that I reckoned the time required for success might exceed my life expectancy.

'I'm from the east end of Glasgow,' I told her. 'I'm already on borrowed time.'

We agreed on the nuclear option: Jennifer extracted the tooth and added the gap to the list of locations for titanium implants. By the middle of 2019 we seemed to be on the home straight. No fewer than five implants had been screwed into my gums and I could finally look forward to a Christmas dinner where I saw myself crunching through turkey bones and grinning ear-to-ear in family photographs. Next to me, a Cheshire cat would look positively miserable.

My time with Jennifer was drawing to a close and, in a way, I would be sorry to say goodbye. Our fortnightly appointments had allowed us to build up a good rapport and she always indulged my dopey curiosity about her experiences as a dentist. She surprised me by telling me that many patients actually fall asleep during treatment and that was without anaesthetic. I wondered what kind of stressful life some people might be living if they thought a trip to the dentist was an opportunity for relaxation and slumber. I asked Jennifer if she preferred it when patients kept their eyes open or closed during treatment, but she didn't mind either way. I thought it might be startling if someone's eyes suddenly sprang open, like the final scene of a slasher movie when the audience realised the killer isn't quite dead. I told Jennifer about the thesis I had written for my psychology degree: 'Tooth Loss Dreams as a Function of Personality'. These dreams are a worldwide, intercultural phenomenon. Native Americans once believed that such dreams foreshadowed the loss of a family member. Evolutionary psychologists would have it that dentists *ought* to dream about losing their teeth in the way that midwives without children often dream about childbirth because it allows them to empathise with expectant mothers. Jennifer thought about this, told me she had never had such a dream and concluded that meant she didn't have much empathy. I didn't disagree. In truth, I liked her matter-of-fact, tell-it-like-it-is approach. There was no sugarcoating from this dentist.

And so, when Anne and I returned from an October break to Lanzarote and I called Jennifer to cancel a scheduled appointment, she asked me what was wrong. I told her I had fallen ill while away, had a stinking cold and some kind of odd blister had developed on my tongue. I'd been smearing it with Bonjela and a few dabs of Germolene. Internet gurus had suggested baking soda, the go-to solution for everything of course. Nothing was working and I could see the blister was getting a little bigger every day. I didn't fancy having Jennifer working on my sixth and final implant while this embarrassing monstrosity was lurking on the other side of my gob.

'Probably best that I skip our appointments until I'm feeling up to it.'

Jennifer disagreed, asked me to come into the clinic so she could have a look at the blister, frowned when she saw it and in her usual manner said, 'You'll be worried that might be mouth cancer, won't you?'

'Well, no ... not until you just put that thought in my head. Surely it's just a blister?'

'That's not like any blister I've seen before,' she said. 'So I'm going to phone the hospital right now and see if they can book you in for a biopsy.'

That's when I really started to think this might be something serious. I was so concerned that I didn't wait for the hospital to get back in touch. I called my GP practice, asked to see any available doctor and was hoping a quick examination would allay my fears and put my mind at rest. Maybe a week on antibiotics would do the trick. It was not to be.

'That's quite a big tumour,' said the doc, as he extracted the ruler from my mouth. 'About four centimetres. Let me call the hospital and see if I can hurry them up about that biopsy.'

It was the first time anyone with medical expertise had described the blister on my tongue as a tumour, but by the time I went for the biopsy, the hospital medics had downgraded it to 'ulcer', as in: 'That's a very sizeable ulcer. We'll take some photographs. Do you mind signing a release form in case we want to publish them in a medical journal someday?'

'As long as you get my good side,' I said, feebly, but the worries remained. Anything that was interesting enough to make medical news was never going to be a good thing. Was this cancer or not?

'It may be your tongue has been rubbing against the rough edge of a filling, but we can't say that for sure. We'll have to wait for the results of the biopsy and get some blood tests.'

The nurse who took my blood was more reassuring.

'Oh, my sister had something like that and it turned out to be nothing.'

That was good to hear, although she kind of blew it when I got up to leave.

'Hope it all turns out well and we'll see you on the other side.'

'The other side? Don't say that!'

'Ha ha. Well, you know what I mean.'

The biopsy involved four injections of local anaesthetic into my tongue and then a scalpel sliced a sliver of flesh from my blister/ulcer/tumour. The results came back in just over a week and I was called back to the hospital to be told the news. A nurse led me into the consulting room and sat beside me, disconcertingly too close. Her job, I guess, was to hold my hand if I broke down in tears, but I was looking for information more than comfort. I kept having to speak over the top of her head as the doctor talked through the lab report. It was definitely a tumour. Squamous cell carcinoma. The seventh most common type of cancer, he told me.

'Usually seen in smokers, but in your case it could be a virus you picked up last month or even years ago, or else it's a genetic thing, you know, just bad luck.'

I would need an x-ray, an MRI scan and a CT scan, and then it would be up to a surgeon to judge how much of my tongue would have to be removed and then find out how far the cancer had spread.

All this had happened in just a few weeks and there had not been much time to take stock and think about the implications of surgery or what might happen afterwards. The full horror only emerged when I had my first meeting with Mr Kishore Shekar, consultant surgeon from the maxillofacial unit at Ninewells Hospital in Dundee, who travelled up to Inverness every few weeks to see out-patients at Raigmore. I warmed to him immediately, not least because of his politically incorrect sense of humour and his air of supreme self-confidence, and, again, because he was someone who told it to you straight. Anne sat with me in the clinic while Mr Shekar looked through my notes and scans and then examined my tongue.

'I think I can fix you,' he said, finally, 'but nothing is guaranteed. This will be a big operation and there can be complications, but it's a procedure I have done many times and I have an extremely high success rate. Ninety-five per cent. That's an official Government figure.'

I suspended my usual cynicism about Government statistics and allowed myself to be reassured.

'You'll be under general anaesthetic for nine hours. Another surgeon and I will operate on you simultaneously. We will remove the tumour and an area around it. One third of your tongue in total. We will then take a piece from your forearm to create a flap and we will graft that on to your tongue to replace the section we have removed. We will also take a vein from your arm to maintain bloody supply for the graft. After that we will take a section from your abdomen to replace the skin we have removed from your arm. At the same time, we will cut into your neck and remove a sample of lymph nodes. That will be sent to a laboratory for analysis. The results will tell us how far the cancer has spread. If it has spread, you may require radiotherapy. Chemotherapy is unlikely. All of this will happen in Dundee, at Ninewells Hospital, and you will be there for about two weeks, maybe a few days less.'

'Oh,' I said. 'I like Dundee. I used to go on holiday there when I was young.' It was the only thing I could think of to say, other than just screaming.

Mr Shekar nodded, ignored my rambling nonsense and continued. 'After the surgery you will not be able to speak for a few days. We may need to perform a tracheostomy – cut a hole in your throat to allow you to breathe, because the tongue will swell up and block your breathing. We'll see.'

'When will this be?' asked Anne, who was taking notes in a little school exercise book, just in case I wasn't absorbing all these details. And I wasn't.

'It will be, let me see, on 21st January. You'll come into the hospital the night before and we'll operate the next morning.'

'That's the day before my birthday,' I said.

'Feel free to bring cake for us,' said Mr Shekar. 'But you won't be eating much for a while. You'll have to relearn how to swallow. You'll start with Weetabix and mashed potato. Then speech therapy so you can learn how to speak with your new tongue. But you will have a lisp.'

Given that I now earned my living giving lectures and speaking at book festivals, a speech impediment of any kind wasn't exactly going to be helpful.

'Any more good news?' I asked.

He smiled. I think he could see I was losing sight of the big picture.

'Yes! The good news is that I intend to cure you of cancer. Cure. Not alleviate or minimise. Cure. And the other thing I tell all my patients is that your problem is now my problem. There is nothing you can do between now and the operation. You have given the problem to me to solve. So, go home, spend time with your family, enjoy Christmas, eat, have a glass of wine and I'll see you in Dundee in January.'

He explained that the surgery might have been happening a week or two sooner were it not for the Christmas holidays. 'Everything shuts down. It's ridiculous. People take far too much time off in this country.'

Anne asked about the likelihood of the operation being cancelled at the last minute, perhaps if he or people in his team fell ill.

'I don't believe in getting sick,' he declared. 'In my twenty-five years as a doctor I have only ever taken twenty minutes off because of sickness. I sprained my ankle in the car park but hobbled into the A & E department and strapped it up myself. Sickness is for wimps.'

We left him, smiling, and went home to follow his instructions – to spend time with family and try not to worry. Christmas came and went, and we counted the days through January. Anne was impatient for the surgery to happen, fearing that my cancer was spreading day by day. I, on the other hand, knew that my life would be changed in some way or other after the operation, so I eked out the remaining days of relative normality. I told myself that this whole cancer thing was just a nuisance and in a few months it would seem like a silly blip. By March it would almost be forgotten and life would go on. All the same, we did some grown-up things like getting our wills in order and arranging power of attorney, which would allow Anne and me medical and financial control over each other's affairs. This was just in case I slipped into a coma and was unable to sign cheques.

'But make sure I really am in a coma before you pull the plug on me,' I warned Anne, 'because I might just be napping.'

The day before my surgery, we drove to a hotel in Dundee, by the waterfront, and Anne checked in for the duration of my time in hospital. We had a late lunch and then we went to the hospital. Mr Shekar greeted us like old friends and told me he had been rethinking a few things.

'I don't think we'll need the tracheostomy,' he said. 'You look reasonably fit and I'm not removing too much of your tongue, just a third. I think you should be able to breathe OK, but we'll monitor your oxygen levels in the intensive care unit.'

He took a marker pen and drew a thick black line on the underside of my left arm. He finished with an oval flourish in the shape of a tongue. This was where he would remove the skin and tissue needed for my graft and the vein that would keep it supplied with blood while he did that. He warned me that my fingers might swell up, so I should remove any jewellery. I slid off my wedding ring and gave it to Anne for safekeeping. It all felt very symbolic, like a religious ritual. Then, oddly, Mr Shekar told us to go back into Dundee city centre and have a good meal.

'Enjoy it while you can,' he said.

We did, and later that night, at about nine o'clock, I went back into the hospital alone, reported to the nurses' station in the surgical ward and was shown to a bed. A man in the opposite bed was nursing a bandaged hand and talking to a woman who, I presumed, was his wife. He was not happy. Apparently his surgery had been cancelled at the last minute because an emergency case had taken priority. That wasn't upsetting him so much as the fact that he hadn't eaten all day. His wife offered him a bag of Starburst from her handbag, but he wasn't interested. He called a friend and, about a half-hour later, said friend arrived with a huge take-away meal from the local Burger King. As he tucked in, the greasy smell of fries and grilled beef wafted around the ward. Things certainly had changed a lot since the last time I'd found myself in a hospital bed. When was that? I shocked myself by doing the sums and working out it had been fifty years since a bad case of mumps had resulted in an ambulance ride to the old Belvedere Infirmary in Glasgow. In those days they didn't mess about when it came to infection control. Visiting hours and numbers were restricted, and any books or comics brought in to cheer up young patients had to be incinerated once read. I couldn't imagine Mum and Dad coming to visit me with a fish supper in hand.

I got a few hours of sleep, but mainly spent the time sending text messages to friends, masking my anxiety with daft comments. I told my friend Richard that, if the worst happened, he should write and read the eulogy at my funeral.

'Be sure to work in a plug for my book,' I told him. 'And no discounts for mourners.'

In the morning I was asked to shower and then dress in a hospital gown. I was wheeled to an anteroom outside the operating theatre. A whole team of doctors was already waiting for me as I appeared on the trolley. There was no sign of Mr Shekar, though. I wondered if the top guys always turned up later, like the headline act in a big show. More likely he was readying himself in the next room, while his team did all the prep work.

'You're probably wondering why I've asked you here this morning,' I said as the medics around me began their work. It wasn't the most original opening, but it broke the ice. A jolly anaesthetist joked with me as he prepared the cocktail of drugs that would put me to sleep for nine hours. He said that as soon as I became drowsy he would ask me to tell him the PIN for my bank card and then go for a night on the town with my wallet. I laughed but the others had clearly heard this schtick many times and ignored him. I had asked the anaesthetist what it would be like to be unconscious for so long. Would I dream? Would I have any sense of time passing? He told me a funny story, which he admitted might be apocryphal, about an unpopular doctor who needed some minor surgery. This was in midsummer. They put him to sleep and, while he was under, decorated his ward with Christmas lights and tinsel. The man's surgery had taken less than half an hour but as they wheeled him back to his ward and brought him round they exclaimed, 'It's a miracle ... you're alive ... after all this time in a coma!'

I laughed. Again, I was the only one.

'So, no, you won't have any sense of time passing, but some people do dream. A friend of mine dreamt he was playing an entire game of football. Ninety minutes plus injury time.'

A junior doctor was given the job of connecting a cannula to my arm. I could tell he was nervous and he was making a botched job of it, but I didn't want to get him into trouble, so I ignored the pain until it became unbearable. When I winced, he drew back and let a senior colleague take over. The syringe was connected to the cannula, the plunger was pressed and I began to feel that relaxed way you do after the first few sips from a glass of wine. Malbec, preferably.

'See you on the other side,' I mumbled, and tiny voices from long ago drifted into my mind.

'Come back, Bobo, come back!'

Then, on the eve of my fifty-seventh birthday, everything went dark.

THE SQUARE

Dark. That was how I imagined my family's life before 'the square'. My parents and brothers told stories that didn't include me, and which had happened in places that sounded so awful I was glad never to have lived there. I could only imagine the soot-blackened Glasgow tenement in Forrest Street – demolished before I was born – but I had seen the ugly grey blocks in Pitcairn Street where the spiked iron railings had been removed to help the war effort, leaving only the metal stumps embedded in the low stone wall that surrounded the entrance to the dimly lit communal close. It was where the stench of the gasworks blended with the bitter smell of chocolate from the Macfarlane Lang biscuit factory. Parkhead, Tollcross, the Calton – these were the places my grandparents and parents had lived through the war years and in the 1950s. It was where my seven older siblings – six brothers and one sister – had been born and had lived as children. But to me, these places belonged to the dark and dangerous past of a tough city that was known for its hard drinkers and razor gangs, for its slum landlords and sectarian rivalries.

I, thankfully, was born in the space-age and into a world of modern flats with indoor plumbing, open countryside and brand new schools. It was a place where the red Marchetti

Brothers ice cream vans chimed their cheery presence day and night. It was where Bert Hogg in his big blue grocery truck sold the boring stuff that only parents regarded as necessities, like soap and vegetables. It was a place where green and yellow buses brought people the six-mile journey to and from the city centre, though not as quickly as the new blue electric trains. It was where, before they built the motorway over it, the Monklands Canal flowed past a purpose-built park complete with a pristine green for lawn bowls. It was where a clump of five trees came to be called 'the forest' and the annual visit of a run-down travelling funfair was hailed, excitedly, as 'the carnival'.

This was Easterhouse, or at least the Easterhouse I remember from my childhood. Maybe it was exactly as I've described or maybe it never was. Maybe your image of the place, if you have one, is very different: boarded windows, graffiti, vandalism and junkies ... a vast holding pen for fifty thousand people, just a fraction of Glasgow's overspill population as the city fathers moved to demolish the slum tenements alongside a great many buildings that should have been saved. Housing schemes like Easterhouse, Drumchapel and Castlemilk provided a quick-fix alternative to the new towns of Cumbernauld and East Kilbride. You could be cynical and suggest the schemes kept grateful voters within the city boundary, within existing constituencies, and, therefore, kept city politicians in power. You could also point out that the speed of construction meant there were plenty of places to live, but few places to find work. You might even put the subsequent rise of street violence down to the lack of local jobs and amenities. There is some truth in all of that, but in the ten years I lived on the square, I simply thought of Easterhouse as home. In my mind's eye, the air is fresh, the grass is green, and morning or afternoon sunshine glints from the bright white blocks on either side of quiet streets.

21

Home, to be specific, was a first-floor, four-bedroom flat in Corsehill Street. We were at number 9. It was known as a 'five-apartment' because you included the living room in your calculations, but not the bathroom, the kitchenette or the veranda. The front room – the living room – was warmed by a coal fire which also heated the water boiler behind it. There was one more fire, in my parents' bedroom, but that was only lit when someone in the family was ill and had to be looked after in there for a few days. Coal was delivered, once a fortnight, by men driving flatbed trucks who heaved the hessian sacks up to the bunker in the stairwell landing.

Our flat was part of a continuous block that made ninety-degree turns to semi-enclose a grassy square populated by three spindly trees protected by wire mesh. That square was the centre of my universe. Like all neighbourhoods we remember from our childhood, it still looms large in my memory. Some of the details have faded, of course. There was a time when I could have told you the name of every person in every one of the twenty-four flats that looked on to that scrappy square. I could also have told you the names of their dogs, which were allowed to roam freely; you knew which were friendly enough to pat and which snarling mutts were best avoided. These days I remember only a few of those dogs and only some of their owners. I see faces, but more often it's just the nameplates on neighbours' doors that I recall: Usher, Melville, Gormley, Maley, Deacon and a few more. Across the landing from us were the Tonners, Frank and Agnes. Frank Tonner was a delivery driver for the House of Fraser store and his wife was one of those people who, at the time, people described as being a bit 'wandered'. Perhaps now we'd talk about dementia or Alzheimer's; either way, she was forgetful and lacked the ability to concentrate on anything for more than a few minutes. If Mum asked me to nip next door and ask Mrs Tonner if she had a shilling for our electricity meter, both the explanation and the conversion of our loose change of pennies and threepenny bits into a silver shilling would be a struggle for our poor befuddled neighbour to comprehend, assuming, of course, she could even remember where she had put her purse.

Below us at number 9 were the Bullens and the Lees. We didn't have much to do with the Bullens, but Mrs Lee was a friendly woman with a gentle Alsatian dog called Sandy. She also had three memorable household gadgets. The first was an electric vacuum cleaner – an upright Hoover with a light to help you search out the dirt. For special occasions, such as Christmas or Hogmanay, my mother would ask if she could borrow this wonderful machine to give our floors the kind of once-over that her brush or manual sweeper could never achieve. Mrs Lee also had a coin-operated television set, which even then seemed somewhat absurd. Imagine *Coronation Street* blanking out during a vital scene and then having to insert half-crowns into a top slot if you wanted to keep watching. It would be many decades before proper pay-per-view became a reality. Mrs Lee, however, did have one very important device that few of our neighbours could match. She had a telephone. This sat on a special table in her hall, not far from the front door and opposite a picture of Jesus – *The Sacred Heart of Jesus*. It's the one where Christ's heart seems to burst from his body, the bloody organ ablaze with divine light. Beside the phone was a small wooden box and this was for neighbours to deposit coins for the cost of any call. I think the scary picture was strategically placed to ensure that everyone was honest with their payments.

In the next close, at number 11, lived the Wards and the Murphys, and both Mark Ward and John Murphy were among my childhood friends. Mark went to the same Catholic school as me, St Clare's, but John went to the nearby Protestant school, Rogerfield, and had cultural activities that were strange to us papists. He was a member of the Boys' Brigade, went to church instead of chapel and, because no one had thought to tell him that Jesus was a Celtic fan, supported Rangers football club. He collected those football cards that came packed with a brittle strip of bubble gum almost indistinguishable from its cardboard backing. Non-Rangers cards would be tossed or traded as he searched desperately for 'Derek Parlane', the one card that was missing from his collection. John's mother, about fifteen years younger than my own, was a door-to-door representative for Avon, and because of that, John's house reeked of those scents that can overpower you near a department store's cosmetics counter. Mrs Murphy wore bright red lipstick and cat eye glasses. She had a sassy manner and when I think of her now, I make some kind of an association with Jackie Kennedy. Mrs Murphy was a sixties gal.

One close along, at number 15 (there was no number 13 because Glasgow Corporation decided that would be unlucky), there was a family that was even bigger than our own: the Palmers. They also lived in a five-apartment flat, but I think they must have slept in a shift pattern because there seemed to be hundreds of them. Mr Palmer was a mountain of a man, barrel-chested and probably overweight, but his height allowed him to carry it. He was some kind of big cheese in the Orange Order and proudly marched wearing his sash and bowler hat every July. We were, in truth, a bit frightened of the Palmers because they seemed like people who had no fear of death – even the younger members like Brian and Jimmy Palmer, who were in our age group. Jimmy Palmer, in particular, thought nothing of jumping from a first-floor landing window to evade an irate relative. He would treat street games with the seriousness and intensity of a wartime mission and happily run through nettled hedges or hitch rides on the back of passing coal lorries. If a group of kids from a rival neighbourhood ever threatened to muscle in on our territory, you could rely on Jimmy Palmer to take them on. Usually single-handed.

At number 17, on the corner of the square, lived my absolute best friend, Danny Pryce. His family was much smaller than ours. He lived with his parents, his younger sister, Suzanne, and his elderly grandmother. The Pryces had Irish ancestry and his grandmother especially talked much about the legends and superstitions of the old country. For a time my sister, Rose, was convinced that Danny was an intellectual giant on a par with Einstein. The evidence for this was fairly thin. Once, when seeing the unusual sight of a Corporation bus drive past our flats – we were not on the bus route – Danny had speculated that this might be what he termed 'an optical illusion'. Rose was unduly impressed by his use of such big words and hence decided he must be something of a brainbox. It didn't seem to occur to her, or Danny, that the bus might have been taking a diversion to avoid temporary roadworks.

That, then, was the cast of the square, or at least those were the principal players. There were others who had supporting roles. Mark Ward's sister, June, was one of our crowd, as were, from time to time, the Maley brothers, Adam and Michael (and Laddie, their bad-tempered Labrador), who lived in the flat above the Wards. And there were the posh girls, Anne Douglas and Catherine Robertson, who lived two storeys above the Palmers but who rarely associated with the rest of us, and whose families were the first to move out of Easterhouse. I think their parents had warned them to stay clear of us street urchins. If you wanted really posh, though, you had to go to the other side of the square and to the corner flat at number 7. There on the second and third floors respectively and respectably lived the Martins and the Grants. Occasionally my mother would find herself invited for afternoon tea with either Mrs Grant or Mrs Martin and, after ensuring I was suitably scrubbed, she would take me along. There I saw how the other half lived. These flats had actual glass doors for all the rooms and fitted carpets in most of them. Not a scrap of linoleum in sight. Even their kitchenettes were tiled in black and white chessboard squares, exactly as you saw on television in those adverts for Flash cleaning liquid. Mrs Martin had a modern gas fire and had therefore converted her coal bunker into a playroom for her two children, both boys, the sort of boys who watched *Blue Peter* on BBC television and collected stamps, wildlife photographs and those plastic coins they gave away at petrol stations. What's more, unlike John Murphy and his elusive Derek Parlane card, they had several complete sets mounted and framed on their bedroom walls. Yep, they were *those* kinds of boys and they didn't play with us either.

The square at Corsehill Street was our playground. In summer it would be a football field or an open arena for make-believe showjumping (we all pranced around holding invisible reins and jumping over cardboard boxes). In winter one of the Palmer boys would throw water on a long stretch of the pavement and create a huge (and potentially lethal) ice slide. On the square we would fly kites, ping arrows from toy bows or simply stand there waiting for the ice cream vans to arrive, empty Irn-Bru bottles in hand, so that we could redeem the deposit from the glassware. The square was the setting-off point for epic bike rides, and it was where we stood to shout up at our friends' windows and ask if they were coming out to join us. It was where football fans – both Celtic and Rangers – sat together in overgrown gardens, listening to the radio commentary and drinking orange crush or cream soda from shared bottles. It was where we played until the sun set, and when the streetlights came on, parents' voices could be heard, calling our names and telling us it was time for bed. Plaintive pleas for just 'five more minutes' were usually ignored.

Evenings on the square could also be a place of fear. There was the night we saw those strange lights hovering in the darkening sky and, huddling together for safety, decided it was either a flying saucer or else the second coming of Christ. (It turned out to be a weather balloon reflecting the moonlight.) On another occasion, during a short-lived bout of mass hysteria, we convinced ourselves that the serial killer Bible John was lurking in every stairwell. I also had my own trio of personal fears: escalators, volcanoes and the Loch Ness monster. Stepping on to any moving escalator was scary enough, but when Mum took me shopping in Glasgow city centre, I demanded assurances that we would not be visiting C & A in Trongate, because the escalator there seemed faster than any other. A queue of frustrated shoppers would build up behind us while I hesitated, watching the metal steps unfold, waiting for the right moment to step aboard. Having managed that, the next worry was about getting off at the other end because I knew, for certain, that if I mistimed my step the escalator would suck me into its grinding mechanism and to a netherworld inhabited by moving mannequins. As for volcanoes, well, I had once seemed rock-solid sure that they only existed in faraway lands and on tropical islands until an older brother told me that Edinburgh Castle had been built on a volcano and that, should it decide to erupt, the river of molten lava could easily cover the forty miles to the east end of Glasgow. I wasted a lot of time worrying about this and thinking about how quickly I might be able to shin up one of those pathetic trees in the middle of our square. Similarly, the Loch Ness monster seemed to be safely out of harm's way in somewhere called the Highlands of Scotland, but again that same older brother put me right. He said that it was so big that it could reach Glasgow in just ten short steps. Serial killers and UFOs were nothing compared to the horror stories I could conjure from my own imagination, cruelly assisted by my mischievous siblings.

You want romance? Well, the square could have been the scene of my first kiss when a pretty fair-haired girl called Maria (or it might have been Mandy or Molly or Mindy) made me a deal: 'If you catch me you can kiss me,' she had said, before laughing and running off like one of those electric hares at a greyhound track. Momentarily stunned by the offer, I was slow out of the traps, but I soon picked up the pace and we ran around the caged trees and through the closes to the back courts, darting playfully around laundry poles and huge iron midden bins overflowing with coal ashes and potato peelings and then back to the square again. I could see that I was closing on her, but I ran out of time. Just as I got within smooching distance, a window opened above and behind me, and Mum was calling me in for the night. I wasn't too heartbroken because Maria (or was it Molly or Mandy or Mindy?) was a passing fancy, a visiting cousin of one of my friends. It was never going to be a serious relationship. Besides, at the age of seven, I had already given my heart to Anne Douglas, similar in height but four years my senior, who tore up my lovesick notes and finally sent 'cease and desist' warnings via my embarrassed sister.

Love, laughter, fear and friendship. That square in Corsehill Street was where, literally, my life began. But discovering how, exactly, that happened, involves another story and other memories.

It also involves a jumping frog.

JUMPING FORWARD

Frankie McGhee had just buried his jumping frog when Big Smiddy brought up the topic of sex and asked us if we knew where babies came from. I'm not sure why these thoughts stay paired in my memory, but maybe it's because, when you are eight years old, a jumping frog seems particularly impressive. It wasn't a real frog so don't fret yourself about the whole burial thing. It was one of those plastic toys attached to a thumb-controlled air pump by means of a six-inch length of rubber tubing. Perhaps it's that umbilical tubing that makes me think of sex because, before Big Smiddy set us straight, I had my own theory about where babies came from and it was all to do with belly buttons. Through close examination of my own navel I had noted its similarity to the knot you tie in a balloon after you blow it up. It stood to reason, therefore, that when babies were ready to emerge into the world, all the doctors had to do was untie the knot in a woman's stomach and gently scoop out the sleeping infant. I'm making that sound easy but undoing one of those knots on an inflated balloon can be tricky. One false move with a sharp fingernail and the whole thing goes pop. No wonder doctors needed so many years of training. I should also say that my theory about the importance of belly buttons seemed confirmed when Mum caught me browsing through the lingerie section in her mail-order Littlewoods catalogue and saw me placing a finger on every belly button on view. I told her that I had been counting the buttons and ranking them in order of best to worst. Mum was not impressed and told me this was a dirty thing to do. I was immediately consumed with unfathomable guilt.

None of that was really at the front of my mind when Frankie put his frog on the ground and squeezed the pump. To our amazement, it leapt forward and it was a big leap. I would say it covered twice its own body length in distance. Big Smiddy signalled his approval with a low whistle and Frankie was chuffed. This might seem like a fairly basic form of amusement, but to us in 1971 this was the kind of technology we assumed had been developed by NASA scientists in collaboration with Victor Frankenstein. One by one we all had a go at squeezing the pump and making the frog move. Big Smiddy went first and then Danny Pryce had a go, and then it was my turn. Frankie then announced he was going to bury the thing.

This all happened on a Friday afternoon, not long after the start of the new school term, when the four of us had been walking home, taking our usual route through the back of what we called the 'new houses' on Forglen Street, past the lock-up garages, down the grassy slope and on to the red blaes playing fields which marked the half-way point in our journey. We weren't in any particular hurry and the sun was shining, so there was time for frog fun and, as it turned out, life-changing discussions about the origins of our existence. Frankie began to bury his toy under a pile of the sharp sand of the football pitch and said that he would memorise its location and then find it again on our way to school on Monday. It was a kind of do-it-yourself treasure hunt and it did have that element of jeopardy. Suppose, come Monday morning, he couldn't find the burial spot? Suppose someone else happened to come across it and took it away? Suppose it was unwittingly stepped on and crushed? We all agreed that Frankie McGhee was a risk-taker, a veritable daredevil. He was also a trainee altar boy and, although some months had passed since Easter, it may be that the idea of a burial and resurrection had some religious significance for him.

It was as we continued our walk home that Big Smiddy asked the question about babies. The lead-up to this had been prompted by the frog talk which had dovetailed into a discussion about favourite toys and on to what we were hoping to get for Christmas. This was August so, naturally, we had already been thinking about our Christmas lists. We talked about the days gone by when we would send such lists wafting up our fireplace chimneys. Our requests for various toys, games and sweets would be scrawled on a page torn from an old school jotter and then floated carefully above the flames of the coal fire so that the heat would carry it upward and thence to the North Pole. It sometimes took a few attempts and the lists could be badly charred before they began their flight. This, of course, explained why you didn't always get everything you had asked for. We imagined the elves struggling to read the blackened corners of the paper before shaking their heads and substituting a Hotspur annual for that Hot Wheels track we really wanted. Our eight-year-old selves were laughing at the days when we were half that age and so young and so foolish as to have done such things. I laughed, Danny laughed and Big Smiddy laughed, but Frankie McGhee was not laughing, only smiling nervously. Big Smiddy pounced on this and accused Frankie of still writing letters to Santa. Naturally, Frankie said this wasn't the case, but his denials were unconvincing and so Smiddy began to chip away at his entire belief system.

'And I bet you don't even know how babies are made?'

'Yes, I do,' Frankie insisted, but we all knew he didn't. As it turned out, neither did Danny nor I, but we said nothing. Besides, if push came to shove, I had my whole belly-button theory up my sleeve. That at least explained how babies got out, if not how they got in.

Big Smiddy, it has to be said, had form when it came to discussing sexual matters. Although he was the same age as us, he was bigger, more muscular, more mature, and, although I know it can't be true, I always picture him as having a thick mane of ginger hair and the beginnings of a ginger beard. Sideburns, even. He was one of those lads who combined academic ability with reasonable prowess in sport. As a result, he was popular with just about everyone ... even girls. And girls were something he talked about a lot. He was also an only child and found it fascinating that Danny and I both had something that he didn't: sisters.

'Have you ever seen your sister with no clothes on?' he would ask, and when we said, yes, sometimes at bath times or when getting changed at a beach, he would demand a more detailed description. Nothing we could say would convince him that brothers really don't think that way about their sisters and that it was too yucky to be speaking about this. Now, on that walk home, he was talking about making babies and, supposedly to help wee Frankie McGhee fill in the gaps in his knowledge, he described the whole process from start to finish, including the bit where your parents got naked, climbed between the sheets and did shocking things with their genitals. As for how babies came out, well, my balloon theory was now a bust. As Big Smiddy brought his impromptu and unrequested lecture to a close, Frankie McGhee, with tears in his eyes, was in a state of near hysteria.

'That's not true, none of that's true!' he screamed and ran off.

Oh, how we laughed at his naivety, and we decided it would serve him right if he couldn't find his stupid toy frog on Monday. I masked my own shock with this kind of cruel bravado until I got home and then I immediately chapped on my sister's bedroom door. Rose was now twelve years old and was going through phases where she couldn't really be bothered with her little brother. One day she would be content to play games with me or skip rope with a friend, the next day she would claim to be a grown-up and too old for such nonsense. It was hard to keep track. In recent days she had seemed preoccupied with, to my mind, stupid activities such as brushing her hair and experimenting with make-up and nail varnish. She now had her own bedroom and it had been hammered into me that I wasn't allowed in there without permission and I should never enter without first knocking and, as now, waiting for her to call me in.

'What do you want?' was her not so friendly greeting.

'I want to ask you something,' I said. 'It's about where babies come from.'

'Come in.'

As I opened the door, Rose turned from her dressing table and told me I could stay for five minutes. I sat on the edge of her bed and recounted what Big Smiddy had said. Rose listened and nodded; aside from a few details, it seemed that Smiddy's version was hideously accurate. Then Rose added to my afternoon of trauma by telling a story of her own, and it was a story that it seemed she had been saving up for this very moment.

'You know how we have six older brothers?' she began.

I nodded. She continued almost as if she were reciting a fairy tale.

33

'Well, Mum and Dad tried for years and years to have a wee girl, but each time a baby appeared it was a boy. Until, after many years and after several attempts, I appeared. A daughter, finally, a beautiful baby girl.'

'So?'

'At that point they were going to stop having children. Seven was enough, they thought. But then Mum got to thinking it would be a terrible shame if I was the only girl. So, after a few years, they gave it one more try and hoped that I could have a little sister.'

I kept listening. I began to see where she was going with this and I didn't like it.

'But then YOU came along,' she said, pointing an accusing finger at me, 'another boy! And everyone was disappointed.'

'What?'

'It's true … you weren't really wanted. You were a big let-down, and that's why Mum and Dad don't love you as much as they love me.'

Suddenly I was channelling my inner Frankie McGhee.

'That's not true, you big liar!' I shouted. 'You're just making that up!'

'Go ask Mum,' said Rose, turning back to her dressing table mirror. I saw her satisfied smile in the reflection.

I found Mum in the kitchenette, peeling and slicing potatoes and dropping them into the chip pan basket. The pan itself was full of set lard which was slowly melting under the heat of the gas hob. We always had home-cooked fish and chips on Friday nights. It was one of the many certainties of life then. Chicken on Sundays, stew on Saturdays, egg and chips on Wednesdays (when the money was running out). I told Mum what Rose had said about me being an unwanted child and my sister was duly summoned into the kitchen to be given a row and told to apologise.

'Sor-ry,' she said, in her mocking sing-song voice, and I could see she didn't mean it. Also, because her row had been so half-hearted, I suspected there was at least an element of truth in what she had told me about the circumstances of my birth. When Rose went back to her bedroom, I stayed in the kitchenette, and that's when Mum, seeing that I needed her full attention, took the pan off the hob and told me about the day I was born and the miracle of my survival. I guess she had worked out that I now knew enough about the mechanics of childbirth so that she could talk about such things. Little did she know that my knowledge was so fresh that it was still making itself at home in my brain in the space previously reserved for balloons and belly buttons.

'You were two weeks early,' she began, 'and there was no time to get to the hospital or call a doctor, so your dad helped deliver you. It all happened right here at home, right there in our bedroom. We lit the fire in there specially. You came into the world a bit battered and bruised because, well, your dad was a bit heavy-handed and when the midwife arrived, she took one look at you and told Dad to go straight down to Mrs Lee's house and phone an ambulance. You were this tiny wee purple thing and we worried that you wouldn't live long. You went to hospital and you were in an incubator for three weeks. It was like a wee glass coffin. Everyone in the family – your brothers, your sister, even Auntie Jean and Uncle Jimmy – came to visit you. They wanted to see you in case it was their last chance.'

'But I did survive,' I said, stating the obvious.

'Yes, you did ... and look how big you've grown.'

She then distracted me by guiding me to the wooden doorframe of the kitchenette, which was where we all measured our heights and marked our skyward progress with the nick of a knife next to which we pencilled our name and the date. I had grown at least two inches since the last time we had done this and it cheered me up enormously. Plus, there was fish and chips to come.

After tea I went out to meet Danny in the square. We had our usual wander around the streets, blew most of our weekly pocket-money on sweets from Tommy's ice cream van and had our regular argument about who would win in a fist fight between Batman and Spiderman. Danny's antipathy to Marvel's (clearly superior) superheroes was the only faultline in our friendship. We wondered whether either of us would be allowed to stay up late to watch the Friday night 'Don't Watch Alone' horror film on television. The TV listing in the *Daily Record* told us that it was going to be a werewolf film. Not as good as a vampire movie, but better than a mummy flick. We also talked about the girls in our class at school and which ones we would be prepared to kiss if someone offered us a million pounds. Danny said he would be prepared to kiss almost any of them for that kind of loot, but wasn't sure about the ones who wore glasses. We often talked about these million-pound offers. We seemed to have convinced ourselves that there was a roving band of billionaires on some crazed mission to give kids a dollop of their wealth if they tackled moral dilemmas and completed absurd dares.

'Would you eat a dog's jobbie if they gave you a million pounds?'

'Would you walk into school scud naked if they gave you a million pounds?'

'Would you start a fight with Jimmy Palmer if they gave you a million pounds?'

The answers to these hypothetical questions, in case you are wondering, were 'Yes', 'Yes' and 'Not even for ten million pounds.'

That night, I *was* allowed to stay up for the horror film, but, as usual, I was dozing off by the time *Late Call* came on, which was the five-minute religious monologue they put on the telly at half past ten at night. A man in a dog-collar would sit in an armchair and tell you some dull story about a friend or a neighbour with a problem that had been solved by some kind of wisdom from the Bible. Given what I had discovered that day about sex and babies, I wondered if any of this stuff about Heaven was true. I was sound asleep even before the first full moon turned the wolfman hairy and Dad lifted me into my bed.

When I woke up the next morning, I thought about Frankie McGhee and his stupid jumping frog and something about his blind faith in it surviving the weekend made me angry. I decided there and then I would steal it from him. I got up, got dressed, had my usual tea and toast for breakfast, and ran down the street and across the playing fields. It only took me a minute or two to find the frog and I carried it home. I knew I had been wrong to take it, so I kept it hidden and only played with it under the cover of my bed. On Monday morning we met up with Frankie on the walk to school and he raced ahead, excited to see if he could find his frog. But, of course, he couldn't. There was no evidence of broken plastic, so he assumed that someone had found it and taken it. Not for a moment did he suspect any of us, his friends, his pals.

'It's been stolen,' he said, finally giving up the search.

'Finders keepers isn't stealing,' Danny told him. 'It's only stealing if you know something belongs to someone else.'

But Frankie was in no mood for these philosophical niceties. He was crushed and I felt my insides churn just watching his sadness.

That evening I returned the frog to its burial ground and the next morning, on the walk to school, I encouraged Frankie to look again. He wasn't enthusiastic, but he made a feeble attempt to move some of the red sand with the side of his shoe and, lo and behold, there was the jumping frog. I had never seen someone look so happy. He took his precious toy to school and, placing it on his desk, demonstrated its agility to the rest of the class, always scooping it back to safety when it came close to the edge. I noticed that even the girls crowded around for a look, and not just the ones who wore glasses, either. The kissable ones too.

'Can't you make it jump backwards?' one of them asked, as for the umpteenth time he picked it up and repositioned it in the centre of his desk.

'No,' he said, looking a little irritated by the girl who had pointed out his toy's shortcomings. 'No, it doesn't jump backwards. That would be stupid. Even real frogs can't jump backwards.'

And he was right. Frogs can only jump forwards and it's the same with kangaroos. It's all to do with the shape of their legs.

You learn this stuff when you're growing up.

THE WRONG FLAG

The day I told Dad that I would never play football for Scotland was one of those days when he had been threatening to electrocute himself. Not on purpose, of course, and nothing to do with any disappointment about my poor prospects as a soccer internationalist. It was because, when I arrived home from school that day, he was crouching behind our old black and white television set and poking around its innards with a long screwdriver. On the screen was a monochrome kaleidoscope of jagged images and wavy lines. Occasionally a picture would form and then roll upwards, accelerating like a turbo-powered elevator. As usual, Dad hadn't bothered to disconnect the set from the mains electricity, so from time to time he would let out a yelp and exclaim 'In the name of God!' in his rich baritone voice accented with that exotic blend of Polish and Glaswegian. These small but frequent shocks never seemed to deter him from trying his hand as a TV repairman. He had no fear of electricity and would regularly mend dead appliances by removing the fuses from plugs and completing the circuit with a wad of metallic paper torn from a pack of Embassy Regal cigarettes.

As a qualified welder, fixing TV sets was really beyond his capability, but Dad was loath to admit defeat too soon before calling in a professional who would undoubtedly remove the set from our home, take it to a workshop and leave us, for up to three days, with nothing to do but talk to each other. This was one such day and so, when the repairman had come and gone, we got blethering about my day at school and how the PE teacher had watched my pathetic efforts on the football pitch and declared that I wasn't likely to be making an appearance at Hampden any time in the near or distant future. Rubbing salt into the wounds, he had added that I wouldn't even make it there as a pie-seller.

'But I'm quite good at art,' I told Dad, hoping this would, in some unlikely way, compensate for my failings in sport. Dad nodded and then lit another cigarette and gazed past me to the empty space where the TV set had been. He looked lost and in obvious need of a distraction, so that's when I told him about the Hitler thing.

It goes without saying that I owe my life to Adolf Hitler. In fact, that probably epitomises the very kind of thing that should *always* go without saying, even if it's true. Besides, I'm not unusual in this regard. Think of the tens of millions of people who were displaced by the Second World War and think of the children whose fathers or mothers got married in countries very different from those where they were born, and to spouses they might never have met had it not been for Adolf's quest for world domination. People like my father.

Dad only ever told us a few details of his life before the Nazis invaded Poland in 1939. He was a teenager (before teenagers were invented), just seventeen, and working as a farm labourer in a little village called Rozprza, south of the city of Łódź, in central Poland. His parents had loaned him out to a neighbour for the start of the harvest season. He worked all day in the fields and, as that summer's heatwave began to wane, slept on the farmhouse floor in front of an open hearth, gaining

40

what warmth he could from the dying embers of the day's fire. A huge cauldron of soup was always suspended above the fireplace. The soup was prepared each evening and would be used to feed the farmer's family and the field workers during the course of each day. As much as he was tempted, Dad was forbidden from taking any of the soup, and the farmer had warned that any theft would be noticed because a congealed crust of lard would form over the cooling liquid, and any attempt to crack through this would be easily detected. Dad, so his story went, discovered that he could carefully lift out this disc of lard, dip a piece of bread into the cold broth, replace the lard and enjoy an illicit supper. He got away with this for weeks until one morning the farmer's wife discovered something was missing, about half a pint of soup to be specific. She also noticed the disc of lard seemed to be floating in the centre of the liquid and not attached to the sides of the cast-iron pot. There had been a thief in the night and there was really only one possible suspect. The farmer had threatened Dad with a beating, so he ran out of the house and would probably have had to return and accept his punishment had it not been for events on Poland's western border.

As the Luftwaffe flew overhead and the panzers rolled in, the poorly equipped Polish army was over-run. Soon, from the east, came the Soviets, who had formed a non-aggression pact with Hitler and would annex their half of the country. Dad's family and their neighbours were trapped between the two, but the Soviets got to them first. They set about seizing farmland, rounding up civilians and deporting those they suspected of harbouring anti-Soviet opinions. That, of course, was just about everyone. Many military-age young men went on the run to avoid capture. They headed south then east, catching rides on freight trains and relying on the kindness of strangers. Like so many thousands of young Poles, Dad was caught by Soviet invaders and sent to a Gulag labour camp in Siberia.

In 1941, when the Soviet Union joined the Allied fight against the Axis forces, the Poles were set free, and after a long journey via the Middle East, Dad made it to Britain. At the age of nineteen he was a sailor in the Polish Free Navy and his battleship, the *Piorun* – which translates as 'thunderbolt' – was stationed at Clydebank unless called upon to escort the North Atlantic convoys to Murmansk. He met my mother in a Glasgow dance hall and married her after the war. Together they had eight children, of whom I'm the youngest. It's sobering to think that when I was born, the Second World War had been over for less than twenty years. Just think: only eighteen years separates the dropping of the atomic bomb in Hiroshima and the release of *Please Please Me* by the Beatles. No time at all. (I mention the Beatles in passing because Dad thought the Fab Four were not so fab and had done more to destroy the fabric of British society than any foreign tyrant.)

Dad didn't talk too much about his time in the war. It wasn't one of those situations where he kept schtum because it was all too painful to recall. Rather, it was because he found it hard to find an appreciative audience. I suspect my older brothers were much more interested in the stuff that defined their own generation – the Beatles, the Stones, motorbikes and flower power – and my sister and I were too young to understand what these grown-ups were talking about when they mentioned bombs and ration books. Also, to be honest, my siblings and I were sometimes suspicious about those few stories Dad did repeat from time to time. We wondered if, consciously or not, he had merged some of his true-life history with the kind of John Wayne war movies he liked watching on television. That stuff about leaping on and off freight trains seemed particularly cinematic.

Even the soup story had the ring of a children's fable about it.

But when he showed us the fading blue tattoo that marked him as a Siberian prisoner, we believed his descriptions of the punishment cells and the ruthless tyranny of Stalin's Russia. He was more circumspect when it came to talking about Germany and he always made a distinction between the Nazis and the wider German population. In fact, he often expressed admiration for the German way of doing things like building roads and cars. 'They build things to last,' he would tell me, every time we drove over a pothole or when another fault developed in his Vauxhall Viva. 'But the British, they fix things and then have to fix them again five minutes later.' Yes, he liked Germany a lot, did Dad, and when we went on holiday there in the seventies, he got on well with local people of his own age. One night in a little village pub, I watched as he downed glasses of beer with old German soldiers and compared war stories. I remember thinking this was very open-minded of him, letting bygones be bygones and all that. It was even more impressive to hear him speaking fluent German which, according to the locals, he did with a Frankfurt accent, just as his English had that strong Glasgow flavour.

All of which is my hesitant preamble to telling you about the incident with the swastikas. I need the long build-up because it's an incident that still makes me cringe. You see, there were a lot of swastikas in my childhood for one reason or another. You saw them on TV in those old war films and on comedy shows like *Hogan's Heroes*. In those kinds of shows, the Nazis were portrayed almost like panto villains and it really didn't matter how awful they were, because you knew the goodies would win out in the end. The comedian Freddie Starr used to clown about with an absurd goose-stepping impersonation of Adolf Hitler, and, far from being upset by this, Dad proclaimed

Freddie to be the funniest man on television. When one of my motorbike-loving brothers went through a phase where he fancied himself as a Hell's Angel, there was a swastika on his leather jacket. Then there was that game my brother Alan played with the dartboard. He would draw a map of a fictional island on a piece of paper and this would show the relative disposition of British and German forces. The British would be indicated by lots of little Union flags and the Germans, of course, by swastikas. The paper would be pinned to the dartboard and then we'd choose sides and take turns throwing darts, aiming to obliterate the enemy forces through punctures in the paper. What I'm trying to say is that we associated the swastikas with Germany, but, taking our cue from Dad, we didn't associate the Germans with the Nazis. Not all of them, at least.

Look, I know I'm still prevaricating, so let's cut to that moment in the art class when the lesson of the day was about printing with paint. The teacher had shown us how to draw a shape on a piece of card, cut it out, dip it in poster paint and then use it to mark up a huge sheet of paper, repeating the image several times horizontally and vertically. Each of our posters would then be added to a massive wall mural of various shapes and symbols. While my fellow classmates created cards shaped like animals or stars and dipped these in bold primary colours, I went for something different and dramatic. I scissored out a swastika, which I then dipped in black paint and daubed on my sheet of paper maybe twenty times.

The effect was certainly bold and eye-catching and, indeed, caught the eye of our teacher as she toured the class, looking over our shoulders to examine our efforts. As she reached my desk I heard a loud intake of breath and it seemed like minutes before she exhaled. Then her shriek of outrage was so piercing it could be heard all the way along the art corridor so that other teachers came running in to see what had happened. I felt a hand on my arm and I was hauled out of my seat and made to stand up while shocked classmates watched as I was bombarded by words coming so loud and fast I could only catch a few of them. Those that I did felt as sharp as those darts my brother had used to pierce his paper maps.

'Nazis ... Hitler ... evil ... Holocaust ... murder of the Jews ... my family ... Hitler ... sick ... sick ... sick!'

Finally she paused long enough to ask me a direct question.

'Do you have any idea what that symbol means?'

A few minutes earlier I would have given my answer with utmost confidence, but now I was no longer sure of my ground. I could feel the tears forming in my eyes and was afraid to speak in case sobs emerged instead of words.

'Doesn't it mean Germany?' I managed to say. It was a half-answer, half-question. I was hedging my bets and hoping I might get the chance to explain that, according to my father, not all Germans were bad and that, in fact, they made particularly good roads and cars and—

'No, it doesn't mean Germany,' she snapped. Her rage was now evolving into a tearful but more subdued fury. 'It means ... it means ... Oh, just go back to your seat and rip up that paper.'

'The card too?' I asked, just to be clear.

'Yes! Rip it all up and throw it in the bin.'

I walked back to my desk and did as I was instructed, the eyes of my classmates following me with a mixture of glee and curiosity, depending on whether they had no idea what I'd done wrong or were enjoying a rare instance of excitement in an art class. An art class, for goodness sake! I mean, you expected this kind of trouble from those crazy maths teachers or that idiot in domestic science who tried to teach us how to sew and make scones. But not in the art class. Things were usually so calm here, so tranquil.

I went home that day with a burning sense of injustice. I knew I'd done something wrong or got something back to front, but did I really have to be screamed at and humiliated in front of the whole class? It was enough to put you off art for life. So, after a suitable half-hour of grieving for the broken telly, I told Dad about the incident, hoping, somehow, he would take my side in the matter. Of course, he didn't.

'That wasn't a good thing to do,' he told me, calmly and simply. 'Those Nazis were a bad lot. Crazy people. Murderers. And the swastika was their symbol. They flew that flag instead of the German flag. The two things are not the same.' This was how my teacher should have handled it. It was what they now call a 'teachable moment', and I began to understand the real difference between the Germans and the Nazis and, moreover, to understand that the Nazis were not really the boo-hiss comedy fall guys that were portrayed on TV entertainment shows.

Still, none of this really explained my father's tolerance towards the Germans, to a people who had voted for leaders who sent armies to run amok over Europe in a war that ultimately robbed him of a homeland. Understanding that came years later while I was helping Dad sort through some of the 'important papers' in his wooden bureau and we came across his naturalisation certificate, the document that guaranteed him British citizenship. He was proud of his British identity and prouder still of being Scottish. Yet he saw no contradiction in also calling himself Polish. He was proud of that too. As I looked at his documents my eyes fell on the section of one form indicating Dad's country of birth. Where I had expected to see 'Poland' was the word 'Germany'. I looked at him, perplexed.

'You're German?' I asked.

He laughed. 'No, no, I was born in Germany. My mother and father were working there when I was born. They moved back to Poland when I was six weeks old. Besides, borders in Europe move all the time. Some parts of Poland used to be Germany; some parts of Russia used to be Poland. It's the politicians and the generals who care about these things. That's why wars start.'

I looked from him to the documents and back again, thinking this was probably the most profound thing he had ever told me.

'Yes, I was born in Germany,' he said. 'So you know what this means?'

I didn't. I was wondering if he was going to ruin the moment with some ghastly revelation about him secretly working for the Nazis. Instead, he came out with something much more fanciful.

'It means you're only one generation down. You can be called up to play football for Germany ... or Poland ... or Scotland.'

And this was true, but by the time I discovered this I was in my thirties and had chosen a different path in life. Not sport and not art. No amount of football coaching now or ever was going to get me into the squad for any of those countries. But at least I had a couple more teams I could support when Scotland failed to qualify for the next World Cup.

All I needed was the right flag.

THE SHOCK OF THE BUNNY

Three years after the Beatles broke up and a few months before the Bay City Rollers broke through, the world was going mad for pop stars Donny Osmond and David Cassidy. In the early seventies, teen and pre-teen girls were expected to choose between one of those two darling 'D's and to festoon their bedroom walls with posters of their favourite heartthrob. But not my sister, Rose, who, at the age of thirteen – so a proper rebellious teenager – gave her heart to Neil Reid.

'Neil who?' you might be asking and that would be fair enough, because Motherwell's most celebrated singing son had but a few years of fleeting fame after winning the 1970s equivalent of *Britain's Got Talent*. The original version of *Opportunity Knocks* was presented by Hughie Green, who, in his mid-Atlantic drawl and with his catchphrase 'I mean that most sincerely, folks,' introduced the nation to an array of acts that must have been idling in a showbiz holding pen since the death of music hall. Alongside genuinely talented singers like wee Neil, Mary Hopkin and Lena Zavaroni, comedians would tell jokes about their mothers-in-law, men in capes would spin plates, a dog would howl while his master played a musical saw, and a man in skimpy underpants would flex his biceps and triceps to the rhythm of a cha-cha tune. Each week six acts would perform for the studio audience and their enthusiasm would be measured by an on-screen 'clapometer'. That element of the format, Hughie would remind us, was 'just for fun' because it was 'your votes at home that count'. Viewers needing that extra incentive to send a postcard to Thames Television at Teddington Lock were offered the chance to win a Government premium bond. Neil Reid with his heartstring-tugging rendition of 'Mother of Mine' stormed his way to the top spot, and Rose, watching this kilted cutie on TV and realising that she and he were exactly the same age, fell in love.

It's not easy following a star who isn't part of the mainstream pop culture. Fans of Donny or David had so much merchandise they could buy to signal their allegiance. There were shirts, bags, watches and the aforementioned posters, but Neil Reid fans had to improvise. A friend of my brother's used permanent ink markers to make Rose an 'I Love Neil' tee-shirt. Our Uncle Jimmy wrote a letter to the young singer's record company, Decca, and managed to obtain a small collection of glossy photographs, and a bloke at the Barras market made Rose a Neil Reid badge with that plastic Dymo tape normally used to label electrical appliances. The *pièce de résistance*, of course, was the live Neil Reid lookalike she took with her to his concerts. That lookalike, I'm afraid to say, was me.

At nine years old, with blond hair and bad teeth, I looked nothing like the handsome young star, except in one superficial respect. Rose had persuaded Mum to buy me a khaki safari jacket which she was convinced was identical to one she had seen Neil wearing in some of his publicity shots. To me it looked more like the jackets I'd seen old men wearing when they tossed bowls down at Blairtummock Park. It had pockets and buckles everywhere and was made from an unyielding synthetic fabric. It had a lapel so stiff and wide that a strong gust of wind could easily have sent me airborne. I hated wearing it but Rose bribed me with Caramac bars and so I agreed to don it 'on tour', as we followed Neil Reid to his various gigs across Scotland. Attending a concert at the Kelvin Hall in Glasgow was easily done. Neil's city centre gig wasn't exactly a sell-out, although the hordes of screaming girls in the audience at least gave me some comfort that my sister was not alone in her crazy devotion. Travelling to his concert in Hamilton, on the other hand, required three separate bus journeys there and three more to get home afterwards. As tiresome as this was, Rose felt it was worth the trip because she entertained the fantasy that my jacket would change her life. I can't remember the exact details of her delusion, but it involved Neil spotting me in the audience, seeing the jacket, acknowledging me as some kind of kindred spirit and therefore inviting both of us backstage for a chat. At this point in the fantasy Neil would take note of my beautiful sister, ask if he could see her again and, blah de blah, they would get married and live happily ever after in his hometown. Not many fairy stories end in a Motherwell dream sequence, but that one did. All that was missing was a happy epilogue where I took a match and lighter fluid to the jacket and watched it burn.

Events didn't quite turn out that way, but we did get to meet the star as he signed autographs after the shows and Rose did end up living with Neil for a time. Not in his house, but in ours, and not Neil the singer, but Neil the bunny rabbit. You see, my sister had taken to naming various pets after her idol. It had started with Neil the goldfish, who went the way of all goldfish, and was replaced by Neil the yellow canary. When Neil the canary fell from his perch for the last time, he was replaced by Neil the rabbit. Somewhere between the fish and the canary there had also been Neil the hamster, but his fate remains clouded in mystery and a degree of guilt. Found cold and still in his cage one morning, the hamster was placed in a small shoebox and given a decent burial in the local woods. When, some days later, information emerged about the hibernation habits of hamsters, there was talk of an exhumation, but that was ruled out on the grounds that it would be just too damn creepy.

Neil the rabbit lasted much longer than all the others and developed a local following of his own. This was not because of any unusual rabbit skills; he couldn't sing or even perform coney gymnastics to the sound of the cha-cha. What made Neil the rabbit a neighbourhood sensation was his remarkable friendship with another pet, the dog that belonged to my sister's friend Liz. It was a greyhound. Just imagine the scene: Liz would put a collar and lead on her pet greyhound and Rose did the same with Neil. Together they walked the streets, allowing the skinny dog to sniff at trees and lampposts and look on happily as the fluffy rabbit nibbled on buttercups and dandelions. It was like something from a Disney movie and it was like that for months, as neighbours would watch open-mouthed from open windows as this unlikely pairing of animals went past.

It didn't last, not surprisingly, and at this point I should warn you to look away if you don't want to know what happened next. Happily, I didn't see it for myself, but I got a graphic description from a small boy who came running up to me while I was out playing on the square. I didn't know this boy, but by association with my sister and her amazing rabbit, he clearly knew me. He broke the bad news with an economy of words and without decorating his sentences with anything approaching tact.

'Your sister's rabbit was murdered,' he told me, with unmistakable glee in his voice. 'Her pal's greyhound ate it.'

That was almost true, but not quite. For some reason, the nervous hound had taken fright when Neil had bobbed suddenly from one clump of grass to another and, before Rose or Liz could react, had taken a fatal bite out of the poor bunny's neck. By all accounts there was a lot of blood and a lot of screaming, but, as much as I might have wanted to, I never did ask for the specifics. I ran home that afternoon to find my sister sitting on the couch with a blanket wrapped around her and Mum administering spoonfuls of sweet tea. It was what they did for shock. There was no sign of Neil or what remained of him. Dad had taken care of that.

Rose got over it, of course, just as she also got over her crush on Neil Reid. Her friendship with Liz became a little strained, though, because it was understandably difficult for my sister to watch Liz out walking with the beast that had tried to devour her own pet. I was sorry to see the two of them grow apart, because I liked Liz a lot; she was like a substitute big sister to me when Rose wasn't available. More than that, she owned the most fabulous gadget I had ever seen: a cassette tape recorder. Not only did this wonderful machine allow you to record pop music off the radio, but you could also record your own voice and conduct pretend news interviews with friends and family. We had enormous fun spoofing TV adverts and putting on silly voices. I perfected my own impersonation of Hughie Green as we improvised an audio version of his talent show. It was a double dose of fun, really, because not only did you suppress your giggles to record this nonsense, but you had the joy of listening back to what you had done and laughing all over again. I'm guessing that, after a week or two, Rose began to miss chumming around with her best pal, but, boy, how I missed mucking around with that tape recorder. Happily, after a decent interval of mourning, Rose patched things up with her pal and Liz even let us borrow her fabulous machine now and then. Have I mentioned how much fun it was? Truly, truly wonderful.

Anyway, Rose's next pet was another rabbit, but this time it was a female and she called it Tina. It wasn't named after Tina Turner or any other famous person; it was 'just a nice name', said Rose. And … it escaped from its hutch one morning and was found dead on the road. You don't need the details, believe me, you don't.

They say the death of a beloved pet is a good thing for children because it teaches them about mortality and how to cope with grief. Just as they say the love teenagers feel for a pop singer or movie star is a harmless way of experimenting with emotions. Those emotions change as we grow older, of course, and perhaps we become a bit more guarded with our feelings and a bit more careful about who or what we love. As the years pass it takes a memory of Rose and her various Neils to remind me of the love I felt for my sister on the day she lost her amazing rabbit. Love that never went away exactly, but maybe got buried with the rest of life's clutter. Love that never died.

It was just hibernating.

Hmm, let me try that ending again. Press the 'play' and 'record' buttons together. That's it. Testing, one, two, three …

Love that never died. It was just hibernating, and I mean that most sincerely, folks.

Nah, scrub that. The first version was better.

TAKE ME TO THE ORPHANAGE

We were nearing the end of the bunk-bed stage of our childhood, Rose and I, when the carving knife incidents kicked off. They began one night about a half-hour or so after we had been tucked in, but before we had drifted off to sleep. Our bedroom door creaked open and a crack of light illuminated the tip of the blade that began to slide ever so slowly through the gap. We screamed, of course, and as the knife inched forward, I made a frantic effort to escape from the tangle of my sheets, blankets and candlewick bedspread and scrambled towards the protection of my sister on the top bunk. As she hauled me up towards her, I could see her eyes, wide and glassy as she watched the progress of the knife that was still moving forward behind me. Then, just as slowly, it reversed course until its steel blade disappeared completely.

Alerted by our shrieks, Mum, in her tartan-slippered feet, padded her way down the loaby – the hall corridor – and demanded to know why we were making such a racket. Dad was on an early shift in the morning, she reminded us, so we had to be quiet and get to sleep *right now*. Rose started to explain. She was the elder by three years and eleven months (not four years, as she often claimed), so I was sure that Mum would listen to her and believe her. To my eyes Rose was practically a grown-up herself.

'There was a knife—' she began, still struggling to breathe between sobs. 'It came through the door.'

'What knife?'

'A big knife. Like the one in the kitchen. The one Dad uses to cut the chicken.'

But Mum didn't believe her. 'Probably just a bad dream,' she said. 'Now go back to sleep. Think of nice thoughts. Like Christmas and chocolate … and, em, *next* Christmas.'

'But we both saw it.'

'Right, that's enough. Sleep. Now!'

And that was the end of the matter until, a few nights later, the knife came again, and again Mum told us to think those nice thoughts and go back to sleep. A week later it happened again, and this time the knife came further into the room. This time we saw its black handle and a thumb, a man's thumb. The thumb of the man who was gripping the knife. It was the scariest thumb I had ever seen, and it still is. Up on the top bunk, we tried to control our hysteria so as not to disturb Mum and Dad. As before, the knife slid backwards and vanished. The next morning, Rose and I discussed the matter and concluded that the knife was not the product of our imagination but was more likely a real knife. And it probably wasn't just *similar* to Dad's big carving knife – it was probably that actual knife. And, if that was the case, it probably wasn't being wielded by some headless ghost or other spectral entity, but by a real live person. Someone who lived among us. Trouble was, we had too many suspects, because we had six older brothers and at least five of them were known for their sinister pranks and macabre sense of humour.

The most likely suspect was Brian. Twelve years older than me, he had already tried to trick us twice, first with a mysterious door that he had built in his bedroom. This was an ordinary wooden bedroom door that he had installed with a hinged frame against his bedroom wall. Opening the door led to a black void which, he told us, was a secret passage to a cellar filled with sweets and treasure. As we stepped forward, however, we encountered only the hard wall where he had painted over the floral wallpaper. An illusion, a nice trick, but not as sophisticated as the time he tried to persuade Rose and me to hand ourselves in to an orphanage. He began casually, telling us that he happened to have been passing the window of the local orphanage and noticed that every night all the kids got to eat strawberry jelly and ice cream. Knowing that this was one of our favourite foods, he suggested a plan where we should turn up at the orphanage just before teatime and claim to have lost our memories.

'They'll give you the jelly and ice cream,' he explained, 'and then I'll come by an hour or so later and collect you. I'll tell them there was some kind of mix-up and bring you home. Just think … free jelly!'

To me, this sounded like a brilliant wheeze, but Rose wasn't convinced. Notwithstanding the fact that neither us had ever seen or heard of this 'local orphanage', she thought the biggest flaw in the scheme was that Brian couldn't be trusted to come and get us.

'You'll forget,' she told him, as he tried to maintain his sincere expression, and then she turned to me, hoping to enlist me as an ally. 'You just know he won't come for us,' she said. 'We'll be stuck there forever.'

'Och, Rose, you're spoiling it,' I told her, huffily, and turned towards my big brother. 'Just take me by myself.'

But he wouldn't. He said it was both of us or no one. For days I was furious with both my brother and my sister. I had lost out on jelly and ice cream because they wouldn't take me to the orphanage.

So, was Brian responsible for the carving knife? No, it seemed he had an alibi, as he had been away on a camping trip on the nights in question. Suspicion fell on another brother: Alan. Just two years older than Rose and also known for dark mischief, he had once arrived home nursing a bandaged arm which he unwrapped to expose a mass of orange scar tissue – the product, he claimed, of a horrific burn suffered during his narrow escape from a freak fire. As we watched in disgust he began to pick at the scabs and peel away large strips of the damaged skin and then, no, surely not, deposit these gooey strips in his mouth and swallow them. Because of course there had been no fire and no burn injury, and the soft scabs turned out to be the sticky yellow innards of Jaffa cakes which he had collected by licking away at the chocolate topping and nibbling away at the sponge beneath.

A carving knife scare seemed like an Alan sort of thing and we confronted and accused him. He denied it, naturally, but then he would, wouldn't he? What with Mum having to settle us after each scare, he wasn't going to own up to something that might also incur the wrath of Dad, who, as we were told, was on earlies at the steelworks and needed his sleep. Despite his protestations, it became the accepted part of family folklore that Alan had been the knifeman. We tried to memorise the look of his thumbs for comparison during any subsequent night frights, but there were no more.

I suppose there must have been something about me and my sister that made people much older than us want to scare the living daylights out of us. People like Auntie Jean and Uncle Jimmy.

Jean was Mum's older sister and Jimmy her husband. They had no children of their own, but Jimmy was like a big kid himself. At thirty stone, a noticeably big kid. He had been a cinema projectionist and loved the movies of Laurel and Hardy and the songs of Al Jolson. He did those tiny magic tricks that uncles tend to do, like finding a coin behind your ear or making his thumb appear to split at the joint. When the local cinema was turned into a bingo hall he found work in a glass factory, but a bad back meant he only ever turned up to hand in a sick line from his doctor and collect his wages. Auntie Jean was a retired nurse and they both lived in a semi-detached house in Tullibody, one of those wee towns in Clackmannanshire on the outskirts of Alloa and Stirling. Their house had a huge back lawn and a strawberry patch covered with netting to protect the juicy fruit from thieving birds. At the front, the house looked towards the local primary school, St Serf's, and beyond that was open countryside, the Ochil Hills and the neogothic Wallace Monument. I thought of the monument as a cross between a clockless Big Ben and a loose spire from Dracula's castle. I could spend hours gazing at it with Uncle Jimmy's binoculars. It was all quite different from Easterhouse, and when, every Easter, Rose and I were shipped off to Auntie Jean's for the school holidays, it felt like a real treat. Or, at least, it did at first.

The one thing our auntie and uncle didn't have was a television set, but they had an upright piano in their front room and Jean would teach us how to read sheet music and play tunes with both hands. Jimmy would haul out a massive cine projector and screen his collection of silent movies and old westerns. During these picture shows, the front room would be darkened, and Jean would appear with a torch and makeshift usherette's tray and serve us ice cream and bowls of fresh strawberries. All of that was good. So too were the day trips into towns like Alloa and Sauchie, where Jean and Jimmy would drive us around in their little Austin Mini and fill our heads with tales of Scottish history. It was from them that I first heard mention of William Wallace, Robert the Bruce and the Battle of Bannockburn. Astonishing as it now seems, we were taught almost nothing about Scottish history in primary school. There was lots about how the Romans invented central heating (whatever that was) and we got instructions on how to make an Egyptian water clock, but barely a mention of the events or people that had shaped our own culture in recent centuries. As might be expected at our Catholic school we learned about the apostles and saints: Andrew, Patrick and the gang. Andrew wasn't Scottish, of course, but our priest had it on good authority that Patrick had been kidnapped from Scotland when he was young, so he was ours, really. As for the rest of Scottish history, well, we fought with the English a lot of the time and we were still miffed about some stuff the Redcoats had done to us. Yet how was it that the older generation knew so much more about Scotland than we did? How was it that my auntie and uncle could take us to places like Stirling Castle and entrance us with tales of its glorious and tragic past? We climbed the two hundred and forty-six steps of the Wallace Monument and stood on its open crown, hoping the wind wouldn't whisk us away.

The attraction of these visits and tours was that the history lessons were interspersed with lunch stops at a variety of cafés and tearooms. There was a famous one in Alloa which had a resident caged mynah bird who would greet diners with 'Hello Cheeky!' I mean, with talking birds in cafés then music and movies back at the house, we hardly missed the television at all. How could we? Not when there was this kind of entertainment on offer.

But then there were the nights, after the film shows and before bedtime, when the ghost stories would be told. Why they thought this was an appropriate way to send children off to the land of nod, I'll never know, but it's what they did. Jean in particular had a deep belief in the spirit world and had even taken Jimmy along to a psychic healer of some kind to see if there could be some supernatural cure for his bad back. The way she told it, Jimmy had to arrive at the healer's house with a half-dozen fresh eggs. He would then strip to the waist and lie face down on a sofa. The healer would then *pretend* to crack the eggs over his bare back, all the while summoning a Native American spirit guide to come forward and inhabit the healer's body. Then in a voice similar to those we had heard in those old westerns the healer would chant various words and lay her hands about Jimmy's exposed flesh. It worked, apparently. Or, as Jean put it, the demon's poison was extracted from her husband's spine and he was good to go for another few weeks. Some cash would change hands and the healer would ask them to 'leave the rest of the eggs'.

Jean and Jimmy told us about the Green Lady at Stirling Castle and various other spooks, but the best of their creepy stories involved a mix of local legend and a now familiar urban myth. We've surely all heard versions of that story where a car/bus/stagecoach stops to pick up a traveller on a lonely country road; the driver and passenger then have a slightly off-kilter conversation, but at the end of the journey as the driver checks their cab/coach, the mysterious passenger seems to have vanished. In some versions of the story, the spooky traveller has been carrying a concealed sword, knife or hacksaw, depending on which era is the setting for the tale. As the bed settee in the front room was made up and Rose and I sat in our pyjamas, Jean and Jimmy assured us that these events had actually occurred on a road not far from where they lived – a country road between Menstrie and Dollar where a bus driver had stopped to pick up a single passenger. As it happens the passenger had been standing near a local landmark called Tait's Tomb, a stone-built mausoleum which was once part of a huge estate. As their story unfolded it became clear that the passenger was the long-dead Tait himself and, of course, by the time the bus reached the terminus, he was nowhere to be seen.

Now, what could make this story-telling even creepier for a nine-year-old and a six-year-old? Well, how about we wrap our dressing gowns a little tighter around ourselves, we climb into Jean's Mini and she drives to the scene of this very incident? Yep, at ten o'clock at night, there we were, parked in a country road, gazing into the darkness and looking at the outline of a structure which we were assured was the very tomb that housed the corpse of Tait himself. And hey, kids, if you're not already traumatised, let's do that trick where we pretend the engine won't restart and, hang on, is that a strange man coming towards us across the field?

Well, it was events like this that might have persuaded our parents to curtail these Easter trips to Tullibody. I don't know if they scarred me or my sister, but we both developed a love of old horror films, and yet nothing could tingle our spine like that night-time trip to Tait's Tomb.

Oh, and a final word about that carving knife. Thirty years later, I confronted my older brother Alan about the incident and told him that he could now own up. He remembered it as a source of injustice, being falsely accused and no one believing his denials.

'But I swear to you,' he said, 'I don't know who slid that knife through your bedroom door, but it wasn't me!'

So, if it wasn't him, who was it? Never you mind. Just try to get some sleep. You might be on earlies tomorrow. So, think of nice things like Christmas and chocolate and, em, next Christmas.

ENTER CAPTAIN HOOPLA!

I think we can all agree that comic-book superheroes stretch our credulity when it comes to that bit in the story where they don their costumes. Or maybe that's just me. Personally, I can suspend my disbelief long enough to allow for super-speed, x-ray vision and alternative dimensions of reality, but I'm easily distracted by the improbability of a hero's attire. No matter how good the origin story – radioactive spider-bite, child from a doomed planet, rich orphan seeking vengeance for the murder of his parents – my attention drifts as I wonder who made those Day-Glo tights and how exactly do our heroes keep them clean. Sure, Bruce Wayne has a butler to do Batman's dirty work, but is there a secret dry-cleaning operation for the Fantastic Four? Perhaps they just pop them into Timpson's on a Monday and rely on the discretion of the staff when they go back on Thursday to pick them up?

'So that's one pair of XXXL shorts for the Thing, one asbestos leotard for the Human Torch, one very stretched onesie for Mister Fantastic and, er, I had the Invisible Girl's costume here a minute ago … now where did I put that?'

Also, how does Spiderman's alter ego, Peter Parker, fit his shoes and street clothes into that tiny backpack while he is web-slinging, and why does no one ever comment that Clark

Kent's suits look rumpled when he's wearing his Kryptonian vest and cape under his office shirt? I speak as someone who has trouble keeping his shirt tucked into his trousers, never mind having to contend with another layer of clothes. And please do not get me started on the Flash and how his ultra-compressed scarlet ensemble springs out of the flip-top lid of his special finger ring. A great idea, but when he is chasing down the latest super-villain, my head is a million miles away trying to figure out how he gets that red suit back into the ring. If you have ever tried to get a sleeping bag back into its original sack, then you'll know the effort it takes. Oh, and in the story, they always skip over the part where the hero actually has to get into the costume. It probably wouldn't look so slick if you saw them hopping about in an alley, trying to sort out the left leg from the right and fiddling with a sticky zip.

These sartorial conundrums were among the reasons for the delayed start to my own career as a costumed crime-fighter in the east end of Glasgow. I had always fancied the notion of having a secret identity, but there was no point pulling your shirt open if, instead of a fancy insignia, all your enemies could see were freckles. If I spotted sticks or pieces of wood lying on the road, I would pick them up, strike them on the ground and hope, like Donald Blake in the original Thor comics, I would be transformed into a Norse god. Nope. No flash of lightning, no roll of thunder. Just skelfs. Then one day, I got lucky. Or rather, I got a lucky bag.

Lucky bags, for those who need reminding, were those treats we kids bought from sweet shops or ice cream vans. Not exactly a pig in a poke, unless yours happened to contain toy farmyard animals, but the same idea. You never knew what might be in them, but you had a fair idea you would get some cheap, tasteless confectionery, maybe a mini colouring book and a plastic toy.

63

Think Christmas cracker novelties but without the snap. You were really paying for the anticipation while absorbing the life lesson of crushing disappointment that would serve us well as adults when lottery scratch cards came along. Yet there was once, just once, that I opened my lucky bag and found something folded inside which would, I knew, change my life, and potentially save the city, if not the galaxy. It was the key to my new identity. It was my very own superhero costume. And it allowed for the birth of Captain Hoopla – would-be enemy of the Easterhouse gangs. Taking on the gangs was a natural objective for me as a born do-gooder. Listen, I was the guy who had won the school's best behaviour prize three years in a row. I'm the boy who picked up other people's litter in the playground. I'm the idiot who thought there was a link between using bad language and jail time. I never swore and in fact I had a bit of a reputation as a curse-free kid. In my head, I was hero material.

The costume, I have to admit, was not specifically designed for crime-fighting. It was, in fact, a facsimile football shirt fashioned in the same thin polythene that's used for supermarket carrier bags but with holes cut for neck and arms. The idea was that you would collect these coloured tabards of the various English top division teams until you had a complete set. Not being a football fan, I had no idea whether my blue top was meant to honour Everton or Chelsea, but I simply realised its potential to strike fear into the heart of evil-doers, especially if I were to make my own adaptations. These included the use of some black duct tape to create a massive 'H' emblem on the front of my plastic shirt. Next came Captain Hoopla's amazing weapon. Yep, you've guessed it: a plastic hula hoop. The clue's in the name, really.

The hula hoop was popularised in the late fifties and early sixties as a funky way to keep fit and lose weight. We've all seen those back and white images of beautiful young women spinning the hoops around their waist with a gyrating pelvis. I really have no idea how I came to own one. I think it was part of the family collection of bits and pieces stored in the dank hall cupboard that housed the gas and electricity meters. It was wedged at the back along with broken Scalextric cars, leaky water pistols and a single boxing glove. But this was to be my weapon of choice, and no one was more impressed than I was with my ability to send it spinning forward with a wrist-twist of backspin before it paused a few yards ahead of me then returned to my waiting fist much like Captain America's shield. I was now ready to venture out into the mean streets of Easterhouse and face my foes. I imagined hunting down the marauding bands of thugs, knocking the chibs and shivs from their hands with my fast-spinning hoop and, with a steely gaze, pointing to the large 'H' on my chest and warning them not to cross my path again.

'Be gone, you oafish yobs,' I might yell, 'or face the wrath of Captain Hoopla, who will show no mercy next time we meet!'

Yeah, well, that's how I imagined it, but it didn't quite turn out like that. Having donned my Hoopla gear and slipped out of the house, I ventured down to the playing fields where it was known that rival gangs would battle it out on Saturday nights. On Saturday mornings, however, things were quite different. The pastoral scene around me was disappointing: boys were kicking footballs and little girls were marking out the shape of a house in the gritty sand and putting dolls to bed in an imaginary nursery. Where, I wondered, could I find trouble to shoot?

The gangs, after all, were not a product of my imagination. I knew quite a bit about them. I knew their names and the territories they claimed as their own. There was the Drummy, the Pak, the Den-Toi and the Skinheads, to name but a few.

Most notorious of these was the Drummy, who hailed from the streets around Drumlanrig Avenue near my primary school. Likewise, the Den-Toi had sprung from Denmilne Street. There had been many sensational and sensationalised newspaper articles written about the Drummy and their rivals, and about the general upsurge in teen violence in Glasgow's peripheral housing schemes. Where once the city's Gorbals area was synonymous with the culture of the hardman, now reporters from all over Britain were writing stories about 'the schemes'. Those stories helped create the reputation that Easterhouse began to gain (and has struggled ever since to shake off) as a place where everyone was stabbing each other just for the fun of it. You could also read about the special Flying Squad of plain-clothed cops that had been created to deal with this social problem; the so-called 'untouchables' were said to patrol the streets after dark and be ready to leap from their unmarked Bedford van and mete out swift physical punishment to knife- and sword-wielding maniacs. That was the myth, anyway, but there was little evidence that this was making a difference. The gangs roamed freely and seemingly with impunity.

Once, in my pre-superhero days, Danny Pryce and I had had a close encounter with two of these gangs – the Skinheads and the Toi – on a late afternoon saunter down by the railway tracks near Easterhouse train station. Climbing the station steps back up on to the main road, we found ourselves trapped in the no-man's land between the two gangs, who were each brandishing an array of weapons including – I swear to you – old cavalry swords as well as hatchets and butcher's knives. We knew not to head towards the Skinheads, because they had taken up position on the road leading out of Easterhouse and up towards Swinton and Baillieston. But our way home was also blocked by the mouth-foaming foot soldiers of the Toi, and although our mop-top haircuts were unlikely to see us mistaken for their rivals, it still felt like a risky move to walk towards and through them. There was no obvious escape route until we spotted an elderly man walking his dog up the hill towards the Toi. We rushed over, making the dog bark, and pleaded with the man for safe passage. He was suspicious but didn't shoo us away and so, with an adult and dog for security, we made it through the ranks of the Toi. At a safe distance we turned to see them charge towards the Skinheads and disappear over the hump of the railway bridge.

Such fear, I now decided, would never chill the heart of Captain Hoopla, and when, that day on the playing fields, I finally spotted a group of lads scrawling graffiti on the white wooden goalposts, I knew it was time for my alter ego to make his debut into the world of righting wrongs and exacting justice. The boys – four of them – were about my own age, perhaps a year or two older, but they were strangers. That is to say, they were not from our street, though I recognised two of them from my school playground. As I approached them, they turned and saw my red plastic hoop and the black 'H' emblazoned on my carrier bag costume, and, I must now admit, it seemed the sight of me did not paralyse them with terror. In fact, they laughed.

'What the ... who are you meant to be?' said the boy with the Magic Marker, pausing midway through inking an expletive on the upright post of the goals.

'I'm Captain Hoopla,' I told them, with my chest puffed out that extra half-inch my skinny frame was capable of puffing. 'You shouldn't be writing bad words like that.'

'Bad words? You mean swear words?'

'Yes, now be gone with you!'

'Why, what are you going to do about it if we don't?'

I gripped my hoop a little tighter and raised it in front of me.

This, I have to say, provoked more laughter, and, incensed, I felt I had no alternative but to let them have a taste of my plastic. I flexed my wrist to achieve the necessary backspin effect and let loose with my mighty hoop. Then, in a move I had not quite anticipated while training for this kind of moment, one of the hoodlums simply reached out and grabbed it.

'Now what?' said Magic Marker thug.

'Return my hoop!'

'Suppose we don't?'

For this I had no quick answer. In the comic books, things did not go like this. Villains were either felled swiftly by the hero's weapon or else they scattered and fled.

'Wait a minute,' said one of the other yobs, one I had recognised from school. 'Are you not that boy? The one that doesnae swear? Aye, it's him. Grab him and we'll make him do it!'

And thus began Captain Hoopla's half-hour of torture as the four of them man-handled me to the ground and one of them sat on my chest demanding that I read aloud the obscenity he had scrawled on the goal posts. It began with an 'F'. You know the one I mean.

'Say it!' screamed my chest-sitter. 'Just say it! Say it or we'll kick your head in!'

Now let me pause the action here for a moment, dear reader, while I say a thing or two about swearing and bad language, and for that I need to fast-forward forty years or so to a point in my life where I wore a shirt and tie and went to very important meetings in London and where metropolitan executives liked to prove they had street cred by (a) *not* wearing a tie and (b) lacing their presentation with the odd F-word. Trouble is, they were usually quite rubbish at doing it, the swearing, I mean. There was always that self-conscious pause while they inserted the shock expletive and then another pause before they offered a false apology. I guess they were trying to suggest that they were so passionate about what they were telling us about, say, market trends in media consumption that they simply forgot themselves and got carried away in the moment. It never rang true. Real swearing, the kind you hear on the streets of Glasgow or Liverpool, is just part of everyday conversation and it doesn't necessarily imply anger or frustration. Sometimes it can actually soften a statement by making it funny. It's just vocabulary after all. Posh executives swearing badly sound as daft as people who try to insert Latin phrases into their conversation without being sure about how to pronounce it. If you can't do it well, don't even try. *Acta non verba*, as you should never say.

But let's return to the action and our hero, Captain Hoopla, being squashed on the ground and forced to abandon one of his sacred principles by swearing. Did he succumb? Did he give in to the subsequent salvo of punches and kicks? No, he did not.

The idiot.

After a while, even the thugs grew tired of this game and offered me a way out by allowing me to say 'bloody' instead of the F-word. I was sorely tempted by this proposal, but Captain Hoopla could not give in. His integrity was at stake.

The idiot.

I limped home nursing my wounds, shedding what remained of my flimsy tabard. I was also, alas, hoopless. At the time, this level of casual brutality was commonplace, an accepted part of Easterhouse life. Rarely a day went past when you didn't see kids thumping each other. Sometimes you saw adults doing the same. It was this undercurrent of menace that had, at some subconscious level, inspired my desire to bring peace to my sometimes unfriendly neighbourhood. So, I told myself that this could not be the end of my superhero career. I also told myself that I had been pretty lucky not to have encountered an actual Easterhouse street gang. And I told myself that I had retained some shred of dignity by holding to my principles. I simply needed to regroup and rethink my strategy.

Captain Hoopla was not beaten. All he needed was a new hoop and maybe a better costume.

He could rise again.

The idiot.

WHERE SEAGULLS DARE

I was eleven years old when I managed to sneak into the American president's bedroom, but I don't suppose he minded. He wasn't there at the time. In fact, he had been dead for five years. Besides, you can blame the National Trust for Scotland for my sneakiness. It was their fault and I still have a chip on my shoulder about that. Just a tiny one. Let me explain.

It all started with a school trip to Ayrshire. It was always somewhere in Ayrshire. On a certain day in June, perhaps a week or so before the end of term, a single-decker bus would arrive in the school car park. It was described as a luxury coach because the seats were covered in a warm carpet-like material rather than the cold vinyl of the Glasgow Corporation buses. We would be transported to the coast for a few hours of fresh air and fun. If we were unlucky there would be some educational content thrown in. The only thing that changed from year to year was where exactly we would end up. One year we might be bussed to Ayr or Saltcoats and the next it would be Troon or Largs, or any of those once-popular seaside resorts which were put into the shade by the advent of package holidays to the Balearics. The actual town of Ayr was the preferred destination for us kids because it had a beach, a fun fair, fish 'n' chip shops, a miniature railway and a number of amusement arcades where shelter could be sought in the event of rain. More often than not, it did rain. We're talking about Scotland in mid-June, after all, and as every Scottish child knows, the really good weather only begins in August and usually on the very day you start back at school after the summer holidays.

This particular June, though, in 1974, the day started bright and sunny and we piled into the bus with the usual haste to grab our preferred seats. Boys made for the back, with the worst troublemakers securing their place at the rear window so they could pull faces and make gestures at drivers in following traffic. Girls tended to sit towards the front of the bus and teachers sat as close as possible to the driver so as to shield him from some of the mayhem. Danny Pryce and I as usual sat somewhere in the middle, but individual seating arrangements had been worked on for weeks beforehand through detailed negotiations and the oft-repeated question 'Who are you going to sit beside on the bus trip?' That seating plan might change a hundred times before the actual day of the trip because huffs, sulks, slights and other temporary breakdowns of friendships would have led to different pairings and partners. We got on board carrying enough provisions to last a week, having neglected to mention at home that the school was providing a packed lunch of actual food, rather than the crisps and confectionery that we had persuaded our parents would be the best things to sustain us on this epic hour-long journey through the wild west of Scotland.

As was our teachers' wont, our destination would not be revealed until we reached it. This element of mystery lent itself to ludicrous speculation as we headed through the south side of Glasgow and past Kilmarnock. 'I bet we're going to Edinburgh,' one boy might say; 'No, I think it's London,' another would counter. Both guesses reveal that, despite seven hard years of schooling, we had no sense of distance nor direction. As the bus made its way through the Ayrshire countryside, a teacher told us that we were about to be treated to one of the most famous optical illusions that Scotland had to offer. This was the Electric Brae – a stretch of road where a quirk of the landscape gave the impression that a downward slope was actually going upwards. To demonstrate this, the driver was instructed to switch off his engine and release his handbrake and, wow, look at that, the bus was actually rolling uphill. Or so said everyone else. I couldn't actually see this myself, but I didn't want to be left out of the whole 'oohing and aahing' moment, so I joined in enthusiastically. Then it was time to restart the engine and head to our destination for the day, which was – pause for drum roll – Culzean Castle!

Now, just to prove that I've developed a certain maturity and hold only the tiniest of grudges against the National Trust for Scotland, I'm going to suggest that you visit Culzean Castle yourself. It's a thing of beauty and its location, surrounded by the country park and looking out to the sea, is stunning. The interior is no less impressive, with a red-carpeted spiral staircase leading to gloriously restored rooms depicting the castle's history and even its association with former American President Dwight D. Eisenhower, who was gifted use of a room at the castle as a thank you for his part in winning World War 2. Just one room, mind you, not the whole castle. In Scotland we obviously don't get too carried away with these gestures of gratitude.

That day, as the bus rolled toward the gates of the grounds, stays forever etched in my mind because it was the day I realised that coming from a place like Easterhouse made us, in the eyes of some, lesser beings. Yep, once the guards and officials at the gate discovered we were a party of some thirty oiks from a Glasgow housing scheme, we were refused entry. At first, sitting

73

on the bus, we didn't realise that this had happened. We saw our teachers, red-faced and angrier than we'd ever seen them before, remonstrating with said officials and pointing to sheets of paperwork and then at the bus and then at the castle, and as things seemed to be heating up, we began the chant of 'fight, fight, fight'. In hindsight, this probably didn't help persuade the castle jobsworths that we were a group of perfectly behaved and academically minded students similar to the coach-load of blazer-clad pupils from the posh school who had been allowed entry just ahead of us. The security guards must have looked at our bus and seen something akin to Barbarians massing at the gates of Rome.

Our chants ceased when the teachers climbed back aboard the bus to tell us of the deal they had negotiated with the officials. We weren't allowed to enter the castle because it was felt we might do some damage to the antique artefacts, but we would be allowed to enjoy the grounds and to visit the small horseshoe-shaped beach below the castle. That sounded good enough to most of us, and there wasn't too much wailing and gnashing of teeth because we had been denied the chance to soak up some architectural history or admire some suits of armour. If all we were permitted to do was run about on a sunny beach, then we'd just have to take that on the chin. We could console ourselves with the fizzy drinks and snacks we had brought along, or at least what was left of them, since most of those had been downed about five minutes after the bus had pulled out of the school car park. But, while my fellow classmates were philosophical about this turn of events, the injustice of such discrimination left me feeling outraged. And it was the first time I realised that the reputation of our home turf would impact on how we might be viewed by outsiders, by authority figures, by people in other parts of Scotland and, in all likelihood, by future employers.

'Oh, so you're from Easterhouse?' I could imagine the question at a job interview. 'Well, we'll just cut this short and show you where the door is. No need to waste time frisking you for weapons.'

These thoughts, these dark and bitter thoughts, persisted in my mind as we made our way down the steep staircase that led to the beach. It had been deserted but for some gulls that scattered as we played football or paddled tentatively in the shallow waves. When some of our sugar-fuelled energy had been depleted, our teachers brought out the boxes that contained the school's official packed lunches and these were handed out bag by bag. Each of these included a cheese sandwich, a chocolate biscuit, a carton of fruit juice and, much to everyone's horror, a cold mutton pie. No one wanted the mutton pie. No one would have wanted those pies even if they had been hot. No one, that is, except Big Dunc, a large boy with broken spectacles who wore the same clothes week in and week out and was known to have come from, as we called it, 'a broken home'. We knew this because Big Dunc's surname changed from month to month and his details were regularly being amended in the class register. Big Dunc, we also knew, had a big appetite, so when one of us offered him their unwanted mutton pie, Big Dunc happily accepted it. Seeing this opportunity, the rest of us surged forward to demonstrate similar generosity. He tried to eat each pie before another was given to him, but even for a boy with such legendary capacity for scoffing, that proved impossible. No matter how quickly he ate, the pile of pies in his hands grew from three to five, and then to ten, until finally he was balancing a column of twenty cold pies.

That's when the gulls began their attack.

Dunc began to run, but the gulls circled him, screeching as one after another they swooped down on his teetering tower of pies. Some birds only managed to peck out a chunk of the pastry, but others, the stronger and greedier gulls, were able to carry off entire pies in their beaks. The sight of Big Dunc, his broken spectacles drooping over his nose as he ran across that beach surrounded by flapping gulls and airborne pies, was one of the funniest things we had ever seen. We all laughed helplessly, even the teachers, and Dunc's ordeal only ended when he headed towards the water, waded up to his knees and threw the pies into the sea.

Thinking back to this incident now, I can see the cruelty in our laughter. We laughed because a boy who had clearly had more than his fair share of problems had suffered the further indignity of being the obvious repository of unwanted food. This was not Billy Bunter and comic gluttony. For all we knew, those pies might have been the closest thing Big Dunc had come to a proper meal in days. We had heard rumours about his family life – siblings in trouble with the cops, parents on the booze – and of course we judged him because of his torn and dirty clothes and his spectacles held together by sticking plasters. The rest of us in that school were hardly millionaires. Far from it. In fact, most of our mothers eked out a household budget thanks to the weekly Government handout that was the Family Allowance. But we didn't regard ourselves as poverty-stricken. One of my classmates had boasted that her parents had just bought a refrigerator with a freezer compartment and she could now make her own ice lollies. Another was having a telephone installed. John Murphy's folks had just rented a colour television and he had been amazed to discover Star Trek characters wore jumpers in different hues. My own father was one of just a handful of parents who owned a car – recently upgraded to a second-hand Vauxhall Viva – so we were clearly better off than some; better off than the likes of Big Dunc, who was *really* poor.

A lesser being. That was our unspoken judgement, just as the castle officials had judged the lot of us because of the school we had come from, the streets where we lived and the absence of smart blazers.

After lunch, a proper massive game of football was organised – boys versus girls and teachers – but my mind kept returning to the castle above the beach. The forbidden castle. I opted out of the game and climbed back up the steep cliff-side steps and joined a line of pupils from another school who were being allowed entry. No one tried to stop me and soon I was inside and admiring the aforementioned staircase, the priceless antique vases and paintings, and the Stars and Stripes adorning the room that had been allocated to Eisenhower. I discovered that, in 1945, the castle had been given to the National Trust for Scotland by its owners, the Kennedy family, as a way of avoiding inheritance tax. That donation had included the stipulation that the American general and future president should be given rooms for his personal use. I continued my exploration, feeling like the kind of undercover agent that Eisenhower himself would have admired, had I been in his service. I also felt a sense of satisfaction that I had in small measure beaten the system and had made it through this particular barrier. I wandered from room to room, imagining how easy it might be to steal some of the artworks or silverware (just to get my own back on the snobs) and losing all track of time. When, finally, I walked out of the castle, smiling at the security guard, I noticed two things: the weather had changed to the usual June rain and all my schoolfriends were sitting on the bus, with teachers roaming the grounds outside calling my name. I dashed across and got back on board to hear the cheering news that we weren't going straight home, but instead we were taking an unplanned trip a few miles up the coast to Troon, where, we were told, there would be lots of fun things to do.

And maybe there is, if the weather is good, but when you are ten or eleven years old, Troon in a downpour does not have a lot to offer, or at least it didn't then. We ventured towards the beach, but the rain ruled out any hope of more games and forced us to retreat en masse into one of those brick-built shelters they had in seaside towns of that era. Then someone spotted the flashing coloured lights of an amusement arcade and off we went – teachers too – to fritter away any coins we might have on one-armed bandits, penny falls or those games where you bet on toy racehorses that chase each other around a circuit within a glass globe.

Two of our teachers had discovered a machine that looked like something from another world and, having exhausted our own cash, we all craned around them to see it for ourselves. It was like a television set mounted within a wooden cabinet and framed in yellow. Below the frame were two silver dials, one for each player. On the black surface were white bars and a moving square blob which travelled across the screen until it was swiped by one of the white bars being controlled by the player at the other side. Back and forth went the white blob, like a slow-motion game of table-tennis. The word emblazoned at the top of the cabinet read 'Pong'; it was one of the first arcade video games ever made and the first we had ever seen. The fact that you could control images on a television screen seemed beyond fantastical. Until then, things you saw on television were controlled by people and powers far away and beyond our ken. We watched our teachers play this game again and again while we waited in vain for the rain to stop. But it only did when we were back on our luxury coach, heading north then east, back to Glasgow, back to Easterhouse and back to reality.

We all had a glimpse of the future that day, but I felt I'd gone one better than the others. By sneaking into a rich man's castle I had, despite the efforts of the National Trust for Scotland, crashed through one tiny barrier of class prejudice. Sometimes the only way to get through forbidden doors is to sneak past the guards.

Like I said, those school trips were usually fun, but they could be educational too.

ROLL OVER, BEETHOVEN

On reflection, I spent far too many of my schooldays suffering the pointless miseries of unrequited love. It was bad enough that I would develop a crush on girls my own age, but the real waste of time began when I started to fall head over heels in love with my teachers. Luckily, I never shared these secret thoughts with the teachers in question, although I came close. Too close. I drew up plans and strategies as to how I could engineer a situation that would allow me to declare my feelings. I then entertained fantasies about what would happen next. In Primary 3, for example, I gave my heart to Miss McGrotty, a nervous young teacher with a surname that made her the object of mockery among my uncouth fellow classmates. Being the sole Jeffrey in a school full of Harrys, Gerrys and Dannys, I was no stranger to such nomenclature abuse, so perhaps it was this that drew me to her and allowed me to imagine the scenario where I met her outwith school hours – a seemingly chance meeting on a bus journey, perhaps – and developed a friendship that would, after she stopped denying her heart's desire, lead to marriage. I knew I could not offer her much, but a name change was something she might want badly enough to accept my proposal. I shared these imaginings with my sister and it was she who brought me back down to earth.

'You are seven years old and she's about twenty-five,' Rose explained, in case this fact had slipped my mind, 'so don't ask her to marry you just yet. In fact, do not, *under any circumstances*, tell anyone else what you just told me. Not. Ever.'

She was right, of course, although I was unaware of such age gaps preventing big Hollywood stars from choosing young brides for a second or third marriage. Hollywood, you see, was the source material for my delusions and Hollywood musicals in particular. If you really want to blame one particular star, it would have to be Gene Kelly. On TV I had seen *On the Town*, *Singin' in the Rain*, *Brigadoon* and many more ... and those movie stories were always about an unlikely love affair that survived multiple missteps and obstacles to reach that happy-ever-after moment. Oh, and those songs! They put a smile on your face for the whole human race.

Yet I was a fickle romantic. By Primary 5 I had transferred my affections to Miss Beaton, whose rosy complexion and sense of humour won me over from the start of term. She could defuse bad behaviour in the classroom with a jokey remark such as a threat to lock offenders in the stationery cupboard and leave them there until the morning. A threat that only I took seriously, imagining that overnight incarceration among the pens, pencils and Crayola crayons might provide a way to move our relationship forward. I imagined Miss Beaton locking me up and then becoming distracted by another teacher just as the bell rang for the end of the school day. She would only remember I was in the cupboard when she got home and then, panicking, would return to the school to release me. There, in that classroom after nightfall, she would offer me a comforting hug and well ...

'You did *what*?' Rose asked.

'I asked Miss Beaton if she would lock me in the stationery cupboard.'

'You actually did that? In real life, I mean?'

'Yes. I did. I walked up to her desk and asked her if she would lock me up for the night. I sort of whispered it.'

'And what did she say?'

'She just laughed. Then she told the whole class what I had said and then everyone laughed. It was ...'

'Humiliating?'

I nodded.

'I think you're going to have to get used to that,' said Rose, with remarkable prescience.

It was around about then that I gave up on my quest for true love among the teaching staff. At least for a while. Instead I focused my attention on the raven-haired goddess who sat opposite me in class. We'll call her Jacqueline and, in the interests of sparing blushes, that's a safe bet because so many girls born in the early sixties were named after Jacqueline Kennedy, just as the Apollo 11 moon landing resulted in a glut of Neils. There was a multitude of Jacquelines in our school but none compared with *this* Jacqueline. Day after day I sat across from her in the cluster of desks known as Group 2 and hoped she would notice me with my toothy smile and mop of blond feather-cut hair. Alas, she only had eyes for the boy who sat next to me. Harry was his name and he also happened to be a star striker in the school football team. He'd won cups and medals and these had been handed around the class for us all to touch and admire. I had given them a cursory glance before passing them across to Jacqueline, who, in my opinion, lingered over them far longer than was necessary. I noticed how she had laughed and laughed at Harry's infantile jokes, jokes he had clearly stolen from TV comedians. By contrast, my own line in original urbane humour and dry wit had provoked nothing but a confused frown. Neither was she impressed when, week after week, I came top in the

Friday morning dictionary quiz – a game in which we had to identify a mystery word before Miss Beaton had finished reading the definition.

All of this happened a long time ago, but I can now say with absolute certainty that I made no impression on Jacqueline whatsoever. I know this because, some years ago, when that precursor of Facebook, Friends Reunited, allowed us all to cyber-stalk our childhood sweethearts, I made contact with my former beloved. She remembered the school, she remembered Miss Beaton, she remembered Harry, of course, but as for me, she said these words in electronic form:

'I'm really sorry, but I have absolutely no memory of you at all.'

I'll grant you this was some three decades after primary school that she told me this, but I was still crushed. I thought at least she might have remembered my unusual name, perhaps my hair? The dictionary champion? But no. Nothing.

By the time I reached secondary school, yet another Jacqueline had caught my eye, but by this time the traditional love letter had given way to mix tapes. When a person wanted to express their emotions to another, all they had to do was record a dozen or so tracks on a cassette tape and hope that would convey both their intentions as well as their taste in music. This, to my teenage mind, seemed a bit hit and miss. Surely it would be better to add some spoken links between each track and hammer home the point one was trying to make. And so, that's what I did. I attached my stereo microphones to my new Waltham music centre and recorded some profound thoughts to accompany each piece of music. You may be happy to know that neither my script nor the recording has survived, but I do recall reading an entire Shakespeare sonnet prior to introducing Gerry and the Pacemakers asking a question worthy of the Stratford bard himself: 'How do you do what you do to me?'

I popped the cassette in an envelope with an accompanying letter of explanation and a suggestion that we might meet up. I made my way to my beloved's doorstep and, with only a moment's hesitation, pushed it through her letter box and ran off. I then returned home and waited by the phone. A day or so later, I received a call, not from my school-age crush, but from a grown-up woman who thanked me for the recording, told me she was flattered, but intimated that I might have got the wrong address. Indeed, I had. The flaw in my plan was not to have undertaken an adequate reconnaissance mission. Getting the wrong address was such a schoolboy error only mitigated by the fact that I was, of course, a schoolboy. Flustered, I told the woman on the phone that I had no idea what she was talking about. I suggested that it was she, indeed, who had got the wrong number. Before she could say any more, I hung up, returned to my bedroom, stuck my head under a pillow and stayed that way for a day and a half. Yep, Rose had been right. I was getting used to these episodes of humiliation.

Music played a big part in my romantic endeavours when, inevitably, I fell in love with another teacher. Despite limited musical ability, I had somehow become a member of the school orchestra and the rehearsal rooms offered a semi-legitimate place to hide and avoid the nightmare of PE lessons. There, instead of kicking balls or climbing wall bars, I would sit with my baritone horn – a brass instrument slightly smaller than a euphonium – and practise my oompah noises. The school orchestra, it must be said, was really a brass band with the addition of a few clarinet players. We'd play at school concerts and give visiting performances to local old folks' homes – setting up our stands and instruments among the armchairs in the residents' lounge and risking a wave of cardiac arrest with sudden brassy renditions of 'When I'm Sixty-Four' or 'Tijuana Taxi'. After each concert or evening rehearsal, the music teacher, Mrs Kerr, would take chosen groups of us to the Little Chef café at Baillieston and treat us to pancakes with ice cream and maple syrup. All of that was good.

Then came the arrival of a young student teacher called Miss Howie and my stupid heart – now conspiring with teenage hormones – began its nonsense again. Miss Howie took charge of the school choir and asked me to audition. She complimented me on my unusual vocal styling and noted that my voice had broken ahead of many other boys my age. What I took then as code for her appreciation of my masculine maturity was, I now realise, her diplomatic way of telling me that my voice was no good for the school choir. But in any case, I was smitten, and while Miss Howie returned to the staffroom for lunch, I walked around those music rooms with a certain swagger and flung on my parka with a swooping flourish worthy of a French musketeer donning his cape. And in that one action came disaster.

The swish of my jacket knocked something from Miss Howie's desk and I heard an ominous crash. A foot-high bust of Beethoven lay on the floor in two pieces. I was aghast. I picked them up and stared at them. Ludwig's fierce expression was no less penetrating when divided in equal halves. The opening bars of his fifth symphony would have been an appropriate soundtrack to my terror. What had I done! What could I do now! There was nothing for it but to come clean, admit to my wrongdoing and hope for a merciful hearing. I made my way to the staffroom door, knocked once and asked for Miss Howie. As I showed her the two pieces of the broken bust, I noted tears in her eyes.

'Oh, no!' she said. 'How did this happen?'

I told her about the accident with my jacket, and her look of incredulity and contempt has stayed with me to this day. There were no words of mercy and forgiveness. Instead, she told me how Beethoven's ceramic head had been a gift from a special friend she had met at music school and it had meant the world to her. She never went anywhere without it, it seemed. It was so, so precious to her. I listened to all of this with my mouth agape, struggling to produce words that would mean anything. I looked down at the broken bust.

'I think I can fix it,' I said, eventually. 'I'll ask the janitor if he has any glue or cement or something.'

At this point in the story you might as well add the soundtrack from *Mission: Impossible*, because our school janitor was not renowned for his willingness to help pupils. He regarded us all as a nuisance and often spoke about how the school would run so much better and cleaner without us lot cluttering up the place. But ask for his help I did, and he grumpily gave me a pot of some kind of industrial adhesive and I returned to the music room, removed my offending anorak, rolled up my sleeves and began my restoration project. Within half an hour the job was done and it really was difficult to spot the crack where the bust had split. Proud of myself I decided I would return to the staffroom to show Miss Howie the result of my labours, hoping to see the happiness return to her young face, and, yes, in that moment of fantasy I again imagined the possibility of a grateful embrace.

'You've done an amazing job, Jeff. That looks good as new.'

'Don't mention it, Miss Howie.'

'Oh, you can call me Cathy. Come here and let me hug you.'

Back in the real world, I placed the bust on her desk, picked up my anorak and, in a swish of misplaced confidence, knocked Beethoven to the floor again.

And this time he didn't just break in two clean pieces. He shattered and crumbled like desiccated coconut.

Stupidly, because clearly the best course of action at this point was emigration, I returned to the staffroom bearing a handful of brittle confetti and owned up to my crime. This time, Miss Howie's look was not one of mere incredulity or contempt, but it was a look tinged with the suspicion that I had actually done this dreadful thing on purpose; that I had a streak of cruelty that bordered on the psychotic. And thus, perhaps accompanied by the imagined strains of the 'Moonlight' Sonata, my quest for school romance was finally over.

This phenomenon of the crush – probably best defined as temporary but intense infatuation – is now well documented by psychologists and sociologists. The positive spin is that it demonstrates the capacity for love. At worst, of course, the infatuation can become an obsession and therein lies a potential route to incarceration that involves more than just a night in a stationery cupboard. But I tell you my stories with one strict caveat. Just as my sister once warned me, now I must ask for your assurance that you will not, *under any circumstances*, tell anyone else what I've just told you.

Not. Ever.

BELIEVE IT OR NOT

My short-lived career as a nun ended tearfully when I tore off my habit, threw it at the Mother Superior and demanded the return of the cash I had given her to buy flowers for the altar. It was, after all, most of my pocket-money for that week, and the habit – one of my sister's old blue polyester nighties – was making my neck itch. It was also the case that Rose, having appointed herself top nun, was getting far too bossy and, in my opinion, the makeshift altar on her dressing table didn't really need expensive flowers. That chipped vase full of buttercups and dandelions looked fine alongside the rosary beads strung from the mirror with Jesus on his cross taking centre stage.

Inspired, I guess, by Julie Andrews's portrayal of Sister Maria in *The Sound of Music*, Rose was going through a religious phase. Always glad to be included in her plans, this whole 'let's play at being nuns' game seemed to me like a good idea to begin with, but, as with actual religion, it all got a bit silly in the end, to my mind. There was too much kneeling and praying and even the singing was dull. There was even some crazy talk of fasting.

'You mean not eating?' I had asked. 'But for how long?'

'A week, maybe more,' said Rose.

'But I'm hungry now. Release me from my vows!'

A life in the convent, otherwise known as my sister's bedroom, was not for me. Fasting sounded bad enough, but it was mainly the money thing that clinched it for me, because that week in school I had already donated an entire sixpence to the 'Black Babies'. I'd done my bit. I'd earned my halo. Now I wanted out.

The 'Black Babies' was a fundraising wheeze run by real nuns, priests and their henchmen schoolteachers who encouraged us to donate a small amount of money each week to help starving children in a part of Africa which was being torn apart by civil war. It was a ridiculous name for a charity and suggested that if children suffering through war and famine were not enough to elicit our sympathy, then the awfulness of being black would put the tin lid on it. A perfect example of good intentions sowing racism. Our donations were tallied on a card, and once you had bankrupted yourself you were given a glossy picture of an infant which you could take with you to Heaven to prove your generosity. This picture disappointed some of my fellow pupils who assumed that their weekly cash donations were part of a hire purchase agreement that allowed you to pay for an actual baby on easy terms.

At school, the nuns and priests were always coming up with new ways to mug you on the way to the tuck shop and guilt-trip you into diverting the money you had earmarked for a bag of Rainbow Drops or a chocolate MB Bar. We once had a visit from a White Father. This was a priest, garbed in white vestments, who was doing missionary work somewhere in Africa. He was running a cash-for-trinkets racket in which your donation was rewarded with a little plastic 'miraculous medal'. This was an oval-shaped silvery gewgaw with a relief impression of the Blessed Virgin Mary on one side. You had to supply your own means of stringing it around your neck; a short length of your mum's knitting yarn would suffice. After being told all about his work converting heathens, we were called out from our desks one by one to receive our medals with the option to hand over whatever small amount of money we had in our pockets or purses.

As with so many roll-calls I endured at school, this one was done in alphabetical order, so by the time I went to hand over my tuck money to the White Father, his supply of plastic medals had run dry. With much ballyhoo, however, and provoking the envy of my classmates, he told me I could have one of his 'special' medals. This was slightly smaller than the others but was made of tin with a blue enamel inset. Checking recently on the website Holyart.co.uk, I noticed that you could pick one up for just over a quid. I got mine for sixpence, but that was back in the seventies. I'm not sure if this deluxe version of the medal granted me extra privileges. Perhaps when I got to Heaven, I would be allowed into a VIP enclosure. If so, it would have been well worth the half-shilling I had paid for it. Imagine me on a cloud, quaffing champagne, angels with supermodel looks draped either side of me, while my newly dead friends looked on trying to conceal their seething jealousy.

But it wasn't only this endless quest to empty the pockets of schoolchildren that put me off religion. I was, for example, quite happy to buy the monthly *Crusader* magazine. The pocket-sized publication contained stories and puzzles and, probably, articles about global do-gooders. The title had obvious connotations with the holy wars of the Middle Ages, and I doubt that a magazine that brought to mind conflict with Islamic forces would be allowed in today's multicultural classrooms. In any case, all that went over my head because I bought *Crusader* for its gripping serialised story about a boy living in a world where time had stood still and everyone but him seemed to be frozen in place. This captured my imagination but left me wondering why the hero didn't take advantage of his situation and maybe break into Woolworths and raid the pic 'n' mix counter. I guess that wouldn't have been a suitable plotline for a readership of Catholic schoolchildren. Still, the magazine felt worth paying for; another sixpence, if memory serves.

At home there were more papal pressures on our family finances. Dad particularly resented the parish priest's occasional unannounced visits and requests for loot to fund good causes or the upkeep of the church. Indeed, a special book of miniature donation envelopes were supplied to every Catholic household to facilitate and record such forced generosity. We made good use of them. To organise the weekly household budget, Mum used the envelopes to separate the cash for food, rent, coal, electricity and so on. Also, lost baby teeth could be sealed in an envelope and placed beneath a pillow. By morning, that very same envelope would be torn open to reveal the tooth had been replaced by a sixpenny bit. It was the kind of deal that had me, for once, thankful about the poor condition of my teeth. By my calculation I had about ten shillings' worth of treasure in my gob, and a little toing and froing with my finger could easily loosen a stubborn gnasher if I ever needed a financial top-up.

The little envelopes were never used for their intended purpose. Ever cynical and suspicious, my Polish-born dad had little trust in the various Irish priests we would encounter and their particular brand of Celtic Catholicism. He would question the destination of church donations and, when told that the priest was saving up to buy a car so as to help him get around the parish and visit 'the frail and the elderly', he snorted and predicted that, once the car was bought, the priest would zoom off into the sunset with the housekeeper and both of them would live in a caravan in Fife. Burntisland, to be specific. This

91

somewhat detailed prediction was based on a story he had read in the *News of the World* about another priest in another parish with a housekeeper who looked rather more the 'running away with' sort than the female Methuselah who looked after our own priests in Easterhouse.

Mention of Mrs Methuselah brings me to the real reason I began to question my Catholic brainwashing and even the existence of God. For all the talk about the power of love, it seemed to me that our religion was powered by fear. There was the fear of committing a mortal sin, fear that God could read your mind, fear of angry priests, fear of statues coming to life, fear of letting babies starve in Africa, fear of going to Hell and, every Monday morning, fear of being caught in a lie when the teacher asked who had and who had not attended Mass on the previous Sunday. There was a two-fold process to this weekly interrogation. Firstly, pupils who openly admitted they had skipped Mass were told to stand up and were then subjected to a bit of a tongue-lashing.

'I don't know why you are even at this school. You might as well put your coats on and walk down to Rogerfield and sit with the … Protestants.'

Although it was never said out loud, we all knew that 'Protestants' was code for 'the damned' and that the poor wee souls in Rogerfield Primary had no idea they were facing an eternity stoking coal in Lucifer's boiler room. Then came the next stage of the grilling. A random selection of those who had remained seated were now asked details about the Mass they claimed to have attended. It was like a game show with hellish consequences if you gave the wrong answer.

'What colour were the priest's vestments? Green, purple, red or yellow? You have no more lifelines. Final answer? Oh dear, you had a purified soul. You've just LOST your state of grace. You're going home with nothing … except a guaranteed stay in Purgatory.'

An encounter with the priest's housekeeper was the incident that finally shook my faith. In Easterhouse, the Priest House at St Clare's sat alongside the church itself – a prime example of block sixties architecture which still stands to this day, despite the demolition of the adjacent school. In front of the church there was a sizeable grassy lawn, bordered by flower beds, and it was always beautifully tended. We children were told that on no account should we put one foot on this lawn. Not a single toe. Given that this was an instruction from the priest, we assumed it fell into the same category as all the other rules and regulations that he had told us about: don't steal, don't kill anyone and don't step on the lawn. That kind of thing. Similarly, we imagined the punishment for infraction of any of these rules would be the same. Eternal damnation awaited unless – thanks to handy Catholic loopholes – you had previously been absolved through a timely confession and penance paid.

So, on that day, when I was nine years old and two older boys grabbed my school satchel and threw it over the high church railings, I watched in horror as it landed squarely in the middle of the sacred lawn. As the bully boys ran off laughing, I gazed through those railings much like I imagined I might have to gaze through the Pearly Gates of Heaven: from the wrong side. I didn't dare walk across that grass to retrieve my bag and the books and pencils that had spilled from it. Not unless I got permission from the priest himself. I wasn't sure how easy that would be. Would the priest have to consult the church hierarchy? Would telegrams have to be sent to the Vatican? Would I need documentation from a papal emissary? Nevertheless, I walked up to the Priest House, chapped on the door and was greeted by an excitable woman in her eighties who was hustling me away from her doorstep before I could get a word out. Mrs Methuselah.

'I wonder if the Father is in …' I managed to say. 'These boys threw my bag on the grass and—'

'Jesus, Mary and Joseph. Away with you, away with you!' shrieked the housekeeper in her thick Irish brogue.

'But you see, my bag is on—'

'The Father is not here. Not here, I'm telling you. Not here! Now, go. Go!'

What to do now? I looked from the closed door to the lawn and then decided I would risk the fires of Hell and go and get my bag. I took one step over the flower bed and then another onto the grass. My heart was racing, my legs shaking, but I ventured further and further towards the middle of the lawn and grabbed my bag, scooped up my books and pencils, and at that point I paused, looked around me, looked skywards and realised that nothing whatsoever was going to happen to me. The carefully manicured ground was not going to open up and suck me into the pit. The sky was not going to darken as lightning bolts sparked towards me. My fears had been ill-founded, nonsensical even, and it began to dawn on me that this whole religion thing might be one massive practical joke. If walking on the church lawn didn't lead to immediate punishment from above, then what about everything else? Did statues really bleed? Was God really watching everything we did at all times? Could prayers really cure the sick? I thought about those long boring Sunday services and about the time I wet myself on the pew because there seemed to be no means of escaping from the church and asking permission to go to the toilet. Again, it was about fear of the consequences. And now? Whisper it, did those wafers the priest placed in our mouths every Sunday really become the body of Christ? Where, I wondered, was the evidence, the concrete evidence? I needed something more than just blind faith. I mean, you could believe in the tooth fairy because there was hard cash in a sealed envelope. No doubting that. But this God thing? Was any of it true?

Still, even as I walked home with my retrieved satchel safely strapped on my back, I wasn't ready to abandon everything I had been taught. I wasn't about to throw out the baby Jesus with the holy bathwater. I still liked some of the spooky stuff. Like how God always won against vampires.

The vampires featured in the old horror movies that my pal Danny Pryce and I liked watching on television on Friday nights. The Hammer Horrors were the best because they featured Dracula, played by Christopher Lee, locked in endless battles with his nemesis, Professor Van Helsing, played by Peter Cushing. Inevitably at some point in these movies the hero would wield a crucifix to push back the Prince of Darkness and, even as my faith in Catholicism started to waver, I still felt a certain amount of pride at being on the same side as the Christian goodies who strike terror into the heart of blood-sucking ghouls. I often imagined our priests watching these flicks and feeling just a bit chuffed. Not that they ever talked about anything as interesting as horror movies. Nope, it was all about saints and their good deeds and other dull stuff. I'm sure a few rattling good tales about ghouls and goblins would have brought in more converts.

The spooky stuff also included the thing Danny had taught me about how to communicate with the dead. No, nothing to do with Ouija boards, he said; this technique was one he had been taught by his Irish grandmother and it involved sitting in a darkened room in front of a mirror. You placed a candle in front of the mirror and peered at your own reflection while thinking of the deceased friend or relative that you wanted to have a chat with. It was important to have a crucifix close at hand just in case some evil demons decided to hijack the conversation. Nowadays you'd compare that to being hacked during an online Zoom conversation. Demons were unlikely to intrude on us in Danny's house, though, because his family seemed to have Jesus nailed to the cross in every room. Another requirement, in order to achieve the necessary amount of solemnity, was darkness. If, as was the case with Danny's bedroom, the room was not dark enough, then a blanket or sheet could be draped over both the mirror and would-be communicators to achieve a proper level of low and eerie illumination.

And so it was, one bright Saturday afternoon, Danny and I sat with a huge orange bath towel draped over our heads, staring into his father's shaving mirror while basking in the glow not of a candle but the flickering light of a bicycle lamp. All we had to do now was intone the name of the deceased party and await his or her appearance in the mirror. That's when we hit our first snag because, for the life of us, we couldn't think of anyone we knew who had died. That's the thing about being ten years old, most of your friends are still above ground and breathing happily. So, we started to think of famous folk who might have passed on. We threw out some names, but in those dark ages before Google, there was no sure way of knowing if they were still in the land of the living. Danny thought one half of Laurel and Hardy had gone to the next world but couldn't remember if it was Stan or Ollie. Then he remembered seeing something on the news about the death of the woman who played 'Granny Moses' in the *Beverly Hillbillies* TV show. Of course we had no idea what her real name was so we had to use her character name. Back under the towel we went, the bicycle lamp eking out the final glimmers from its drained battery

96

as we stared into the mirror and Danny spoke in funereal tones.

'Can you hear us, Granny … Granny Moses from the Beverly Hillbillies … can you hear us? Come to the mirror, Granny Moses … come to the mirror!'

Then it happened. The dim reflections of our own faces appeared to dissolve and out of the gloom there formed the face of the actress who, I now know, was called Irene Ryan and who had died just a few months earlier. Poor Irene would have been fresh in her grave when we started disturbing her with our no smoke and soapy mirrors antics. Not that we lingered long under cover. As soon as we saw an image in the mirror, we threw back our makeshift shroud and Danny reached for the crucifix.

'Wow!' he said, breathing hard. 'Did you see her?'

'I saw something,' I said, hedging my bets, 'but maybe it was our imagination playing tricks.'

'Or an optical illusion,' said Danny, who had remained fond of that phrase since my sister had complimented his vocabulary years before. He let his breathing steady before adding, 'But let's not do that again.'

I nodded in agreement and we passed another half-hour or so talking about anything other than dead actresses or spiritual communication. We often mused over the big philosophical questions. Where did we come from? What was there before the universe was created? If you tear a sheet of paper in half, what happens to the bit in the middle that was keeping them together? How can we be sure that we all see colours the same way? If it's raining in Glasgow but not in Edinburgh, is there a place between the two where you can stay dry but stick your hand out and get it wet? As I say, the big questions. Eventually, though, we turned our attention back to the mystical mirror and Danny came up with a brilliant idea.

'Let's try and reach someone who's not dead.'

'Like who?'

He mentioned a girl in school that we both thought was worth trying to impress with our unearthly skills, but Danny was still wary of playing with the dark forces, so I agreed to go it alone. I threw the towel over my head, stared into the mirror and called out her name.

'Come to the mirror,' I murmured. 'Come to the mirror!'

This time I had to describe what I was seeing to my pal, who was now regretting his decision to stay above ground, as it were.

'She's there,' I assured him. 'She's looking gorgeous.'

'What's she doing?'

'Not sure. She's in her own house, I think. Oh, look. Look!'

'What? I'm not seeing anything. What is it?'

'She's running a bath.'

'What?!'

'Yes, she's running a bath and now she's taking her clothes off and—'

At this point I realised I'd pushed the joke too far. Danny whipped off the towel and punched me hard in the shoulder. It was sore, but I was laughing too much to protest. Now that the bike light had finally given up the ghost, I was amazed that Danny had actually thought, even for a moment, that I could see anything in that mirror. It just goes to show that people will believe almost any old nonsense, if they want it badly enough.

THE SUMMER HUT

If you could avoid being hit by a golf ball or a high-speed train, the next worry was unexploded ammunition. Such was a walk to the beach in my childhood. The beach in question was part of the Barry Buddon army camp at Buddon Ness, that wide peninsula where the Firth of Tay meets the North Sea. Find Dundee on an Ordnance Survey map or Google and trace your finger along the coastline, past Broughty Ferry and Monifieth. If your finger skips towards Carnoustie and Arbroath, you've gone too far north, so go back. Okay, now that you've hit the right spot I need you to come slightly inland, away from the beach, through the army camp and the assault course, and follow the marked right of way over the stile, back across the railway line and to the other side of the golf course. It's there you'll find a piggery, a famer's field and, on one side of a quiet road, a line of ten well-spaced detached houses. Behind those houses there's now a site for storing caravans, but there once was some open land with a scattering of wooden huts. Ours was the big green one with the black felt roof, red brick chimney stack and white painted window frames. If you were posh you might call it a holiday chalet and if you were couthy you might call it a but 'n' ben. We called it simply 'the hut'.

Dad had bought the hut some time in the mid-1950s. He had come upon the site by chance during those post-war years when he roamed the country picking up any work he could find to provide for a growing family back in Glasgow. The hut made for cheap winter accommodation while he toiled as a labourer and then a semi-skilled metalworker in various gasworks and factories around Dundee. When he eventually secured permanent work as a welder in Glasgow, he and Mum decided the hut would make an ideal holiday home for the family, which, by 1963, numbered seven boys and one girl. By the time I came along my oldest brother was just fifteen, so the hut had to accommodate two adults (Mum and Dad), two teenagers (Frank and Ian), one infant (me) and five other brats (Billy, Brian, Michael, Alan and Rose). The cramped conditions were the price of freedom, away from the dark tenements and sooty skies of Glasgow.

The hut chiefly consisted of one long main room with a double bed at either end. In the middle there was a fireplace and a large mirror above the mantelpiece. There was also a set of drawers, a compact dining table and an assortment of chairs. There were two adjoining rooms, separated by curtains hung above the narrow doorways. One of those rooms was used to store coal for the fire. It also contained a tin bath full of sun-bleached toys – half-deflated footballs, skipping ropes, buckets, spades and a frayed cotton kite. There was a tiny kitchenette which had a sink, a dresser and a two-ring hob powered by bottled gas. Rooms were lit by a gas mantle connected by a rubber hose and a switching valve attached to the same kitchen cylinder. Shadowy nooks could be illuminated with wax candles or paraffin lamps. Fresh water came in buckets from a standpipe a hundred yards away and toilet facilities comprised a wooden outhouse or else, in the case of us boys, a quick dash into the bushes.

In the early days, Dad would take his two weeks' leave from the steelworks to coincide with the start of the summer school holidays. After that he would go back to Glasgow and would rejoin us at weekends. He would transport us en masse in a second-hand Dormobile. This was the precursor of the modern campervan and was really just a converted Bedford van like the kind you see in those old Ealing comedies about bank robbers. It had sliding doors at the driver and passenger side and two swing doors at the rear. These were particularly useful because Dad's Dormobile had a dodgy braking system, with no reliable handbrake to speak of. Dad devised a system, therefore, when climbing steep hills in stop–go traffic. Frank or Ian would be entrusted with a house brick tied to a piece of rope. As the Dormobile ground to a halt on, say, that notoriously hilly stretch outside Perth, he would give the command 'Stopping!' and one of my brothers would leap out of the back, run after the vehicle until it came to a standstill and then place the brick behind a rear wheel to prevent us slipping backwards. Then, as the traffic began to move on, Dad would give the warning 'Moving!' and the brick would be hauled back inside and, with any luck, my breathless brother would be pulled in too. There's always the possibility that I had many more than six brothers but that some were left behind on that Perthshire hillside and never spoken of again. Actually, as family legend has it, there was only ever one accident, and that had happened on a bend on the outskirts of Monifieth and involved a slow head-on collision with a sign welcoming visitors to the town. No one was hurt.

Today, a car journey from Glasgow to Dundee takes about an hour and a half, even allowing for rush-hour. Fifty years ago, that same journey would have taken more than twice as long as cars, buses and lorries crawled through tiny towns like Dunblane and Auchterarder and got snarled completely in the centre of Stirling and Perth – all of which have now been by-passed. This was a time when car radiators overheated and when drivers had to pull to the side of the road and lift the bonnet to allow the steaming engines to cool. You saw numerous such breakdowns along the route, with car occupants often using the occasion to have an impromptu roadside picnic and drink tea from tartan flasks. I suppose, in a way, the length of that journey and the sheer ordeal of travelling in a hot van without air conditioning made the trip to our hut seem like an epic adventure in itself. Even Dad's habit of chain-smoking his Embassy Regals while driving didn't dull our enthusiasm.

By the time I was old enough to read, I joined in the family excitement of watching the mileage signs count down from 100, then 50, then 30. At the first glimpse of the coastline there was just ten miles to go and we all craned forward to peer out of the windscreen for that last stretch through the outskirts of Dundee and along the Barry Road. We held our noses as we passed the piggery then, a quarter of a mile before the riding stables, Dad steered through a gap in the line of houses and we bumped and bounced across uneven grassland, weaving through other huts until we parked at the back of ours. There were yells of elation as we piled out to breathe the fresh country air and run hither and thither to see what might have changed since we had left the previous summer. Would the man who kept chickens in his back yard have added more to his flock? Would the boy who built the den in his back garden have added yet more extensions to his makeshift structure? Would the big board nailed above the standpipe still have that grim painted notice from the landowner warning children not to trespass on the nearby golf course?

We would all help to unload the car and Dad would produce the big iron mortice key that unlocked the hut for another summer. As he opened the door we inhaled that wafting odour of warm wood and coal dust. Luggage was brought inside, curtains were opened and a bucket of water was fetched from the standpipe so that Mum could make the first big pot of tea. She insisted we have a drink and a sandwich before we were let loose to properly explore the surrounding countryside, visit old friends from other huts and ignore previous warnings about straying on to the golf course. For the seven weeks of our school holidays, we only ever returned to the hut for meals and for sleep. Dad would put fingers to his teeth and produce the most piercing two-note whistle that acted as our summons to regroup. Daytime meals tended to be simple fare such as cereal, sandwiches or soup, but at night, to ensure Mum had a break from the cooking, Dad might head into Carnoustie and return with half a dozen bags of fish 'n' chips and several bottles of Irn-Bru or the tasty Pola-Cola that they sold in that part of Scotland. We would guzzle by the fireplace, under the glow of the gas lamp, our heads nodding with exhaustion after a day of fun in the sun. We children slept three to a bed and there were the inevitable moans and giggles about who had the best pillow or whose toe was jabbing into whose foot. Mum would call out for us to be quiet and we'd sleep until we were woken by the early morning squawk of hens and the squeal of pigs.

There was plenty to occupy us when the sun was shining. Mum seemed content to sit in the garden, sipping tea and catching up with the mothers of other families. Dad would survey the roof of the hut and decide if it needed a new coat of tar and felt. On rainy days, he would drive us to Arbroath and we would park at the harbour, eating the town's famous smokies – smoked haddock – from their newspaper wrappings. For many years I only ever thought of Arbroath as a place where it rained and smelled of fish. Only in my adult years did I discover such delights as Victoria Park and the nearby cliff-side trail.

There were trips to the other nearby towns. Mum did her grocery shopping in Carnoustie or Broughty Ferry. Monifieth was close enough that you could walk there and, until they were swept away in a bad winter storm, settle for the day in one of the deep grass-fringed dunes at the beach. There was a beach at Broughty Ferry too, but trips there also included a visit to a wonderful ice cream café that sold novelty rock confectionery in the shape of mermaids or baby soothers. Broughty Ferry had a cinema, as did Carnoustie, and it was in these picture houses that we watched those dreadful summer comedy films based on popular TV shows. There were movie versions of *Nearest and Dearest*, *Steptoe and Son* and *Please, Sir!* but you could tell the prints had been in circulation for a little too long. There were frequent jump cuts where snapped celluloid and hasty repairs had led to jarring edits and gaps in the storyline that made a nonsense of the plots.

Carnoustie's Gala Week dovetailed with the Glasgow Fair holiday and scores of our fellow citizens descended on the town. They swelled the audience for events such as the weekly talent show which was held on Saturday nights in the Beach Hall. Here an array of local and visiting amateur performers would strut their stuff on the stage and then a panel of local judges would decide the winner. Performances ranged from mature adults singing opera to tiny infants being ushered into the spotlight to charm us all with their rendition of 'Twinkle, Twinkle, Little Star'. There was a raffle too and the 'lucky Telegraph' competition. Here the trick was to spot a note or doodle that had been added to a page in one copy of the Dundee *Evening Telegraph* which audience members could purchase from a stack at the entrance to the hall. One year I found myself on stage being handed my prize of a small plastic torch, having, seemingly by chance, selected the doodle-doctored copy of the paper from the tall stack. This left me consumed by guilt because luck had played no part in this win. Rather I had noticed that one copy of the paper was sitting slightly askew in the pile to which it had obviously been hastily returned after the doodle had been added. I had pulled this paper from the pile and then feigned surprise and delight when I was called up to receive my reward. I take this opportunity to apologise and would gladly hand back the torch if required.

As the summer wound on, there was easy cash to be made by picking berries for local farmers. Dad would drive us to the raspberry fields early on a Sunday morning and we'd be allocated a dreel and instructed on how to pick the berries clean from their green foliage and deposit the intact fruit in plastic baskets. We were also warned against eating any of the delicious fruit ourselves as this, of course, would amount to stealing. By lunchtime, with our faces stained with incriminating red juice, our filled baskets were taken up to the farmer's van to be weighed and small change payments were doled out. On a Sunday there was only one place open where you could spend this newly acquired loot and that was at Barry Stores, an old-fashioned shop that stood on its own in the centre of the village, selling eggs, milk, bread and – let's cut to the chase – chocolate bars. Four hours of picking was quickly transformed into four Mars Bars.

On other days, assuming there was no red flag warning of artillery practice at the firing range, we could walk to Barry beach or to an area of the army camp where model plane enthusiasts were permitted to fly their radio-controlled aircraft. Watching them was fun for a while, but you easily began to despise these overgrown kids with their expensive toys, and it was a source of concealed satisfaction and mirth when one of the planes crashed to the ground and the owner had to shovel up the pieces and put them in the boot of his car. More exciting were the times when the army hoisted a massive barrage balloon carrying half a dozen squaddies per flight and then kicked them out into the fresh air. Happily, they were wearing parachutes and it was quite a sight to see the silk canvasses billowing into life and then carrying these real-life action men safely to the ground.

As the years passed and my siblings grew older, they would get jobs and girlfriends and would no longer be part of the family entourage making those summer journeys to the hut. My older brothers preferred to stay behind in Glasgow enjoying a different kind of freedom afforded by the absence of parents. Eventually it was just my sister and I who came north in the car, but we managed to keep ourselves amused with games of badminton or by cycling into the nearby towns. Once when biking back from Monifieth I tried to outstrip my big sister by pedalling faster and more furiously than I had ever done before. I kept looking over my shoulder to make sure she wasn't gaining ground, and as we reached the Barry Road with its high grass verges I was confident I would make it back to the hut well before her. But it was that last backward glance that became my undoing, because as I looked behind me, the bike steered into the hard verge and I somersaulted over the handlebars. As I hit the ground, chin first, the momentum kept me moving forward, scraping along the tarmac and leaving a small trail of skin and blood. By the time my sister reached me, I was already struggling to my feet, glad that I could actually do that and that no bones appeared to be broken.

Then Rose looked at my chin, peered upwards and, eyes wide, uttered the memorable words: 'There's a huge hole ... I can see all the way into your throat!'

I don't remember much more until I was sitting in the casualty department of the old Dundee Royal Infirmary with a doctor asking me to tell him my name and a nurse unbuttoning my trousers so she could give me a tetanus shot. Apparently, Rose's reaction had sent me into shock and I had a blank face and glassy eyes while my parents rushed me first to the local Monifieth pharmacist to have a look at my injury who then recommended a speedy trip to the hospital. Things were not as bad as my sister had described. The hole in my chin was deep and bloody, but there was no way you could shine a torch in there and illuminate my tonsils. It was a flesh wound, easily stitched together and leaving, until this day, the tiniest of scars.

Another year or two passed and then even Rose – now an independent seventeen-year-old – opted to stay behind in Glasgow, and so trips to the hut involved just Mum, Dad and me. For the first few days I was lost without a sibling companion and I wondered if I should also have stayed behind. Then a curious thing began to happen. I found a new playmate in, of all people, my father.

It's fair to say that Dad had mellowed over the years. The twenty-something Polish seaman who had married Mum had tried to be a strict disciplinarian when their brood of boys began to multiply. He had firm views about behaviour and punishment inspired by his own upbringing in rural Poland. He would threaten to take a belt to his children's backsides if they stepped out of line, and sometimes followed through on his threats. By the time my sister was born, though, he was older and gentler, and by the time I came along he had only to touch his belt buckle to remind me to stay on his good side. At the same time, perhaps realising that with me being the youngest in the family his role as a father was coming to an end, he would spend more and more time with me, taking me on late-night car journeys to spot nocturnal wildlife. During our summers at the hut he taught me to shoot, skin and cook rabbits. We went toadstool picking together and he showed me the difference between the ones you could fry for a tasty meal and the kind that would fry your brain.

One day, in his efforts to keep me amused, he salvaged the broken kite from behind the coal bin, repaired the struts and added a long tail weighted by bows of twisted newspaper. He attached a length of string and sent it aloft, and there was something about the way he looked at that kite in the sky that made me think he was, somehow, up there with it. What had started out as a fun pastime for me soon became something of an obsession for him. He found more string to allow the kite to fly even higher. When Mum called us into the hut for tea, Dad stayed outside, watching his kite fly high above the golf course and out towards the army camp. Finally, succumbing to Mum's warnings that his tea was getting cold, he tied the string to the hut porch and came inside, but continued to watch the kite from the window as it soared and danced and swooped and dived. He gulped down his tea, eager to be done with it so he could go back out to play, and that's exactly what he did. I had never seen him in such a mood. It was as if he had suddenly discovered his own childhood, perhaps the one that had been curtailed first by being sent to work as a farmhand and then by the war.

Frustrated that he had no more string to add, he summoned me to the car and we drove into Carnoustie, heading for the little haberdashery shop that sold everything from airgun pellets to washboards. It also sold those little packs of tricks and novelties beloved by children everywhere – fake dog poo, whoopee cushions, the kind of thing Dad had warned me never to waste money on – and of course string. Dad scoured the shelves and bought enough balls of it to wrap a million brown paper parcels. The journey back to the hut was hair-raising because Dad had difficulty keeping his concentration on the road ahead. He rolled down his side window and kept one eye, if not both, on the kite, which was still flying high on the horizon. Once back at the hut he lost no time in unwinding the new string, but just as he did that, the atmosphere changed. You could feel it. The wind dropped, and high in the sky the red and yellow kite began to fall. Soon it was below the tree line and out of sight, and the string connecting Dad to it went loose. I looked to him thinking I would see sadness or at least disappointment on his face, but there was only weary acceptance. It was as if the trance had been broken as soon as the kite fell.

With no alternative, Dad marched off to retrieve it, following the trail of string that was now entangled in yellow gorse bushes and the branches of tress. The sun was low in the sky by the time he returned. The kite was still in good shape, but the string was in separate balls as he had had to cut it free in several places on his trek. He handed the kite to me and I took it back to its resting place beside the coal, and when I went back to Dad's side, he said we should now drive to the beach. There was no sign of a red warning flag, he said, so we could drive up through the army camp and go to the beach there. It was always quiet and, with nightfall just two hours away, we would probably be the only ones daft enough to go there. But the evening had turned mild since the wind had dropped and he hoped we might find enough driftwood to light a fire.

That night with Dad on Barry beach remains one of my most vivid memories, not least because of what he told me and about what happened after that. We did indeed build a camp fire near the dunes, and once it was lit, we sat together watching the sparks fly into the night sky, looking out across the Tay towards Fife, to the glow of lights from St Andrews behind Tentsmuir Forest and to the red aircraft warning lights on the big television transmitter. Dad lit one cigarette after another and began to tell stories about my brothers when they were young and their various bouts of mischief. As he spoke the darkness crowded around us. The light from the fire was glistening in his eyes and the red glow from his cigarette indicated the gestures he was making to emphasise points in his stories. He laughed as he described practical jokes he had played on shipmates during the war, including one that involved putting pieces of cork into a kettle of tea which caused uncontrolled flatulence among the ship's crew. I had never thought of Dad as the practical joker. He had never seemed to have time for such nonsense. This was a man who saw no artistry in the classic whoopee cushion or the trick pack of chewing gum that clamped fingers in a sprung trap. Now he was telling me fart stories?

As the flames started to die down, Dad suggested heading back, but I pleaded for us to stay a little longer, so he went off to find more wood to keep our camp fire ablaze. He went alone, telling me it wasn't safe for me to search in the dark because this was the army beach, of course, and I might pick up something I shouldn't, like a live hand grenade or an unexploded mortar shell. He wasn't gone long and came back carrying two logs the length of his arms. He threw them on the fire, and when the flames again became tall and orange he sat down and reached for the pack of cigarettes he had left on the sand, pulled one from the pack and lit it.

'You know,' he said, his voice suddenly quiet and reflective, 'I used to cry a lot when your brothers were wee.'

I was just thirteen years old and felt awkward with this turn in the conversation, and, for reasons that were soon to become obvious, I felt full of regret.

'The boys were scared of me when they were young,' he told me. 'And I would come home from a late shift and they would all be in their beds. Hiding from me.'

'Maybe they were just tired,' I told him, trying to sound reassuring.

'No. They were scared. I scared them a lot. Shouted at them too much. I was trying to keep them out of trouble. Didn't want them joining gangs, especially when we moved to Easterhouse. You know what I mean?'

I nodded, but doubted he could see that.

'So, I'd come home, have my dinner – stew and potatoes – watch some telly and then your mum would go to bed. I'd sit alone in the living room and have a wee cry to myself, like a stupid daftie. Such a big family, but they didn't talk to me like you do.'

I nodded again. Dad took another puff from his cigarette.

'It's fine now,' he continued. 'They're older, so we go to the pub and have pints and that makes the talk easier. Men always need the beer to talk, I think.'

I tried to interrupt him.

'Dad,' I began, 'there's something I need to tell you—'

I never got to give him the warning before the explosion. A small explosion. Not so much a bang, more like a pop, and then there was a sudden flare from the end of the tattered ciggy. He took it from his lips and stared at it, baffled.

'Dad, I'm sorry. I pushed something into the end of your cigarette. A joke thing. I bought it at that shop where we got the string ... you weren't looking, so ... It makes cigarettes explode.'

He looked at me and then back at the remnants of his cigarette. I thought my timing could not have been worse. Just as he was opening his heart to me about his feelings and his

111

perceived failings as a father, I was setting off pyrotechnics in his face. If only I had chosen a better moment. Maybe just after the stuff about the cork in the tea. That would have worked.

'Well,' he said, a smile beginning to crease his tobacco-splattered mouth, 'that will teach me not to smoke so much. And a warning to you too – don't ever smoke. It's bad for you.'

I promised him I never would, and I stuck to that. We sat by the fire a little longer, eventually dousing the embers with wet sand. Then, like two best friends, we walked off the beach, back to the car and back to the hut.

BOY ABOUT TOWN

In 1975 Glasgow was celebrating the 800th anniversary of its founding and every schoolchild was given a commemorative mug to mark the occasion. There were *Glasgow 800* events staged all over the city, and Easterhouse was not forgotten. There was a special fortnight of fun that included concerts in local schools, street performers and army parachute drops. Soldiers spiralled down from the sky trailing coloured smoke from ankle canisters. Three of them made it safely on to a tarpaulin target, but a fourth was blown several hundred yards off course and into our five-tree 'forest'. Oh, how we laughed, even before we knew the poor guy wasn't injured. It was one of the highlights of that summer. In the festival's printed programme, the popular newspaper columnist Frank Skerret had been asked to contribute a few hundred words and he quoted that old joke, 'You can tell when a letter has come from Easterhouse just by looking at the stamp. The Queen is holding her nose.' I laughed at that too, but not everyone joined in.

People can be very defensive about their home turf. It's fine for insiders to moan and criticise, but woe betide anyone else who has a go. One evening, some weeks after the summer festivities, there was a feature about Easterhouse on the TV show *Nationwide*. This was a teatime magazine programme that was beamed across the UK on BBC1. The journalist, filming his report in black and white and framing it much as though he had macheted his way through the steaming jungle to discover a savage tribe, described all the problems of 'this notorious housing scheme' before cutting to interviews with local residents as they emerged from the shopping centre and into a light drizzle of rain. Among them was my sister-in-law Anne, who, like the others we saw on camera, vigorously defended her neighbourhood and said it was 'not as bad as some people make out'. That's always going to be true, of course. If 'some people' described your home as a 'rat-infested cesspit of broiling excrement' then, hopefully, you could legitimately say that it's 'not as bad as they make out'. But, when you think about it, it's not exactly a ringing endorsement. 'Okay,' you might say, 'the broiling excrement is a given, but you're wrong about the rats.'

By the time Glasgow was celebrating its 800th birthday, Easterhouse was just twenty years old and our flat in Corsehill Street was surplus to our requirements. There were now too many bedrooms and not enough family members left to fill them. All of my older brothers had left home and five of them were now married with children of their own. By the time I was ten years old, I had become an uncle several times over. Two of my brothers still lived nearby in Easterhouse; the five others, those who had joined the army, were scattered across Bahrain, Germany, and Cyprus. Regular airmail letters described their new lives and how, year by year, they were being promoted through the ranks. Clearly an upbringing in Glasgow equips you well for a life in combat fatigues.

At home there was now just Mum, Dad, Rose and me, and Mum wanted to move. I did too. Things had started to change in the square. Much-loved neighbours and friends had skedaddled, some to the new towns and others to the thirty-storey tower blocks that had been another genius solution to the city's housing shortages. The posh Grant family moved out and so did the equally posh Martins. Many of the newcomers were what were termed 'problem families' with 'antisocial behaviours' and symptoms of 'multiple deprivation'. Yes, there was a whole new jargon for poverty, crime and boozing. In the square, the children from the new families began to dominate and intimidate us old-timers, and the frequently hurled question 'Do you think you're better than us?' would be the prelude to sudden violence. The antisocial behaviour that I encountered stemmed from a boy who delighted in ambushing me on the stairwell, grabbing both my ears and pulling them like the ends of a Christmas cracker. It was his idea of fun, and the fear of encountering him any time I left the flat made me miserable. Flitting, moving to a new house, seemed like one way of escaping his clutches for good. It was either that or hiring a hitman, but my weekly pocket-money would only stretch so far.

Aside from my own personal battles with a bully, there had been a noticeable deterioration in the look of our streets and gardens. Graffiti was more prevalent, garden fences were broken and never repaired, litter clogged the kerbside drains and stanks. There were the broken bottles of Lanliq and Eldorado wine and, marking a pathetic trail from the shattered glass, the bloody paw-prints of roaming dogs and cats. The three trees in the middle of our square fell victim to the vandals, but it hardly mattered because the roads department turned up one fine day and simply tore out the stumps and tarmacked over the muddy grass. There had been no warning or consultation about this. Like something from a Joni Mitchell song, it just happened.

There were also more reports of house and car break-ins, and on Saturday mornings, if you walked across the grass rugby fields of Lochend school, you were bound to come across the body of a grown man. Not dead, just dead drunk after the excesses of a Friday night. These were men who had spent too many hours in pubs like the Casbah, the Brig or Griers, and had either forgotten how to find their way home, or else had been kicked out at some point during the night and had decided to sleep it off in the open air. Sad as it was that this was all happening, perhaps what was worse is that we gradually came to regard it as normal. We came to accept a level of squalor, threat and brutality because it hadn't happened overnight; it had crept up around us gradually with quiet menace and slow decay.

Mum had always dreamt of living in a house with a garden and with her own front door. But was that dream affordable? With just two children left at home, weekly Family Allowance payments had been much reduced. In 1975 it was £1.50 per child. Dad was working at the British Steel plant in Cambuslang, and Mum – working as a 'dinner lady' in school kitchens – had moved from a £10 a week part-time job at Rogerfield Primary, doubling her wages by working full-time in Westwood Secondary. She was also able to sneak home the odd platter of 'excess' food, and we often dined well on beef stew, salmon loaf, and sponge cake and custard. Dad never revealed his earnings, but Mum told him she would contribute to any increase in the rent if necessary. There were new waves of council housing being built at Commonhead and Craigend – both areas still technically regarded as 'Greater Easterhouse', although Craigend was over a mile away from what we regarded as the edge of our scheme. Dad was won over, an application was made to the housing department, our pristine record of rent payments was taken into account, and we were allocated an end-terrace house in Craigend in one of the many new streets that had been built under the shadow of two immense concrete water towers that looked like spaceships on stilts. This was Jerviston Road.

Our new house not only had a front door, it had a back one too. It had four flights of stairs with the bedrooms, kitchen and living room located on different levels. It had fancy air-blown central heating which quickly proved too costly to run and was substituted with electric bar fires. There was a postage stamp of a back garden dominated by an industrial size whirligig for drying laundry. This had been roughly cemented in place at an angle you would describe as anything but perpendicular. The front garden was a mass of rubble and broken clay pipes, left over from the construction phase. This was Glasgow council housing, after all, and you could not expect the niceties of a snagging process or luxuries such as topsoil.

Rose and I resisted the suggestion that our new address meant that we needed to move schools. To be fair, her argument against moving was much stronger than mine. She was in her final years at St Leonard's Secondary whereas I still had two years left at primary school, albeit having already been moved once from St Clare's to a brand new school in Commonhead. St Colette's, as it was named, had been built, hastily, to accommodate the ever-growing population of families with young children. It was a modern, pre-fab construction with an open-plan layout which allowed classrooms to be connected or separated with the aid of giant concertina-style partitions. In the playground there was a small brick castle and a huge concrete pyramid which sloped down towards the playing fields. Our new teacher, Mr Nevin, was the progressive sort, as happy to talk to us about his love of David Bowie as he was teaching us about binary numbers and the meaning of onomatopoeia. I liked him, I liked the school and I was still classmates with many of the people I had known at St Clare's. Staying there, though, would mean both my sister and I would have to get a bus to and from school each day. That would be another drain on

Mum's purse but, having achieved her own dream of a house with a garden, she was inclined to take pity on us, and agreed to give us the daily bus fare and some lunch money too.

It seemed to me that our family life began to change after we moved house. First came the news that my Auntie Jean and Uncle Jimmy had been in a car crash and that Jimmy had not survived. A young and careless driver had crossed from the other side of a dual carriageway and hit them head-on. Auntie Jean was in hospital for weeks with her injuries. While she was there, I went with Mum to help sort out her house in Tullibody, to get it neat and tidy for her eventual homecoming. We stayed for a few days as Mum gutted rooms, hoovered carpets and polished furniture. As we set about cleaning the front room, we came across dozens of chocolate bars that had slipped down the side of armchairs and the back of the settee. More were found in the magazine rack, tucked between pages of the *People's Friend* and the *Weekly News*. Yet more lay under the sheet music in the piano stool. We piled these squashed and misshapen treats on the coffee table: Mars Bars, Dairy Milk, Turkish Delight – about two hundred items in total, and some bars in wrappings that the manufacturers had long since updated. None of it looked safe enough to eat. Not even I was tempted. I told Mum about the many times I'd gone shopping with Jean and Jimmy and how Jean had warned her husband not to buy chocolate because of his diabetes. I guess he had found a compromise solution. He'd bought the chocolate but hadn't eaten it, or else he had tried to hide it from his wife and then had forgotten about it. There was something immensely sad about that pile of confectionery on the table. A dead man's secret stash. In many ways, Jimmy had never seemed like a proper grown-up. He was more like a pal. I really missed him.

Back in Craigend, just as we were getting used to our new neighbourhood and new neighbours, some unexpected visitors arrived. One Saturday morning, a taxi driver knocked on our door and said he had two women in the back of his cab who were unable to pay the fare. They spoke little English but carried a letter with our address on it. The women, one elderly and one middle-aged, turned out to be Dad's mother – my grandmother – and his brother's wife, Teresa. They had travelled from Poland and the letter which would have given us notice of their arrival had never made it as far as Scotland. Polish authorities – even in those days of Soviet control – were now allowing more citizens to visit the West, but they took care to ensure that husbands and wives did not travel together, for fear they might never return. Hence my grandmother and my aunt had been the permitted pairing. They stayed for the three weeks their visa allowed, and Mum and Dad took pride and pleasure in showing them around Scotland. They went to Largs and had lunch at the famous Nardini's ice cream parlour. They toured Edinburgh Castle and other tourist hot-spots, but what impressed my grandmother most of all was the Easterhouse shopping centre and the supermarket there. She was clearly astonished to see shelves laden with goods and no sign of queues or panic buying. Compared to the shortages in Poland at that time, Scotland must have seemed like a land of plenty.

Having these Polish relatives stay with us was an unsettling experience. Until then, our Polish roots had felt like something distant, something from Dad's rarely mentioned past or when he sang the Polish songs he had learned from his wartime shipmates. Only occasionally would he hook up with two of those old pals and spend an hour or three in Glasgow's Sikorski Polish Club for ex-servicemen. That, and the appearance of *wiejska* pork rings and *kabanos* sausage at Christmas, was about the limit of our Polishness. Dad didn't even like vodka, preferring beer and whisky. Now, with our Polish granny and auntie as house guests, we began each day with a cheery 'Dzień dobry!' and our fridge filled up with strange smoked meats marbled with fat. Egg and chips on Wednesday was replaced with greasy potato and onion pancakes, and there was always a big pot of chicken soup on the hob. Our Polish relatives went to Sunday Mass and signalled their disapproval when we didn't join them. It all felt like tiny pieces of our family history were catching up with us. For me it accentuated that feeling of being different, of being not quite Scottish enough compared to friends who spoke proudly of their clan heritage, and whose parents sang songs about glens and lochs and described ancient battles with the English as if they had wielded the claymores themselves.

As the days passed my grandmother continued to educate us about our heritage and even debunked some of the things that Dad had told us about his childhood homeland. Even that song that Dad would sing at the drop of a whisky cork – a song about the river Volga sung to the same tune as the Seekers' hit 'The Carnival Is Over' – was dismissed as not being Polish at all. It was a Russian song, Granny told us, about a Russian river. (This was a bit like a Scot going to America and telling a clan gathering that 'Scotland the Brave' was a pantomime song and that the tune for the bagpiper's favourite 'Highland Cathedral' was actually German. It may be true, but what good does it do you to know it?) Over those three weeks, Rose and I gradually picked up a few Polish words and phrases. We learned how to offer our visitors cups of tea – *herbata* – and asked if they wanted more *mleko* in that. Dad found his role as the translator mentally exhausting, and you could see the stress on his face as he smoked one *papieros* after another. There were tears, of course, when he took the two women back to Glasgow airport and watched them board the flight to Warsaw, but there was also relief.

The Polish connection was reinforced the following year when Dad's younger brother, Uncle Józef, came to visit us. This time we had been given adequate warning and he had even sent a photograph of himself so that we might spot him as he arrived off the train from London. The photo showed a fairly handsome young man, debonair even, with a full head of rich black hair. As we gathered in Central Station watching passengers alight from the Euston train, there was no sign of such a man. Just as we were about to give up hope, an older, balder man approached us and, in a frenzy of hugs and a babble of rapid-fire Polish, introduced himself as Józef and apologised for not wearing the wig he had worn in the photograph. It was in his suitcase, he assured us, but we took his word for that and brought him home.

Uncle Józef's first shock news was that he had a three-month visa, which he immediately arranged to have extended for an additional three months. For half of that year, therefore, he became part of the family. He was not so interested in seeing the sights of Scotland. Instead he made contact with fellow Poles in Glasgow and found himself a job working night shifts in a petrol station at Parkhead, not far from Celtic Park. This was illegal under the terms of his visa, of course, but no one blabbed. We were tempted to, though, because the novelty of having him stay with us soon wore off and there was growing friction between my dad and his younger sibling. Dad was questioned by his brother about his decision not to return to Poland after the war. Why had he not come back to support his parents on the farm? The answer, as those who served in the war could have explained, was that Soviet-controlled Poland was not a place that welcomed those who had fought with the Allies. Many who did return were seen as a threat. Thousands were imprisoned and hundreds executed. Uncle Józef, however, was fifteen years younger than Dad and had grown up in Communist Eastern Europe. He had known nothing else.

The longer Józef stayed with us, the more he grew strident in his criticism of the Western lifestyle and my father's apparent lax attitude to family discipline. He noted that money was being wasted on luxuries and fripperies – records for me, make-up for Rose – money that could have been sent home to Poland. I became embroiled in one of these arguments because of a pen I had been given as a Christmas gift. It was a Parker ballpoint pen, now fairly commonplace, but then one of those pens they displayed in glass cases in fancy shops. I had been warned that this was such a good pen that I should never take it to school because I was bound to lose it. Sure enough, I did exactly that and Mum was justifiably annoyed when I admitted my carelessness. Word of the lost pen also reached the ears of my Polish uncle, who told Dad that I should be soundly beaten. Dad explained that wasn't how they did things in Scotland, at least not how *he* did things, not any more. A row ensued and I searched every crevice of my Adidas sports bag looking for that damn pen. I felt responsible for the toxic atmosphere that now pervaded our home, and that if I could find the pen, everything would be sorted.

Of course, Dad and Józef argued about other things too, mostly about money. Józef had come to Scotland with the clear intention of earning as much hard currency as he could and taking it back to Poland. He did not, therefore, make any contribution to the housekeeping budget or offer to pay for the odd treat; instead he asked that my dad should top up his ever-growing pile of sterling banknotes with contributions from his own weekly wages from the steelworks. This would compensate for his years of absence from the farm. It was even suggested that Dad should buy his younger brother a second-hand car which he could then drive back across Europe. The tense atmosphere built and built and began to impact on Mum's mood too. There were arguments late into the night, sometimes made worse if Dad had been drinking. Rose was now engaged to her boyfriend, Vince, and would spend more time at his place, so I felt very much on my own as I sat in my bed, hearing the voices in my parents' bedroom get louder and angrier. I would turn up the volume on my bedside radio to drown them out and I would tune to stations in foreign countries to take my mind far from home.

I was lonely. Recent visits back to see Danny Pryce and the others had not gone well. My old pals now had new friends. On one trip back to the square, Danny and I encountered John Murphy. I wanted to ask him if he had ever found that Derek Parlane card to complete his collection, but I held back. He had looked at me suspiciously and the crowd he was standing with pegged me as a stranger who had breached the boundaries of their territory. Among them was the bully who used to pull my ears. Danny and I beat a hasty retreat. Eventually my hook-ups with Danny became less frequent and then stopped completely. Had I bitten the bullet and switched schools when we had moved house then I, too, would have made new friends who lived locally, but now I was in the wilderness.

With my parents arguing into the early hours, I slept poorly at night and then overslept in the mornings. More often than not I would get to the bus stop just in time to see the green double-decker shrink into the distance belching black smoke from its exhaust pipe. By then I was in my second year at secondary school and my punctuality became an issue. Teachers, the smart-ass ones at any rate, began referring to me as 'the late

Mr Zycinski'. It was the era when corporal punishment was still allowed in schools, so latecomers had to report to the deputy headmaster who would belt us on crossed hands with a leather strap. It was usually just one whack for a first offence, but repeat offenders like me would get 'six of the best'.

One morning, having overslept for the third day that week, I walked to the bus stop, thought 'Sod this,' crossed the street and boarded a bus going in the other direction. It took me into the middle of Glasgow and to the brand new Buchanan Bus Station with its brightly tiled concourse resembling an airport departure lounge. From there I wandered the city streets, killing time until I caught another bus back home. The next morning, I crossed the street again, but having done a lot of exploring the previous day, it was more difficult to fill the hours. I used the weekend to devise a better plan and drew up an itinerary for myself. I also decided to forego the bus completely and walk the five miles into the city. This had two advantages: it would eat up more empty hours and it would leave me with money to spare.

Once in town, I would consult my itinerary, which involved visits to the city's free museums and libraries, or I would locate famous buildings so as to gaze up at them and admire the architecture. One afternoon I walked up to the West End, to the top of Byres Road, and there on Queen Margaret Drive was the headquarters of BBC Scotland. I had often wondered what it looked like, but as I walked towards the entrance doors, a uniformed security guard, eyeing this dishevelled teen in his damp parka jacket with a battered sports bag slung over his shoulder, suggested I should turn around pretty pronto and clear off. 'There's nothing to see here, son,' he told me, which I thought was an odd thing to say about a place that made television shows. Unlike my storming of Culzean Castle some years back,

I could see no easy way of slipping past this guard. If I was ever going to infiltrate the BBC, it was going to have to be a long campaign.

I had never intended this pattern of truancy to last indefinitely, but when those first few days became an entire week and then a month, I felt there was no way back. There had been letters from the school asking about my non-attendance. Since both Mum and Dad left the house before the postman called, it was easy to intercept these letters. I replied, forging my mother's signature, and explaining about a long and serious illness. How, then, could I suddenly reappear back at classes looking as fit and as healthy as anyone would if they now walked ten miles a day, five days a week? After two months of this absurd life, I got busted. A truancy officer had called at our house just as Mum had come home from work. As I walked through the back door that afternoon, she was waiting for me in the kitchen and her uncharacteristic frown should have told me all was not well.

'Where have you been?'

'Em ... school?'

'Tell me the truth.'

Naturally, after such an intense interrogation, I caved in, I buckled, I fessed up and apologised again and again, but could offer no rational explanation for my behaviour other than to say, 'I don't know, I just didn't feel like going to school.' Then I produced what I thought might be my trump card, my get-out-of-jail-free card, my royal pardon. Fishing in my Adidas bag I produced the Parker pen I had lost all those weeks ago. Not the same one, of course, but a replacement I had bought with all those saved bus fares. I had gone to the stationery counter at Lewis's department store and handed the sales assistant a quid's worth of loose change. As crazy as it now sounds, I thought this pen could restore some kind of harmony to our disrupted family and bring us back to happier times. I was wrong. Of course I was. The rows between Mum, Dad and Uncle Józef were about many things, but it was never about the pen and there had been no change in the gravitational pattern of the solar system; the world did not revolve around me.

Teary-eyed, I went to my room, threw myself on my bed and did what I always did when I wanted to escape reality: I buried my nose in a book. It was a book I'd borrowed from the library, a western, a novelisation based on the old *Bonanza* TV show, and it was a story about the tight-knit Cartwright family – Ben, Hoss and Little Joe – fending off attacks from rival ranch owners. I liked the idea of a tight-knit family and wished I still had one. A few hours later, my bedroom door opened slowly, and Dad came in to check on me. In as soft a voice as I'd ever heard him use, he asked if I wanted to come back downstairs and watch television, but I told him I was happy to stay in my room and finish my book. He nodded and then, after a while, asked me exactly where I had been all those days when he and Mum thought I was at school. I told him about the museums and libraries and the warmth of the new bus station waiting room, but I'm not sure he believed me. I'm not sure anyone did. It would have made more sense if I owned up to being in friends' houses, playing music, drinking cheap cider or sniffing glue. That's what delinquent teenagers were supposed to do, wasn't it? Whoever heard of a boy going so far off the rails that he ends up touring art galleries?

Mum and Dad were called to an evening meeting at my school and talked to the headmaster and the principal of the English department. Apparently they had a note of my IQ score and said that I simply wasn't reaching my true potential. When they were asked if there were any problems at home that might be affecting my behaviour, Mum and Dad looked at each other and shrugged. There was nothing they could think of, nothing that immediately came to mind. Nope.

I had missed a lot of schoolwork and, by third year, poor exam results meant I was dropped down into the lower grades. I now found myself sitting among fellow pupils who spoke not of plans for university, but of football, football and football. My reputation as a chronic truant did gain me some credibility among my less academically gifted classmates, and in telling my tales of my city centre wanderings I may have invented a few incidents about shoplifting and meeting girls. I left out the stuff about the museums. There was one other unexpected bonus. PE teachers noticed my weight loss and new-found fitness, tried me out on the athletics track and picked me for the school relay team. So, it hadn't been a complete waste of time. True, it would take a year of nightclasses to get me exam passes good enough for college, but I had gained a particular appreciation for the art and culture that Glasgow had to offer. In back-of-my-hand style, I now knew the layout of city streets as well as any taxi driver. That would stand me in good stead, when, many years later, I was working as a radio news reporter in the city and driving from location to location to cover stories.

At home, things calmed down almost as soon as Uncle Józef boarded the plane back to Poland. Rose got married, and she and her husband moved in with us for a while as they saved for their own starter flat. At Christmas, Dad sang his song about the Volga and we all joined in. Who cared if it was a Russian song? Not us. We were a family again, not quite the Cartwrights, but we were getting there.

YOU'RE IN THE BOOK, MUM

Excuse my lips puckering because I'm about to issue a clarion call for us to come up with a new marketing strategy for one of my favourite institutions: public libraries. To be specific, we need a snappy slogan to encourage readers – young and old – to venture back into the world of free books, free knowledge and free fantasy. I might be on to something with that whole 'triple free' thing, but I'm sure, if we all put our heads together, we can do better. You see, I love libraries and always have. Take me to a new place – a town, a village – and the first thing to catch my eye will always be the public library if it still has one. These days many are housed within a massive community hub alongside a theatre or swimming pool, but some still stand alone in their original Victorian setting or, at worst, in some 1970s monstrosity with bright orange signage and an exterior bike rack sufficient for one or two Raleigh Choppers. Local libraries are one of the few public buildings you can still enter without being interrogated at the door, so, like a spy from another council area, I experience a secret thrill in wandering among unfamiliar shelves under the unforgiving lights of those fluorescent strips which, more often than not, illuminate bizarrely patterned carpets and those backless couches that beckon you to sit, but never relax.

There's so much fun to be had on these cloak-and-dagger expeditions. I've noticed that librarians can have a quirky sense of humour when creating table displays. Once in a very posh suburban library I spotted a cluster of true-life stories of childhood neglect arranged under a handwritten placard that read, with uncalled-for flippancy, 'Read 'em and Weep'. I also recommend reading the posters on the community noticeboard, because those haphazard displays of pinned announcements beg so many questions. Is there really a demand for clog-dancing lessons? Why are there quite so many slimming clubs – and the equivalent number of coffee mornings offering home baking? Am I alone in spotting the link? While we're at it, does the Church of Scotland's £2 per person cuppa really hope to compete with the Catholics' half-price gig with the added offer of a free fruit scone? That's obviously being underwritten by the Vatican or else subsidised by those slimming clubs as a way of sabotaging diets and drumming up future business.

I became a besotted book borrower at a young age. It was my sixth birthday when Mum took me by the hand and led me to a long wooden hut that would serve as the temporary library in Easterhouse until they built the new one within the big shopping complex. That wouldn't happen for four more years, and in the meantime this hut was put in place as part of Glasgow Corporation's anti-crime strategy. Violence and gang culture in the peripheral housing estates had been making the city look bad, and so, for that population of fifty thousand people, they provided a wooden library slightly smaller than a single-decker bus. You can just imagine the leader of the most notorious gang – the Drummy – throwing down his weapons and telling his fellow thugs it was time to put an end to territorial vendettas and get down to some serious reading.

'And make sure we get to the effing encyclopaedias before those animals in the Den-Toi Young Team get their filthy paws on them. The scum!'

In the hut, Mum helped me fill out the required paperwork and I was issued with three small pieces of yellowish cardboard which, I was assured, guaranteed me free access to the junior section. It was a sweet deal: I could borrow three books at a time, keep them for two weeks and – get this – take them *home* to read. I couldn't believe my luck, and even as I was walking towards the exit, books in hand, I half expected sirens to blare, lights to flash and to feel the firm grip of the librarian's hands hauling me back inside for a sound thrashing and a visit to the police station.

For most of my early childhood we didn't have many books at home. Available reading material, besides the *Daily Record* and the *Sunday Post*, amounted to a copy of *The Highway Code* and a road atlas so old that blue motorway routes were annotated with the words 'under construction – opens 1959'. Aside from that there were the 'special books' kept in a locked glass cabinet alongside family birth certificates, rent books and Dad's coupons for the football pools. These books – there were four of them – were the school prizes awarded to my older brother Michael for various achievements in academic excellence. The cover of one actually became the source of my night terrors as it showed two boys creeping through a moonlit forest with the disproportionate face of a large screech owl gazing down at them. Years later I realised this was one of the Hardy Boys adventure stories and, as by then I had proved myself as a responsible reader, Mum allowed me to take it from the display case, read it and return it in much the same way that historians and archaeologists are given special permission to handle rare artefacts kept hidden and preserved within temperature-controlled archives of prestigious museums.

Back in my early days in the junior library, I tended to borrow big picture-books or else the cartoon adventures of Tintin and *Asterix the Gaul*. But I do recall the first time I read an actual book – a book with just words – all the way through. It was *Reach for the Sky*, the gripping story of Douglas Bader's days in the RAF and his attempts to elude Nazi guards as a prisoner of war. My own imaginary escape from the occasional brutality of my surroundings came when I discovered Jennings. Anthony Buckeridge's boarding-school stories of Jennings and his friend Darbishire transported me to a place far removed from the streets of Easterhouse. Jennings inhabited a world of midnight feasts, of steam train journeys through Sussex and cross-country adventures on the South Downs. Buckeridge was the J.K. Rowling of his generation, and though the high jinks at Linbury Court Preparatory School contained none of the mystical menace of Hogwarts, the schoolboy's fear of being caught outside the dorms after lights-out seemed no less terrifying than being chased by dragons and dementors or, like Douglas Bader, being pursued by the Gestapo. The best thing about the Jennings books, though, was that they were funny. Laugh-out-loud funny. So funny that, if I came across a passage or sentence that was particularly mirth-inducing, I would be keen to share it with Mum.

'Listen to this bit,' I would begin, before dissolving into giggling incoherence, unable to utter more than a few words of Buckeridge's hilarious prose. It would take four or five attempts before I had regained sufficient composure to complete my reading, at which point Mum would smile kindly and say, 'That's very good,' and then return her gaze to the television set for the latest goings-on at the Crossroads Motel or down Coronation Street.

Time marches on and so came the big day – I was ten or eleven – when I was told I was now old enough to borrow books from the library's senior section. My infantile yellow cards were withdrawn and I was issued with five new ones in a mature green. Five cards! That meant I could borrow five books at a time and that's when I developed a slightly morbid interest in crime fiction. I loved Raymond Chandler's novels more for their use of language than for their plots, and I became fascinated with the police procedural as exemplified in Ed McBain's 87th Precinct stories. Senior membership also coincided with an odd period in my life – pre-puberty – when I became overemotional about so many things, including inanimate objects and neglected books. Perusing the shelves, I would examine the return date-stamp within some of the less appealing titles and realise that such books had not been checked out for many years. Feeling unfathomably sorry for the poor things, I started borrowing obscure volumes such as *Office Organisation* and *Teach Yourself Serbo-Croat*. Oh, if only I had actually read that book instead of letting it languish unopened by my bedside for two weeks. Maybe it would have led me into a career as a translator or a diplomat. Perhaps I, single-handedly, could have prevented the break-up of Yugoslavia and the subsequent war. If only! But on the plus side, I like to think that fresh date-stamp guaranteed the book's survival on the library shelf for another year or two. So, you win some, you lose some.

There was another library that played a minor role in my childhood and that was the school library at St Leonard's, my high school. For some reason, we were rarely allowed into that library, which is probably why the place remained so pristine and explains why the school librarian always looked so terrified whenever actual school pupils entered her inner sanctum. She had an unpopular 'naming and shaming' policy when it came to overdue books. Each week a typed memo would be circulated and registration teachers would read out a list of the overdue books and the names of the offending borrowers. As one who never ever breached the rules, I was horrified one Monday morning to hear my name added to this list of sinners. Not only that, but the book I was alleged to have borrowed – *My Friend Flicka* – concerned a boy's relationship with a wild filly. This, to my mind, was the kind of reputational damage that would make me an obvious target for verbal and physical abuse from the school bullies. However, I happened to be a bit of a big deal on the school magazine – *Fulcrum* – and abused my position to publish an excoriating exposé of the librarian and her haphazard approach to record-keeping. I went on to point out that I had never borrowed nor read *My Friend Flicka* and, what's more, my current reading habits included the works of Franz Kafka and Carl Gustav Jung. Naturally, this pompous outburst backfired and provided ample ammunition for the bullies. On reflection, I can understand and almost applaud the subsequent ridicule and beatings.

When, happily, my schooldays came to an end there was a new library to explore as I began life as an undergraduate in what is now Glasgow Caledonian University, but was then known simply as 'Glasgow Tech'. The campus library had three massive floors where tables and reading carrels nestled among shelves stocked with the required texts for the various courses on offer. That, in itself, proved distracting. The set reading list for my own course in social sciences included tomes on economics, psychology and sociology, but I hankered after those unread treasures on the upper floors: books on architecture, engineering, photography, but these would have to wait. Essay deadlines dictated the avoidance of such displacement activities, but come the summer break, things were different. I'd cycle back into the city centre and, with the college library now almost devoid of swotting students, indulge my curiosity and roam freely on the previously unexplored top floor.

Once, when reading a book about the British film industry, I came across a chapter about British Lion Films and there was a picture of Mum. Or, at least, I could have sworn it was her. In her teenage years in Glasgow, the years before she met the Polish sailor who was to become her husband and my dad, Mum had worked for the distribution wing of the company. She toiled in a department that repaired the reels of film which had snapped after multiple screenings in the many cinemas and picture houses that were dotted around the city. She told me how she used strong celluloid glue to clamp the films back together before they were sent back out on the circuit. Inhaling fumes from the glue made her 'feel funny', she said, and I still wonder if she was high as a kite when she decided to throw in her lot with Dad. The black and white picture in the book I had found showed a young woman engaged in the kind of repair work that Mum had described, and it certainly looked similar to those I had seen of her in the big black bag that served as the repository for all our old family snaps.

I checked out the book and hurried home to show Mum the photograph. She examined it for a long while before concluding that 'It might be me, but maybe not,' because she didn't have so many teeth then. This led to her telling me how, as a treat for her eighteenth birthday, her parents paid for her to have her remaining decaying and unaligned teeth removed and replaced with dentures. This, she said, was a common occurrence at the time. It cost a lot of money to have this done, so it was the 1940s equivalent of a nose job or Botox treatment. She believed those new dentures completed her look and gave her confidence when she went to city dance halls a few years later. So it was the teeth that got her stuck on the young Polish sailor, not the glue.

We looked again at the pretty young woman in the photograph and concluded that her teeth were real but too perfect. It wasn't

Mum, but the book got us into another conversation about her love of going to the cinema, especially in her youth in 1930s Glasgow. She talked about the Saturday morning matinees and the serialised adventures of Superman and Flash Gordon. She saw Shirley Temple movies and remembered singing songs made famous by the Hollywood child star. One was 'The Good Ship Lollipop'; Mum sang the first few lines and then stopped, confessing that she couldn't remember the rest of the words. To be honest, brats that we were, we didn't encourage Mum to sing much. Whenever she began her rendition of 'Bonny Bobby Shafto' or 'I'm Forever Blowing Bubbles', we would yell out in protest and cover our ears with our hands. As I say, horrible brats we were. But we shared her enthusiasm for the cinema, and when old enough to be admitted to more than just Disney flicks or the likes of *Chitty Chitty Bang Bang*, we'd tag along to picture houses like the State in Shettleston or the Parade in Dennistoun.

A love of books, though, came late in Mum's life and I only realised it had happened when I saw the shelves in our wall unit fill up with red faux-leather volumes. Mum had been seduced by the newspaper adverts for Heron Books and by the glossy pictures of bound volumes lining wooden shelves. Perhaps she imagined their addition to our 1980s décor would transform our living room into a Belgravia gentleman's club or a Sherlock Holmes style study. She sent off her postal orders and signed up for the complete collection of Dennis Wheatley novels because she liked the blood-red bindings. Then she added the library of Catherine Cookson books in Sherwood green. I don't think she ever read the Wheatley stories, but she developed a love of Cookson and devoured one after another in her armchair alongside family bags of Russian caramels.

One day, though, she found she was struggling to see the words on the page, and went off to the optician's to check her prescription. When that didn't help, I made for the college library and pored over books on ophthalmology and optometry, discovering that cataracts or a detaching retina might be the source of Mum's eyesight problem. In those primitive years before Google, I believed the answer to anything could be found in a book. So when Mum began to experience headaches – severe and debilitating – again I went to the library to bone up on migraine and related conditions. When her speech faltered and she began to jumble her words, I brought home books on speech therapy, but it was to no avail. A hospital appointment was made and a consultant diagnosed a tumour in the centre of her brain, and that led to my worst ever day in a library.

Armed with the Latin name of said tumour, I opened books on neurology and brain disorders and discovered that Mum's tumour was prevalent in women of her age – mid-fifties – and was (at that time) inoperable. Steroids could restore a few weeks of normal functioning – and a chance to say our goodbyes – but life expectancy after diagnosis was likely to be less than six months. Six months! I remember reading those words, closing the book, replacing it on the shelf and walking away from it as if sheer distance would make the information become untrue.

But the book was not wrong. Dad and I nursed Mum through those last months and my sister-in-law Liz moved in with us for a while to help out. We moved Mum's bed into the living room and gradually she spent more hours asleep than awake. Then one night she suddenly seemed to revive, and though she was now too far gone to understand what we were saying to her, she astonished us all by starting to sing. She sang in a voice we had never heard before, sweet and gentle. The tune was not one we recognised, but that took nothing away from its beauty. She sang for a minute, maybe two, and then drifted back to sleep. It never happened again, and within a few weeks she was gone. She was fifty-nine, just two years older than I am now as I write these words.

It makes me a little sad to remember how excited I got about thinking I'd seen her photograph in that book, sadder still that I had raised her hopes about it too. I'll add that to the list of regrets, the kind of regrets we all have when a parent dies and we remember the thoughtless things we might have said, or the thoughtful things we should have said but didn't.

But I can make amends about one thing. Look, Mum, here's this book, and you're in it after all.

WHEN I GROW UP

Once, when they didn't realise I was listening, I overheard my children talking about what they wanted to be when they grew up. Alan, who was eight at the time, was posing questions to Sarah, who is two years older. She was answering in a fairly distracted manner until her brother finally asked her something that really caught her attention.

'What do you think you'll *eat* when you grow up?'

Sarah answered without a moment's hesitation.

'Sandwiches.'

'Sandwiches?'

'Yes. Sandwiches.'

'Me too.'

That, it seemed, was the extent of their plans for the future. I don't think they came to any fixed idea of what job they might do, where they might live or whether they might have children of their own. But the food issue was decided and, as far as I know, they still like sandwiches. I do too and I also liked them when I was Alan's age, only we didn't call them sandwiches. That would have been far too posh. We called them pieces. You could have a piece and jam or a piece and butter. It was always best if you made it with a slice from a plain loaf, because its long oblong shape allowed you to plaster the bread with your chosen filling and simply fold it in half to give you a decent-sized snack. The square slices of a pan loaf were too small to fold and you'd need to mess about with two slices, one on top of the other and then cut that in half with a knife. This was all too much of a faff if you had simply dashed back into the house for a carbohydrate boost between street games.

There were also the 'playpieces' you took to school, although, to confuse the issue slightly, a playpiece didn't always have to include a bread sandwich. It could simply be a chocolate biscuit tucked into your leather satchel to be enjoyed at morning break along with the carton of free milk. Those cartons arrived fresh and cool from the dairy each morning and were delivered to the classroom in big plastic crates. These were then left by the radiator so that, by the time the cartons reached our desks in the middle of the morning, the milk would be lukewarm and have the taste and texture of emulsion paint.

The best pieces, though, were the chunky ones that Dad sometimes brought back from work. These were the pieces that Mum made for him and were usually filled with thick slices of cooked meat or corned beef. They were heavily salted and then wrapped in greaseproof paper torn from the original loaf, and Dad would stuff this parcel into the side pocket of his black woollen donkey jacket as he headed out the door. When he returned, some eight or nine hours later, his pieces might still be in that pocket, unwrapped and untouched and available to the first child who asked for them. It was surprising how nine hours in a jacket pocket could improve the taste of something. That kind of warm and crispy bread was like the forerunner of toasted ciabatta. It was great to have that extra supper treat, but I used to wonder how Dad survived a hard day's toil in the steelworks without a bite to eat. Then came the day I discovered the truth: he had been seeing other women.

Dad's changing shift pattern sometimes meant he worked weekends and had rest days during the week. If he was at home on a payday, he would have to drive back into the work to collect his wage packet. On one such day he asked me if I wanted to come along with him and see where he worked. This sounded more interesting than the activity Mum had scheduled for me – retrieving scattered Lego bricks from under my bed – so I jumped at the chance and into the car, and Dad drove us the four miles to Cambuslang and to the Clydebridge works where, in the mid-seventies, he worked alongside more than three thousand others.

The Clydebridge works supplied steel plates for ships, among them the big Cunard liners like the *QE2*. Dad gave me the tour, passing through the main gates and stepping between the railway tracks that allowed freight trains to bring coal and other supplies right into the heart of the plant. We walked into what he called a shed, but this shed was bigger than an aircraft hangar and was full of noise and machinery. A gantry crane moved overhead ferrying sheets of steel that looked, to my eyes, like massive guillotine blades. The heat came from a massive oven at the other side of the shed, and all around us men worked in blue boiler suits, some with black welders' masks obscuring their faces as orange sparks showered around them. The sound of grinding, cutting and hammering echoed through this vast space, and above all that was Dad's voice shouting a description of what I was looking at and what his job entailed.

When we stepped outside, the noise stopped and the mild summer breeze now felt like an Arctic blast compared to the baking temperatures inside. As we walked towards the wages office we would encounter one or other of Dad's workmates and each man would make the same joke, asking if I was the new apprentice and whether I could do the night shift. Having secured the requisite smile or laugh, he would shake my hand and deftly palm me a coin – usually a ten-pence piece. Apparently this was a bit of a tradition when you met one of your mates' kids for the first time. I'd blurt a shy 'thank you' and drop the coin in my pocket, and was soon jingling with silver treasure as I walked. Dad collected his pay, opening the little brown packet there and then and counting it to make sure no shift payments had been overlooked. Satisfied, he put the notes in his wallet and gave me yet another ten pence from the loose change. I was becoming richer by the minute.

Then we went to the place that explained why Dad didn't go hungry on the days he didn't eat his pieces: the works canteen. We each had a bowl of soup and a cup of tea, and I was impressed that so many people seemed to know Dad and, from what I could tell, liked him. It was as if I was eating with a famous person, and my pockets became so laden with coins that I feared my trousers would slip down when I stood up. Even the canteen ladies came out from behind their counter to come and see us to chat with Dad and ruffle my hair. These were the 'other women' who had led him astray with their tempting tureens full of mince and tatties. I could see the attraction. As they gathered at our table, Dad described me as the 'baby of the family' and this earned me more hair ruffles. It also gave Dad the excuse to remind everyone that he was the father of eight children. He was proud of that, proud to show me off as his seventh son and proud to show me where he worked. It was a great afternoon and it convinced me of one thing: I never wanted to work in a place like that.

Did he really hope that one of his sons would follow in his footsteps? Maybe, but none of us did. My older brothers tried out various jobs as milkmen and van drivers, and then five of them signed up for the army. Our parents were proud to hear

141

of their various successes as they rose through non-commissioned ranks as privates, then corporals and all the way up to becoming regimental sergeant majors. As a war veteran himself, Dad understood that world and the importance of all those military promotions.

My career progression in radio, however, was not something he could relate to. To be fair, I know he boasted when I first started reading news bulletins on Radio Clyde because people he knew listened to that station and had heard me on air. My move through management positions at the BBC, however, left him unsure of what I actually did for a living and how I spent my days. He wasn't alone. A lot of BBC staff wondered the same thing. In any case, Dad must have known I wasn't cut out to be a welder when I brought home the stainless steel ashtray I had made in the school metalwork class. With its uneven base and corner gaps filled with enormous blobs of solder, it was a triumph of effort over functionality. Dad took one look at it and I could see what he was thinking: I would never be collecting wages in the steelworks.

This was just as well, really, because soon there would be few jobs left to apply for. Britain's nationalised steel industry was being outcompeted by foreign rivals and faced one round of cutbacks after another. There was a prolonged strike and Dad found himself on the picket line as unions campaigned to save jobs. It was all in vain. When a redundancy package was offered, Dad did the sums and took the deal. The one-off payment was more than enough for him to buy our council house in Craigend, and the British Steel pension payments just about made up for his lack of a weekly wage. He also had some rainy-day money left in the bank and he talked about getting another job, but, as he was in his early sixties, I assumed it was no more than talk.

Then came the day Dad told me about his big plan for us to go into business together. It was while I was living in Inverness with Anne and the kids but travelling to Glasgow for two days a week to attend BBC meetings. I had just been given the job running Radio Scotland. That had meant nothing to Dad, but I had tried to impress him by telling him about all the deadlines I had to meet and all the incredibly important decisions I had to take. Nevertheless, martyr that I was, I made it a point, every Wednesday night, to drive to Craigend to visit Dad and check he was eating well and taking all his prescribed medication.

As I walked through the back door and into the kitchen, he was sitting, as ever, nursing a mug of tea. He had a twinkle in his eye and a question on his lips.

'Did you see it? Outside. Did you see it?'

'See what?'

'The van. Parked outside. The big van. Did you see it?'

'Oh that? Yes, huge thing. I had to park across the street. It's right outside your back gate.'

I assumed this was Dad's point; the van was parked in his spot and it was annoying him. But no, that wasn't it at all.

'I bought it,' he said.

'Bought what?'

'I bought the van. It's mine. It's ours. Come and have a proper look.'

He got up and went out the back door, and I followed him out into the street where he was now gazing at this van with nothing less than adoration. It was a blue Ford Transit, one of the bigger ones. The registration plate suggested it was eight years old, but it looked twice that. The paint was scratched and there were patches of rust over the wheel arches. The back doors were closed and tied together with a piece of string. The windows were caked in dust, and on one of them someone had scrawled a message about the Pope suggesting that the Holy Pontiff should be forced to abandon his vow of chastity.

'What do you mean, you bought it?' I asked.

'Six thousand pounds. Cash. I went to the bank this morning. Cleaned out my account.'

'But why? What are you going to do with it?'

He turned to me and put an arm around me.

'You mean, what are *we* going to do with it? It's obvious. Fruit and veg.'

'Fruit and veg?'

'We'll get up early, go to the market, buy the stuff cheap and sell it for twice the price. We'll be working together. I drive and you sell. You are good with people. You have the gift of the gab. And no more BBC meetings.'

Now it was all making sense. My boast about my busy career had given Dad the impression that I was stressed out and hating every minute of it. He had sat in his kitchen, sipping tea and thinking about what he could do to help out his poor son. Running a fruit and veg van also made some sense because Dad was a regular customer down at the fruit market. He'd often come home with crates full of apples and satsumas which would then be distributed to friends and neighbours. I felt awful. To think he had blown the last of his savings on this scheme and I was going to have to tell him that it was a non-starter. He would be hurt, horribly hurt, and I wondered if we could resell the van as soon as possible and salvage something from this disaster. But then, just for a few minutes, I began to seriously entertain the idea. Maybe it wasn't so crazy after all. Working with Dad, a life on the open road. Wouldn't that be so much more fun than those stuffy meetings at the BBC? Maybe we'd make a success of it and build up the business. We could have two vans or more. It would be something I could pass down to my own children. A legacy.

No, no, this was nonsense.

'Dad, I'm sorry, but—'

I never got to finish what I was saying. At that point, the man who lived next door emerged from his back gate and gave Dad a nod.

'Sorry!' he shouted. 'I'm just about to move it. It's my brother's van.'

Then he climbed into the driver's seat, started the engine and manoeuvred it ten feet or so further along the street. I looked at Dad, who was already laughing.

'Had you going there,' he said. 'You should have seen your face. It was a picture.'

I was stunned. It took me a few moments to find my voice.

'So, it's a joke. It's not your van. You haven't spent your savings?'

'No, of course not. I was just sitting waiting for you when the man next door parked it there. It made me think of the old fruit and veg vans we used to see. Good joke, eh?'

Yes, good joke, Dad, I thought. Then I wondered if we had any ripe satsumas left in the house, so I could throw them at him.

THE DAY I DIDN'T DIE

The preponderance of beds is misleading. Hospitals are not good places if you want to sleep. They're great if you want to surround yourself with people who can save your life, but hopeless if, after being spared by the Reaper, you're looking for a bit of shut-eye. Ward lights are never fully dimmed and there is always noise of some kind. During the day there is the bustle of doctors, nurses and cleaners. Set visiting times are a thing of the past. Strangers come and go at all hours. Whereas your own friends and relatives delight you with their good wishes and intelligent conversation, those who sit at others' bedsides outstay their welcome with their inane drivel and raucous laughter. At night there are the buzzers and intermittent alarms of patients requiring medication or help getting to and from the toilet. Sometimes the calm is shattered by the arrival of medevac helicopters on the pad outside. Then there's the gossipy whispers of the overnight staff sharing their plans for the weekend, complaining about rota changes or mocking the latest absurd email from clueless administrators. Always, there is the cough, cough, cough of sick people. Sometimes that turns out to be yourself.

It was the cough, my own cough, that kept me awake for three days solid after my surgery. The tumour had been fully removed and the graft was looking good. A small Doppler device

146

was pressed against my tongue to detect blood flow and the regular whooshing beat indicated all was well. There had been some kind of 'breathing and blood pressure incident' during my surgery and my oxygen levels had been giving some cause for concern, so, once I was awake in the intensive care unit, a nurse fitted a mask over my nose and mouth. A few hours later this was swapped for a nasal cannula. The roof of my mouth felt parched and was caked with dried blood which had to be scraped and suctioned. But my only real complaint was the cough, because any time I drifted towards sleep, the chesty convulsions would snap me back to full consciousness. This might have been a side-effect of a drug they had given me during surgery when my blood pressure had soared. I never did get the full story about that, but a warning was added to my notes saying that this particular drug was now on my list of allergens.

I was ensnarled in a spaghetti-like tangle of tubes, one of which drained fluid from my neck into a clear bag hung from my bed. Others offered a route in for liquidised food and medicine. Naturally, another tube offered an exit route. My forearm was tightly bandaged, as was the scar below my belly button. I had no pain; a morphine drip and regular top-ups of paracetamol took care of that. In the coming days I would come to liken the fizzy paracetamol to a freshly mixed G & T and enjoy the sensation of the cool, effervescent liquid as it flooded through my neck. I was given a button to press so that I could self-administer more morphine. I never felt the need, but I pressed the button once or twice because, well, give a man a button to press and that's what happens. It's too tempting to resist. It's why they should never put men in charge of nuclear weapons.

Anne came to visit, which cheered me instantly. Unable to do much more with my voice than make grunting noises, I communicated via a miniature wipe board. Anne wished me 'happy birthday' and I wasted no time in correcting her, telling her, in a scrawl of marker ink, that she was twenty-four hours too early. She then reminded me I had lost an entire day. I scrawled an apology. It was, indeed, my birthday. I was getting older, adding another year to life's short tally, but as they say, that's a lot better than the alternative. My spirits lifted again when, the following morning, they told me I was well enough to be moved out of intensive care, and I was wheeled through corridors towards a general ward. To get there, I was trundled into a huge elevator which had a mirrored wall. It was my first glimpse of myself since surgery and for all that I was scarred, bruised, bandaged, pale and unshaven, it wasn't too much of a shock. I've looked worse with a hangover.

The next seven days on the ward settled into a regular pattern. Patients lucky enough to have slept through the night were awakened at eight in the morning and given their prescribed medication. The cleaners would arrive, two women with the loudest Dundonian voices you had ever heard, who conducted high-decibel conversations from either end of the ward, with no apparent thought about what they were saying or who might be listening.

'Did you see that on the news about that virus in China?'

'Oh aye, I did. And they built an entire hospital in one day.'

'Aye and they've filled it already.'

'Just as well I've got my over-fifty funeral plan sorted.'

'Did you, aye?'

'Aye, got it sorted at Christmas. So that's me good to go any time I like.'

When the cleaners had finished mopping the floor, the nurses would return. Blood pressure readings were taken and then the consultants, with their gaggle of junior doctors, would begin their rounds, talking briefly to the particular patients on their own list and ignoring the rest. I always looked forward to seeing my own consultant, Mr Shekar, because he would inevitably utter some remark that would make me laugh. Now that my voice was able to sound out basic syllables, I told him how well I was being looked after on the ward and how impressed I was by the professionalism of the nursing staff. Mr Shekar replied in his usual deadpan style.

'I'm so sorry that your previous experience with hospitals has been so bad that you think this is a good one.' He then spent the next few minutes apologising to the nurses and making sure they understood that this was just his little joke.

'Now, open your mouth and let me see your tongue,' he would say, getting back to the serious business of my health. Satisfied, he would then instruct the duty nurse about my treatment for the next twenty-four hours. Most days he would decide that one or other of my tubes or drains could now be removed. It was a cunning psychological ploy, because it gave you the feeling that you were making progress, and as each piece of apparatus was taken away, you began to feel a little more like your old self. One morning, however, there was no sign of my jolly consultant and another doctor took the lead in my examination. As he did so, I suddenly spotted my Mr Shekar milling about near the nurses' station. He looked downcast.

'Are you okay?' I called over to him.

'No,' he called back, 'I'm not very well. I have man flu. That's why I'm staying well away from everyone.'

Remembering what he had told me weeks ago about never having taken time off for illness, I decided to tease him.

'You should throw a sickie,' I said. 'Have a duvet day.'

'Never!' he replied.

By the next morning, his theory about simply ignoring an illness seemed to have been proven right, when he appeared at my bedside looking fit and healthy.

'I'm so much better,' he said. 'Completely recovered.'

'I'll be the judge of that,' I told him. 'Open your mouth and let me see your tongue.'

His subordinates gasped at the impertinence, but he laughed and ordered the removal of another one of my tubes. I was glad of that, because it was almost the weekend and that was when Sarah and Alan said they would be coming up from Glasgow to visit me. With one less tube tethering me to the bed, I was able to get up and – after a few practice circuits on a Zimmer frame – walk unaided to the bathroom, have a shower and put on a brand new pair of pyjamas. I even managed to shave, but only half of my face, because the skin on one side of my neck was completely numb and I was worried about slicing my own throat. Still, I managed to make myself look reasonably fresh and presentable, and hoped my appearance would not be too much of a shock for my offspring. I needn't have worried. For starters, Sarah, who now works as a radiographer, is well used to seeing patients in various states of distress. Alan, a journalist, knows how to hide any emotion long enough to get the story.

They arrived, with Anne, on a Saturday afternoon. She had warned them that I might look a bit different, but I could see the relief on their faces when they realised I was not the hideous gargoyle they had been steeling themselves to see. After the inevitable hunt for chairs, they huddled around my bedside, brought me up to speed with their own news and then, towards the end of their visit, we talked, as a family, about what we might do when I was fully recovered. We made plans to rent a cottage on the west coast and enjoy a week of doing nothing much but eating, sleeping, walking the dog and being together again. At that time, we had no inkling that such plans would have to be put on hold because of the pandemic. Nor did we know then that, as I thanked them for coming to see me and hugged them, it would be the last time Anne or I would be able to hug our children for many months. But it had been a good day.

My worst night in the ward happened just a few days before I was allowed to go home. As usual, I had struggled to get to sleep, given up trying for a while and decided to watch an awful drama-documentary I had downloaded onto my phone. It purported to tell, in ludicrously repetitive detail, how Adolf Hitler had actually survived the war, escaped from his bunker in Berlin and lived for another twenty years in Argentina, plotting the rise of a Fourth Reich. One particularly grim scene depicted the Führer sitting upright in his eventual deathbed, staring into the middle distance while a hospital ventilator helped him breathe his final breaths. That was enough for me. I turned it off and tried again for sleep. When I awoke a few hours later, I was sobbing so loudly that a nurse came to my bedside to ask if I was in pain.

'No,' I managed, 'just sad.'

'But you're doing so well,' she said. 'Everyone's been impressed by your progress. You've been up walking already, and your speaking is getting better.'

I couldn't tell her what was making me cry. It was a dream, a stupid upsetting dream in which I'd been back at Craigend, talking to my father in the street, and he was telling me that no one needed me any more. My children were grown up, he had reminded me, and I had left my job and, now that I couldn't speak properly, no one would ever want to hear what I had to say about anything. Honestly! What kind of way is that for a dead dad to talk to his son, even in a dream? Until that night, my dreams had been bizarre, but nothing too traumatic. I'd had dreams about those old days in Easterhouse and, probably because I was hearing so many Dundee voices in my waking

151

hours, I dreamt about those summer holidays near Carnoustie and Monifieth. Occasionally those true-life memories would be enlivened with guest appearances from fictional characters or I would find myself in locations I had visited over the years: Paris, Prague, Boston. But now I was getting grim, demotivating messages from beyond the grave. I mean, what the heck?

I was given another fizzy paracetamol – no ice or lemon was offered – and then I lay awake thinking about the last time I had spoken to Dad before he died. At the age of ninety-two, and terminally ill, he had been transferred to a nursing home in Glasgow. I continued to see him once a week on Wednesday nights, after finishing work for the day. Those early visits were pleasant enough, and we'd talked about the fun times we'd had at our holiday hut and how one of my older brothers had chased a rabbit across a field and then disappeared from view as he fell into a hole. Dad always liked retelling that story and could barely reach the end of it before his laughter triggered his smoker's cough. As the weeks passed and his condition deteriorated, it became more difficult to fill the time with small talk or to prompt him with stories he hadn't already covered a dozen times.

There was one exception, the tale my sister and I referred to as 'the pipe story'; whenever he started to tell it, we settled in for the long haul, wondering if the seasons would change before he reached the end of it. It wasn't the substance of the story that was the problem. It was a perfectly good tale about how Dad had gained his qualification as a welder by working on thirteen metal pipes, each of which had to be inspected in turn by a supervisor before he could move on to the next one. The snag, though, was that if one of his welding joints failed to pass muster, he would have to start again from the first pipe. As Dad told the story, he would describe the welding of each pipe in intricate detail and might get to the fourth pipe before telling us how he had had to start again.

'No good,' he would say. 'Start again. Pipe one ...'

Then it would be back to detailing the challenges of the first pipe, and so on. Sometimes he got as far as the eleventh pipe, and my sister and I would begin to dream of a life beyond the pipe story, but then our hopes would be dashed as we heard how he had failed with pipe number twelve.

'No good. Start again. Pipe one ...'

So on one of my last visits to the nursing home, when Dad was still able to sit in a chair and talk, I asked him to tell me the pipe story and I sat beside him, soaking up his words, fixing in my mind the rich sound of his voice and understanding, perhaps for the first time, the pride he had felt in becoming a qualified welder and realising why he had always taken such care to relay every detail of that final exam.

Thinking of that as I lay in my hospital bed I cried again, but this time my tears were silent and then, dreamlessly, I was asleep.

The next morning Mr Shekar, hearing about my overnight meltdown, said it was time to cut off my morphine, but as a special treat I would be allowed a few sips of tea to test my ability to swallow liquid. I can't tell you how happy this made me, and when I managed to down an entire cup the 'Nil by Mouth' warning was wiped from the board behind my bed. Now when the cheery young woman with the trolley came round offering not just tea, but coffee and hot chocolate too, I was the first to put my hand up. The next challenge was food, and so a hospital nutritionist ordered me up a small smorgasbord of purees. Julie, a speech and language therapist, came to watch me eat. I could easily manage the instant mashed potato, but the pulverised bananas were still beyond me.

'Give it time,' she assured me. 'You'll be having steak and chips before you know it. Also, we're arranging for you to see a speech therapist in Inverness when you get home.'

'An Invernessian speech therapist?' I exclaimed, reaching for another pathetic joke. 'But have you heard the way they speak over there?'

'I'm from Inverness,' said Julie.

'Oh.'

That night the trolley woman sneaked me a custard cream which I was able to dunk in my tea and suck to oblivion. I was on my way back.

Ten days after I had checked in at Ninewells Hospital, they redressed my wounds, handed me a big bottle of soluble paracetamol and told me I could go home. Anne arrived with some of my clothes, which all felt far too baggy when I put them on. I had lost more than twenty pounds in under two weeks. 'Cheaper than a fancy health spa,' I told the nurses as I went round as many as I could find and told them how much I appreciated their care and compassion. I wanted to shout my thanks from the rooftops but neither my legs nor my voice were up to it; instead I later wrote to the Scottish Government's Health Secretary and asked her to pass on my gratitude, thinking my words would have more weight if they trickled down from the powers that be. Meanwhile I would not be saying goodbye to Mr Shekar, as I still had to wait for the lab results from my lymph node tests. Those would take another week to come through. It was a week in which I read up on the effects of radiotherapy and braced myself for the next stage of my treatment.

'Your results are fine,' Mr Shekar told me as Anne and I returned to his clinic at Raigmore. 'No spread and there's no need for radiotherapy or chemo, but I'll see you once a month here in Inverness just to keep an eye on you.'

'And the cancer?' I asked, needing him to say it out loud.

'You are cancer-free,' he said. 'You don't have cancer. You are cured.'

Cured!

We walked out of the clinic feeling not simply happy, but imagining how we could now get our lives back on track and do all the things we had planned before I had gone to the dentist with that mysterious blister. But we remembered to use the hand sanitiser on the way out, because this was late February 2020 and the writing was already on the walls. There were posters warning us about the coronavirus. Soon the television news programmes would depict frenetic scenes from hospital wards in Italy, France, Spain and then, of course, in Britain. Sarah would find herself on the frontline, scanning patients at Glasgow Royal Infirmary. Alan would be covering the story as a journalist, popping up on television himself now and then as he posed questions to Scotland's First Minister, Nicola Sturgeon. Anne and I followed all the rules on social distancing, and we agreed I had been lucky to have had my cancer treatment before the crisis had begun. In the lockdown hours, I thought of those doctors and nurses at Ninewells and Raigmore. I wondered what might be happening in that intensive care unit in Dundee.

And, in the quiet moments, I thought about my life, and how glad I was to still be living it.

PART TWO
MAKE-BELIEVE

THE TARTAN TRAVELLER

Only my wife knows for sure that I was involved in the old man's disappearance, and she won't be telling anyone. Now that the police have stopped asking questions, Alice thinks it's time we started spending some of the money. If we do that, there's no going back. Not for us, anyway. Besides, even if we told people what happened, I'm not sure anyone would believe us.

Sometimes I fantasise about that, about telling the truth. I think I'd give the story to Nicola at the *Gazette*, because in a way she was the one who started the whole chain of events. I was the paper's editor then, and she had come into my office to pitch me a story about some volunteering initiative. Nicola was twenty-three years old, one of our fresh-faced trainees. I was trying to decide if I should sack her. She was on the list, but I hadn't told her that yet. I had been waiting for the right moment.

'It's called Highland Helpers,' she was saying as she flipped through her notebook. I noticed the scrawls and squiggles split over two columns on each page. Teeline shorthand. It was good to know the colleges were still teaching that kind of stuff. I put my list to one side and listened.

'It's run by a lady called Maureen Sinclair—'

'I know Maureen,' I said. 'Inverness do-gooder. Finger in every pie. All the worthy ones, anyway.'

'They match skills with needs. Let's say you enjoy cooking and want to learn more about it. Maureen's group puts you in touch with an older person with knowledge to pass on. A retired chef, say. The younger person gets a tutor and that older person gets a friend.'

'Sounds like a Meals on Wheels dating agency.'

I caught the cynicism in my own voice, hated it, but gave myself a break. It had been a bad morning. The bean counters at Head Office had told me the *Gazette* was still losing money and I had to cut the wages bill by a quarter before the end of the month. That gave me just two weeks to decide. Last in, first out, was the usual way of doing these things, and that put Nicola in the frame for a sad goodbye. She would have company on her way out the door. Another young reporter and Bob, my deputy editor, were also facing the axe. Bob was married with two kids and had just extended their mortgage so they could escape their two-bedroom flat.

'Tell me this, Nicola,' I said. 'Why do you care so much?'

'What do you mean?'

'You keep coming to me with these kinds of stories. Hospital shortages, homeless shelters, refuges for battered wives. Do you think people want to read about that?'

'I hope so,' she said. 'It's important.'

I agreed, it was important, but Head Office research suggested people were more interested in celebrity junk. Showbiz nonentities escaping some scandal in London would often hide out here in the Highlands. Our network of contacts and tip-off merchants at local hotels would help us track them down. That would give us big numbers on social media, but it wasn't doing much to bump up sales of the actual paper. It was all very sad, but there was no point living in the past.

'I was like you once, Nicola,' I said, 'but I had a boss who gave me a piece of advice and I listened to it.'

'Which was?'

'If you're so worried about the poor and the downtrodden, go and win the lottery, buy a plane and drop five-pound notes from the sky. That would make the front page. In the meantime, give me copy that sells papers.'

'And that's your advice to me?'

'Nope. My advice to you is to go and write your story about Highland Helpers. Get going. I have a phone call to make.'

'Thanks, Jack,' she said, and left my office with a smile on her face. It was the last time she would do that, because that call I made was to Head Office. I had made my decision.

'Give me a deal and I'm out of here,' I told them. 'I've done my thirty years and more. I've got my savings and my pension and a house that's bought and paid for. Bob can run the paper. He's a good man. What you save on my salary should keep everyone else in a job. For a while, at least.'

By Friday there was a cake, some nice speeches, a jokey plastic gold watch and far too much booze. On the Saturday morning I woke up with a sore head and nothing to do but read that week's edition of the *Gazette* and get used to the idea it was no longer my baby.

After a month of daytime TV and jigsaw puzzles, Alice noticed I was going stir-crazy.

'That Highland Helpers story was interesting,' she said, over breakfast. 'Why don't you pay them a visit? They have an office on Church Street.'

'You just want rid of me for a few hours,' I said.

'More than that, please, Jack. I don't want you moping around at home all day. You're disrupting my routine.'

I didn't need telling twice. Alice and I had been together for as long as I had worked at the *Gazette*. I had met her during my first week on the job. She was a student nurse at the old infirmary and I'd been sent there to write up a filler piece about a charity bed-push. That was thirty years ago and when you've been married this long you know when to give each other some space. This was one of those times. I jammed one last corner of toast into my mouth and spent the usual half-hour looking for my car keys.

'First of all we'll do a simple audit of your skill set. Can you cook?'

This was Maureen Sinclair, the office manager who had spotted me hovering outside the converted shopfront that served as the base for Highland Helpers. She had hauled me off the street at the very moment I had changed my mind. I had actually started walking away when the glass door opened and she grabbed me by the arm. In no time she had sat me down and produced her two-page questionnaire to find out if I was going to be of any use to her.

It didn't go well. I couldn't cook, was rubbish at DIY and had no experience working with sick or disabled people.

'Tell me, Mr Cameron,' she asked, finally setting aside her pen, 'why do you seem so scared?'

It was a perceptive question. I tried to explain.

'It's Jack,' I said. 'I was a newspaper man. I ran the *Gazette* before the cutbacks.'

'I know.'

'But now I think I'm going to end up like that bloke on the telly. The one on the adverts. Old guy in the cardigan. He wanders around telling his neighbours about over-fifties funeral plans. That's all he does. Makes plans for his own death and encourages everyone else to do the same. It's like he's pimping for the Grim Reaper. And another thing, he boasts about having more than one of those policies. I mean, how many times is he planning to die?'

162

I paused. I realised I was ranting.

'I'm sorry,' I said. 'Look, I won't waste any more of your time. Besides, I'm parked on a meter—'

'Aha!' said Maureen, smiling and picking up her pen. 'You drive! And you have a car! Do you know much about motor mechanics?'

'Sorry. I know how to top up the screen-wash, that's about it.'

'Then it would be useful for you to know more?'

'I suppose so, but I thought I was supposed to be offering my skills to younger folk?'

Maureen smiled.

'You're fifty-five, Jack. In my world, you are one of the younger folk.'

And that's when she first told me about Old Lachie. Lachlan MacPherson, to give him his Sunday name. The man who would change my life forever.

'He's a widower,' said Maureen. 'He lives a few miles outside town. Just where Loch Ness meets the river. Not far from the wee village pub there. You know it?'

I nodded.

'He's been looking for a bit of help with his garden and for someone to collect a few parcels for him now and then. You drive and I presume you can push a lawnmower?'

'Yes, I think I can manage that.'

'I'm sure he'll be happy to teach you a few things about engines, and of course we'll reimburse you for any petrol costs and so on. Shall I give Lachie a call and say we'll come and see him tomorrow?'

I hesitated, and then I thought again about how keen Alice had been to get me out of the house and how pleased she would be if I told her I'd signed up as a Highland Helper.

'Okay,' I said. 'You can count me in.'

Next morning, I picked up Maureen in my Dacia Duster and we drove the five miles out of Inverness and along the country road that runs towards the south side of Loch Ness. On the way, she gave me a potted biography of Old Lachie. He was in his eighties, she said, but was still reasonably fit and active. He liked tinkering with cars and machines.

'I think he was some kind of engineer before he retired. He's not a local, really. He only came to live here about three years ago. He bought the cottage on the hillside, which is not very practical when you're getting on in life.'

'You say he was an engineer. What kind? Railways?'

I was lapsing back into reporter mode, asking questions.

'No, not trains. Planes, I think. Jet engines. He worked for Rolls-Royce. He was a pretty big deal in his day, but now his mind has wandered a bit. Let's just say he's—'

'Not firing on all cylinders?' I suggested.

Maureen gave me a stern look.

'You'll have to watch that,' she said. 'People with dementia don't tend to get jokes or sarcasm.'

'Sorry, I didn't realise ...'

'Oh, we're not sure, but he does tend to say some odd things at times, so we've been keeping an eye on him. But we're mostly worried about his mobility. He had a bit of a fall last week and he's not happy being told to rest up. He gets about the house no bother, but I think the garden's a bit much for him. That's why he finally asked us for some help. That's quite a big step for a man with his kind of pride and sense of independence.'

'And that's where I come in?'

'Yes, if he'll have you. I'll introduce you and let him give you the once-over.'

'I didn't realise this was going to be an audition.'

Maureen gave me that look again. No jokes, no quips, no sarky remarks. I got it.

Lachie's cottage was set back from the shoreline and was a good few hundred yards uphill from the village pub where most of the coach parties and other tourists stopped off. The pub car park and the nearby pebble beach were usually teeming with day-trippers hoping to get a glimpse of the loch's legendary monster or else just enjoying the scenery.

The cottage had a great view of the loch and the surrounding hills. The front garden looked to be in fairly good shape. The lawn had been cut recently and rose bushes on either side of the path had been neatly pruned. It left me wondering what chores actually needed done, but perhaps the six-foot fence at the side of the cottage was shielding a jungle at the back that would require my attention.

Lachie himself was not what I had imagined, either. Maybe, despite all that Maureen had said about him being fit and active, I still half expected a frail, grey-haired old man sitting in a bath chair, covered in a tartan rug and using an ear trumpet to catch snippets of our conversation. I'd clearly read too many Beano comics in my youth and I guess my notion of being eighty was probably similar to a teenager's idea of being fifty. As he came out of his front door, Lachie looked to be in the prime of life, a short, stocky man whose checked shirt and dungarees gave him the look of a diminutive lumberjack. I saw no sign of a bad leg, no limp, no hobbling, no ill-effects from the fall that Maureen had mentioned. When she introduced me, I could see him sizing me up, too; in fact, he did more than just look. He grabbed each of my doughy arms in turn and squeezed, and then he looked at my hands.

'You're a strong-looking lad,' he said. 'But these look like office hands.'

I smiled. 'Yes, but some of those pens and pencils were pretty heavy. It took four of us to lift the stapler.'

Two minutes in and I had already forgotten Maureen's warning about daft jokes, but it didn't seem to matter. Lachie let out a hearty laugh.

'Och, you'll do,' he said. 'Now will you be for a wee whisky?'

That sounded like a good idea to me, but Maureen refused on behalf of us both and volunteered to put the kettle on for some tea. She went off to the kitchen, leaving me alone with the old man in his front garden. He was staring down at the loch, watching another tour bus pull in to the car park.

'Germans this time,' he said. 'They come here from all over the world. Sometimes they wander up here to get a better view. Looking for something that's not there.'

'I take it you're not a believer? Better not say that out loud. You'll scare off the tourists.'

It was a jokey remark. Alice and I had often thought that people in Inverness were part of an unspoken conspiracy to keep the myth alive and the money rolling in. I didn't expect Lachie to give me a serious answer.

'There is no monster in that loch,' he said. 'No mysterious creature, no oversized sturgeon. Nothing. Not any more.'

I nodded and decided this might be a good time to change the subject.

'Your garden's looking good,' I said. 'Is it the back of the house you need a hand with?'

This seemed to confuse him, so I explained what Maureen had said to me about pushing a lawnmower.

'Och, not at all,' said Lachie. 'I do all my best thinking while sorting the garden, but I do need some help in the back. Come and I'll show you.'

He led me through the house and out the back. The grass here, too, was neatly cut, but at the far end there was a long wooden garage that looked wide enough and tall enough to house a double-decker bus. Lachie walked over and swung open the wooden doors, flooding the inside of the garage with sunlight, and there, facing us, was something I hadn't seen up close since my childhood. It was an old Bedford camper van.

'It's a Dormobile,' I said.

'That's right, Jack,' said Lachie. 'And this is what I need your help with.'

It was the kind of van my father had owned way back in the late sixties. It was the British equivalent of the VW Camper, but of course, being British, it was much less stylish and much less iconic. With its fat, squashed face, it was to the VW camper what the Morris Minor was to the Beetle. The one I was looking at now had seen better days. Its powder-blue paint had large patches of rust, the back wheels were missing and the headlight on the passenger side had come loose from its fittings, dangling from the front of the van like it had been punched in the face and left with a dislocated eyeball. Across the top of the windscreen was a strip of red translucent plastic printed with the words 'Tartan Travellers' in sun-bleached yellowed lettering.

'I picked this up a few years ago,' Lachie was saying. 'It's had a fair few owners, but I bought it from that backpackers' hostel at the back of the bus station. I think they were using it for guided tours and what have you. Cost me fifty quid, but they were glad to be shot of it. It's a death-trap.'

'My dad had one of these,' I said. 'He would take me and my sister on road trips around Scotland. Every summer he'd just follow the coastline until we ended up back where we started. Living on the edge, he called it. What are you going to do with this one?'

It wasn't a difficult question and, thinking back, I should have noticed then that the old man took his time in answering it.

'I'm doing some work on the engine,' Lachie said, 'and I could use a strong pair of arms. But yours will have to do.'

I immediately felt the need to confess my inadequacies.

'I did once change a windscreen wiper,' I said. 'It stayed on until I made it to Halfords and the boy there did it properly.'

'It doesn't matter,' Lachie said, 'I'm the engineer. I just need your help with some of the heavy lifting. And maybe you could pick up a few parcels for me from time to time. I order a lot of them from specialists, and they go to that depot near the train station. You know it?'

'Yes,' I said. 'It's where they park the big shipping containers.'

'Aye, that's right. So you think you could spare me a few hours, once a week?'

I looked at Lachie and looked again at the old van. We were at the height of summer; the air was fresh and clean and the views were spectacular. It was great to be out of the house and not stuck in an office. More than that, I realised I was actually needed by someone and could be useful again. And Lachie was a far cry from the bent-over geriatric I had thought I might be meeting. I stretched out my hand and he shook it.

'Deal,' I said.

'You two boys seem to be hitting it off,' said Maureen, as she emerged from the cottage with a tray of steaming teacups. 'Is this going to work out?'

'Yes,' I said, turning to Lachie. 'I'll be glad to help.'

We decided that Wednesday afternoons would be the best time for me to come to the cottage. This also suited Alice, because that was when she hosted her book group; that's what she called it, anyway, but I doubt they read more than the labels on the Prosecco bottles. I took to arriving at Lachie's place about noon and working with him until half past four or five o'clock, maybe longer if the sun was shining.

We'd usually finish up with some tea and sandwiches in his front room. It was a good place to unwind. It had that fantastic view, of course, but I also liked perusing the books and magazines on Lachie's shelves. There were dusty tomes about engine manufacturing and aircraft design, but the periodicals looked up to date. It was obvious that Lachie like to keep abreast of new developments in his former world of science and engineering.

There was a single framed photograph on the bookcase, a woman with long dark hair and pink glasses. She was smiling in the way you don't often capture in a photograph. Not forced or posed, but open and authentic.

'Your wife?' I asked Lachie.

'Aye, that's Jean. Gone twenty years now.'

'You must miss her,' I said, because that's the kind of daft thing you say to bridge the awkwardness of these moments.

'Miss her? I do in a way, but I don't think of her as dead. She's just in another part of my life, and I can see her whenever I like.'

'See her?'

'Memories, you'd call it. I like to think of the mind as a time machine. I can go back and forward as often as I like. Remembering takes you back, imagining takes you forward.'

'That's a lovely thought,' I said.

'Not an original one, though,' said Lachie. 'You can blame Einstein and his pals.'

Time, as I understood it, moved on. As the summer edged into autumn, Lachie rigged up some halogen lamps so we could spend more time in the wooden garage. He was usually bent over the engine of the old van or else tinkering with components on his workbench. Some afternoons I would arrive to find him wearing a welder's mask and I would stay well out of his way while the sparks flew around whatever piece of metal he was working on. My duties involved fetching and carrying. From time to time he would ask me to lift a crate or a wheel or help him rip off some of the rusted exhaust piping. Sometimes I'd help him move a metal tool trolley from one side of the garage to the other. He showed me some of the basics of car maintenance, enough to get me going again if I broke down on the A9 or had a flat battery on a winter's morning. The tools he used were unlike any I'd ever seen before.

'I started out as an aeronautics engineer,' Lachie explained. 'De Havilland, Rolls-Royce, even a wee spell with Boeing. These precious babies are designed for fixing jet engines, but they'll do just as well on this old heap.'

'Do you think you can get her to fly?' I joked.

'No chance of that, I'm afraid,' said Lachie. 'At least, not in the way you mean.'

That, I suppose, was another clue, and the journalist in me should have pursued it. But, like the old Dormobile, I was getting rusty too. I should also have noticed that Lachie had more affection for the tools in his trolley than the 'heap' of a van that he was trying to restore. Of course, that was when I thought that what we were involved in was a restoration project. I was wrong about that as well. In fact, the only time I came close to wondering if something was amiss was the time he asked me to go to the freight depot near the train station where I had to sign for three wooden crates addressed to Dr Lachlan MacPherson.

The customs and excise dockets that came with these crates described the various parts that were inside, but they meant nothing to me. As I loaded the crates into the back of my car, I was more interested in the exotic origins of these despatches

– India, Florida, Kourou – and the paperwork detailing the monetary value of each item. Those figures sometimes exceeded two thousand dollars. It made me think that Lachie would have been better off buying a Dormobile that had already been restored by a collector, but I guess there would be no fun in that. I reasoned that Lachie, like me, had been looking for something to occupy his time in retirement. He had landed on the old van; my hobby had become Lachie himself.

I called Maureen at Highland Helpers and told her that I was concerned about the money Lachie was spending on the van. I wondered if he was being exploited by some online hustlers. She told me that she couldn't betray a confidence, but that I shouldn't worry about that too much. She had discovered a few things trying to work out what state benefits or allowances he might have been entitled to. He had plenty of money in the bank, it seemed, and it was up to him if he wanted to waste it.

'How's the Tartan Traveller looking these days?' Alice asked me one morning, as she tried to distract me from a piece of toast that she had designs upon. 'You got it running yet?'

'Not as far as I can see,' I told her. 'Lachie spends most of the time fiddling with tiny bits and pieces. Fuse boxes I think.'

'Fuse boxes?'

'Something like that. Don't ask me. But he's got all the wheels on now, so that's progress. Maybe tomorrow I'll see if he can start her up.'

'You can't tomorrow,' Alice reminded me. 'You have that dental appointment. You've put it off twice already.'

'Blast it, so I have.'

I looked out of the window. It was a fine day, one of the last good days in September. Not a cloud in the sky and just a gentle breeze jostling my pyjamas drying on the backyard whirligig.

'I think I'll take a run out to the cottage this morning,' I told Alice. 'I'll tell Lachie I can't come tomorrow, and see if he needs any help today.'

I didn't call to warn Lachie I was on my way. I didn't think there was any need, but when he opened the door to me he looked confused and slightly out of sorts.

'This isn't Wednesday,' he said. 'You can't be here. I have visitors.'

'Oh, sorry, Lachie, I didn't realise. It's just that I can't make it tomorrow.'

'Well, you shouldn't have come all this way.'

'I know, but—'

'Well, goodbye then. I'll see you next week. Wednesday. It's always Wednesday.'

Then, not to put too fine a point on it, he slammed the door in my face. I got back in my car and sat there, feeling the anger build. What a way to be treated after all the help I'd been giving him. I had a good mind to knock on his door and tell him he could go to Hell. Ungrateful old … But I didn't do that, because just then, as I watched from my car, the cottage door opened and two men came out. Young men in suits and with briefcases. Japanese. I watched as they made their way through the garden, out the front gate and then back down the hill towards the pub and the loch. They might have got into a car or climbed on one of the tourist buses. I couldn't tell because I lost sight of them after that. I was curious, but my indignation at Lachie's rudeness towards me soon returned and I drove home to tell Alice all about it.

'Well, you have to make allowances,' she said. She always does that. She tries to see things from the other person's point of view, no matter how wrong they are. Bloody nurses. Too much compassion for their own good, if you ask me.

'What allowances? He slammed the door in my face.'

'He's an old man,' said Alice. 'Old people get into a routine. It's how they cope. They get a bit frightened when they get confused.'

I said no more. There's no point arguing with people when they are right. They can ruin a good sulk. I decided I would make my feelings known by skipping a few Wednesday visits and waiting to see if Lachie called to say he was sorry.

It was a childish ploy, I'll admit, but it worked. And eventually I got more than just an apology. I got an explanation too.

One morning well into October there was a call from Lachie. 'There are things I should have told you a long time ago,' he began. 'But I don't want to explain on the phone. Can you come over tonight, Jack? I know I can trust you with the truth.'

'That sounds intriguing,' I said. 'And, sure, I'll be over tonight. Seven o'clock?'

'Perfect, Jack.'

It was dark as I made my way out of Inverness and along the country road. The wind was howling in the trees and some loose branches were already flying past the windscreen. I should have turned around and called Lachie to tell him I'd come back in the morning, but curiosity was getting the better of me. I felt like my old self, an intrepid reporter on his way to an exclusive story. Okay, maybe this wouldn't be a story I could sell to a newspaper, but I had to know it anyway. For my own benefit.

'Take a seat,' Lachie said as he ushered me into his front room. 'I've already poured myself a whisky. Will you have a dram yourself?'

'I've got the car,' I reminded him, 'so just a tiny drop and some water.'

He nodded and I sat down as he handed me my drink. It had the aroma of a good Speyside malt, but the taste of Highland tap water. Not unpleasant, but neither one thing nor the other. Lachie was on the hard stuff. He took a sip from his glass and fixed me with a look that suggested he was still hesitating about telling me something important, but then he began.

'Do you mind that story that was in the news last year, about those scientists looking for the deepest part in each of the world's five oceans?'

'Vaguely,' I said. 'Some billionaire was funding it. They built a special submarine or something.'

'That's right,' said Lachie, 'a submersible. Capable of going deeper than anyone has gone before. And there was another story around about the same time, Jack. The one about the scientists in Antarctica with their balloon experiments. They found particles they couldn't explain.'

I shook my head. That one had gone under my radar.

'They were looking for particles from outer space, from the Big Bang, the origins of the universe, no less. They sent balloons up into the stratosphere to collect them.'

'And did they find them?'

Lachie thought about this for a moment.

'Very good question, Jack. They found particles but not the right kind. They were coming *from* the Earth and heading *into* space. It didn't make sense. So, they came up with a theory.'

'Which was?'

'A parallel universe, Jack. One that was going backwards as ours was going forwards.'

I wasn't sure where he was going with this and wondered if it was the whisky talking. He drained his glass and, instead of reaching for the bottle, changed the subject again. Or at least I thought he did.

'You remember those visitors I told you about? That day I sent you packing?'

I nodded.

'Well, I did that to protect you, Jack. I didn't want them to think you were part of my business.'

'Who were they?'

'Two men from Japan. One was a scientist, an engineer like me, and the other was a money man. Made me an offer. I turned them down, but they were back again this morning. They wanted to buy our old heap in the garage.'

'What? The Dormobile? The Tartan Traveller?'

He nodded.

'And do you want to know how much they offered me? Take a guess, Jack.'

I shrugged and then I thought about all the time and money that Lachie had spent on the old van. Maybe that would have hiked its value beyond the fifty quid he had paid for it. I took a stab in the dark.

'A thousand pounds? Or Japanese yen.'

Lachie smiled.

'Actually, their offer was in dollars. American dollars. Ten million Yankee dollars. Cash. They had it with them. Two briefcases stuffed with Uncle Sam's finest lettuce.'

'You're joking,' I said, but I could see that he wasn't. That's when he offered me another drink, a proper one this time, a ten-year-old Glenfiddich. I took it. I needed it for what came next.

'I knew someone would find me eventually,' Lachie said. 'I was expecting the Russians, or the Chinese, but fair play, I've eluded them for three years. I sourced all my components from different people and from different parts of the world. But someone in Tokyo finally put it all together. It's like a jigsaw puzzle, Jack, they found one piece, then another. Just like I had done, back in the day.'

'I'm not following you. Can you back up a bit?'

He laughed at that. It was the same hearty laugh I remembered from the first time I had met him.

'I can back up more than a bit, Jack,' he said. 'That's really the point of all this. It's about going backwards. Backwards in time.'

'You're not telling me you've built a time machine? That Dormobile?'

'Of course not, Jack. That old heap was just a decoy. I knew that if and when they came looking for me, they'd expect to see some kind of machine or vehicle. They were probably looking for a mini-submarine, but the Dormobile was my little joke. And they bought it. They literally bought it. Daft lads.'

'You mean?'

'The cash is in the garage. They collected that old heap this morning. It's probably on a cargo plane right now. Seems like I got it to fly after all. The machine I've really been working on all these years would fit into one of those empty briefcases I left them with. That's why I needed to see you tonight. I have a day, two at most, before they realise their mistake, but I'll be long gone by then.'

'Gone where?'

Lachie poured himself another dram and explained the science to me in terms that a man who struggled to open the bonnet of his car might understand. I was that man.

'Those scientists, the ones going deep in the oceans and the others in Antarctica, they're both looking at the same thing, but they don't know it. There are points on the Earth where those weird backward particles bubble up. The magnetic poles, north and south, and deep ocean trenches too. But here's the thing:

the trenches don't have to be that deep. There's a point that divers talk about, it's below six hundred feet, just below the reach of sunlight. They call it the twilight zone. But there are sources of light down there. Bioluminescence it's called. Light from living organisms perhaps, but also from those same particles that confused the research team at the South Pole. And those tiny flashes are like windows opening between our universe and the one that's running in parallel, the one that's going backwards.

'Imagine you're on a train going north and you pass another train going south. Just for a few moments on that particular point on the line, you get a glimpse through the windows of the other train. It's over in a flash, but you see the other people, the other passengers. You see people who've been where you are going, but they're also going where you have been.

'Tell me, Jack, did you ever stop to ask the question: why am I here?'

'You mean, why do I exist, the meaning of life and all that?'

Lachie laughed again. 'No, I'm no philosopher. I meant, why am I *here*? Why am I, Lachlan MacPherson, brilliant engineer that I am, why am I here, back in Scotland, living in a cottage by Loch Ness? Why, Jack?'

'Tell me. I'm guessing it's not just for the fresh air. Is it the whisky?'

That got another laugh.

'It's because it's deep. Loch Ness. It's seven hundred and fifty-five feet at its deepest point. Or one hundred and twenty-six fathoms, if you prefer. Deep enough to reach the twilight zone. Deep enough to be a site where those strange wee particles might appear, deep enough to create windows into the past. It's like that point on the line where the trains pass each other.

'So, tell me, Jack, if you went out on to the loch with my machine, a machine that provoked enough of those wee particles to come to the surface and that opened up a window to the past … what would we see? Let's say we looked back, say, sixty-five million years, what might you see?'

'I don't know. Trees, different from the ones we have now. Ferns. Maybe glaciers? Volcanoes? I don't really know.'

'Think, Jack, sixty-five million years ago. The Jurassic period. Does that give you a clue?'

'Dinosaurs?'

'And what around here reminds you of a dinosaur?'

I didn't even want to say it out loud. It sounded so absurd, but I said it anyway.

'The monster. The Loch Ness monster. Nessie.'

Lachie was clapping his hands.

'Well done, Jack. You got there in the end. And it's my theory that those sightings of the monster, the genuine ones, have been flashes into that other universe. Perhaps the weather conditions or atmospheric magnetism provoked the particles just as my wee machine will do. There's a way of opening a window into the past. That's what I need to prove tonight.'

'Tonight?'

'Yes. Drink up, Jack, we've got a boat waiting.'

Soon we were setting off for the beach. Lachie carried his machine in a simple Adidas sports bag. He told me he had come up with the basic schematics after working at all those different places: Rolls-Royce, Boeing, even a stint with NASA. He had learned something each time and, again, he compared it to a jigsaw puzzle. He was the only man who happened to have seen all the pieces, so he was the only one who could put it all together. It inspired me to think that this man at his age was still using his brain and still making things happen. What could I do with another three decades of life, if I was that lucky?

The weather was still wild and wet as we walked along the pebbles. Lachie had given me a small plastic torch to light our way, but it was barely up to the job. It took us another ten minutes to find the wooden boat with its outboard engine. I helped Lachie climb into it and was about to join him when he put up his hand to stop me.

'This weather is foul,' he said. 'No sense in both of us risking our lives. You wait for me here. If I don't come back, head to the cottage. I've left a note for you in the garage. It will tell you what to do.'

I tried to protest, but it was hard to make myself heard over the noise of the wind and the waves crashing against the shore, scraping the pebbles back and forth. Conversation became completely impossible once Lachie pulled the cord to start the boat's motor. All that was left was a few hand gestures, a shrug, a wave and a thumbs-up. He powered the boat out into the darkness. I waited and watched. Five minutes became ten. Then there was a flash far out in the middle of the loch. I saw the little boat for less than a second and then it was gone. Within that flash there had been something else. A shape? A head? A creature?

I stood for a while and then walked back to the cottage and opened the big wooden doors of the garage. It was odd to see the place looking so empty now that the old van – our Tartan Traveller – was gone. On Lachie's workbench was a black bin bag stuffed with dollars. I found his note: I was to report him missing, but not tonight. I should wait a few days, try to call him, visit the cottage, discover he wasn't at home and then share my concerns with Maureen at Highland Helpers. There might be a search and rescue operation, but it would all be a waste of time. If they found his boat, it would be empty. 'My machine doesn't open a window,' he had written, 'it opens a door. I'm going to go through it.'

The note ended with his words of farewell: 'The money is yours. Do with it what you want. Put it to good use. Tell people you've won the lottery. You're ready for your next adventure. I've started mine.'

I picked up the bag of dollars, walked out of Lachie's garage and closed the doors behind me. Alice would know what to do with the money, I thought. She was forever talking about good causes and people in need. Maybe we'd keep a little of it for ourselves. We could buy a camper van and do a bit of travelling. A road trip, a bit of fun, life on the edge.

Hopefully, like Lachie, we had years ahead of us.

NEGOTIATING POSITIONS

By Mo's reckoning, she was the third new finance executive in as many months, but management were still no closer to reaching a deal on the downsizing project. As she studied the agenda and waited for the others to arrive, she had little confidence that today's meeting would move them forward. She watched as her own team – all men, all in identical suits and ties – took their seats and arranged their folders and paperwork in front of them. They were, she thought, such a feeble bunch and she suspected most of them just turned up for the tea and biscuits. They all had that pale, nervy look about them and that wasn't going to help. Especially not today. The other side would have their claws out, they would smell blood and, if she didn't play this carefully, they would be eaten alive. As everyone settled down and the small talk subsided, she cleared her throat and began.

'I'd like to address the elephant in the room,' she said, looking directly and she hoped, fearlessly, at her opposite number at the other end of the long conference table.

'Thank you,' said the elephant. 'And on behalf of my members can I formally state our gratitude to you for inviting us here today and also express our regret at the way negotiations broke down at the last meeting? We do hope your predecessor, Mr Smedley, is recovering well.'

181

'It was just a flesh wound,' Mo lied, playing down the incident to avoid immediate tension. 'The doctors say he'll be back to work in a month or so.'

'I would also like to apologise,' said the lion. 'I acted out of instinct and when he made that annoying thumbs-up gesture that he does, well, I sort of pounced before I knew what I was doing.'

Though the lion looked sincere, Mo noticed the hyena was snickering. The elephant admonished this with a flouncing swish of his trunk and continued.

'But I must reiterate,' he said, 'the downsizing plans for the zoo remain unacceptable to our members and we won't tolerate any further cuts to enclosure spaces or the forced sharing of habitation areas. The pandas in particular need their own privacy.'

'I understand that,' said Mo. 'But I hope you also appreciate that we do have to find savings somewhere. Visitor numbers have fallen drastically in the last year. If I could ask you to look again at the Excel spreadsheet in your pack—'

'We don't need spreadsheets to tell us what we already know,' said the polar bear, stretching two white furry paws on the table in front of him in the style of a bad actor in a melodrama. 'We're on the frontline. We can see what's happening. It's not like the old times. Some days there's just a handful of kids looking down at me. I still do my daily swim, back and forth, back and forth, but I miss the applause. It's not the same if you don't hear the laughing and the clapping. Breaks my heart, I tell you, breaks my heart.'

His voice cracked slightly and everyone felt a bit awkward until the tiger spoke.

'It's the same here,' she said, with that silky purr that left you guessing about what she was thinking or feeling, 'and some of those children have absolutely no manners. There's one child, the one with the peculiar odour – we all know him – he's here every Saturday morning with that spoon-faced father of his. Divorced of course. The father gets weekend custody and he always brings his brat here to the zoo. Every single Saturday. No imagination. And that brat drops litter and shouts the most obscene things. But I've been watching him. Watching and waiting and one day, if he gets just a little bit too close to the bars, if he leans in just an inch or two more …'

A hush fell over the room while everyone thought about this and then the elephant tried to get things back on track.

'From the point of view of our members, we don't see why we should suffer for the poor management decisions that have led to this fall in revenue.'

'It's also the whole animal rights thing,' Mo explained. 'Zoos aren't politically correct these days. There are those who would have you all sent back to the wild.'

She had chosen the remark carefully, but she knew it would ruffle a few feathers, especially the penguin's. It didn't take much for him to get into a pointless flap.

'If you ask me,' said the bird, though no one ever would, 'it's time to confront a few hard facts. There are some star names around this table. People still turn up for our penguin parade, for instance, and who doesn't love a giraffe?'

At this, the giraffe sat up a little straighter in his chair and knocked out one of the ceiling tiles. The penguin ignored this and continued.

'But some folk, mentioning no names, are freeloading. Maybe it's time to let them fly free.'

The elephant looked annoyed at this break in the ranks.

'Solidarity, brothers and sisters,' he said. 'And creatures.'

'I'm just saying,' the penguin continued, 'some brothers and sisters aren't earning their keep.'

He had tried to mime little quotation marks around the words 'brothers and sisters' but his wings were too short and stubby.

'Are you talking about the parrots again?' asked the lion, with a long yawn.

'Well, since you mention it, yes. I mean, people keep parrots at home. Why would they want to see them in a zoo? Now, if we let them fly, we could add an extra feeding time for us penguins—'

Mo had heard enough. She stopped him in mid-flow, and everyone seemed glad about that.

'It costs more to feed a penguin than a parrot,' she said.

'Well, I don't know what that has to do with the price of fish,' said the penguin, huffily. Mo rolled her eyes.

'I'm just saying we need bigger ideas. Bolder.'

'I'd get shot of that so-called petting zoo,' suggested the polar bear. 'Pigs, donkeys, lambs. Not zoo animals at all. More like scab labour, if you ask me. Amateurs.'

'Or appetisers,' said the tiger, licking her lips.

By bobbing his head up and down, the giraffe indicated that he had something to say. Mo hoped he wouldn't begin with his usual daft joke. But her hope was dashed.

'If I could stick my neck out,' he began and then paused, looking around the room for even the hint of a reaction. But no one laughed. Not even the hyena. They had all heard it too many times before.

'Please go on,' said Mo.

'Well, I think we need a bit more fear. Yes, fear. Families are giving us less than twenty minutes of their time here at the zoo, but they're spending more time and more money over at the theme park, and you know why that is?'

'The new roller-coaster.'

It was the first time someone other than Mo had spoken up from the management side of the table. The voice belonged to Fergusson, one of the accountants.

'It's pulling them in big time. It's called the Drop to Hell. One of the biggest in Europe, they say. It's turned over three hundred thousand pounds in the first six months. The projection to year end looks amazing. It's a real money-spinner.'

'Exactly,' said the giraffe. 'I think I'm one of the few that has a good view of it from my enclosure. Of course, I get a good view of most things, ha ha, but I'm sure the rest of you have heard all the screaming.'

There were nods and grunts from around the table.

'So I say we need a little bit of controlled fear ourselves.'

Mo was intrigued. 'What were you thinking, exactly?'

'Staged escapes,' said the giraffe. 'Just once or twice a month. It would get us some press coverage – telly, even. Social media at least. And we'd have that element of risk. We could put up signs warning people that they were liable for their own safety. That would spook them. Give them a cheap thrill.'

'I like it,' said the penguin. 'We could start by letting the parrots loose.'

'No one is scared of parrots,' said the lion, yawning.

'What about the chimpanzees?' asked the polar bear.

'Too comical,' said the elephant.

The tiger, who had been listening quietly, saw her chance.

'I'm happy to volunteer,' she said. 'Leave a gate ajar and I'll wander out for a few minutes, just enough time for people to take photographs. I'll be back in my pen before you have time to fetch the tranquiliser gun. Promise.'

Mo could see that the idea was winning favour on both sides of the room and was happy that, after the weeks of stalemate, some kind of consensus was being reached.

'Perhaps we could start this very weekend,' said the tiger. 'Saturday morning good for everyone?'

Before the tiger's release plan could be discussed further, the door of the conference room burst open and Irene from catering came in pushing a trolley brimming with tea, water, biscuits and bamboo shoots. There was also a small trough of leaves and a bucket of horse meat. A feeding frenzy then ensued as the suits in Mo's team fought over the chocolate-chip cookies and shortbread fingers.

The animals, by contrast, were much more civilised.

They always were.

JUST RIGHT

The old woman adjusted her half-moon spectacles and carefully set aside her knitting as, with some trepidation, I entered the room. The first thing I noticed was her hair. It was more silver than blonde, still long and beautiful in its own way. The second thing was the bowl by the side of her bed. Was it too much to hope that it contained porridge?

'It ain't what you're thinking,' she told me, seeing my glance. 'One of the nurses here is Scotch and she keeps pushing porridge on me, but I can't stomach that oatmeal crap. Too many bad memories. You understand?'

I nodded and that one gesture turned out to be my way in. She motioned for me to sit down and I pulled up a chair by her bedside and flipped open my notebook.

'Shall we start with the basics?' I asked. 'Your name?'

'Sure, why not? It's Goldilocks, of course. Otherwise you'd be wasting your time, wouldn't you?'

I smiled. 'But your real name?'

'Oh, who knows! You'd have to ask my grandparents and they're long dead. I guess it was Goldberg or Goldstein or something like that. But I had those curls, so I was always Miss Goldilocks, or just plain Goldie to my friends. Like with Cinderella. It was only the fans who ever called her that. We just called her—'

'Cinders?'

'Nope. Ella. She was a good pal, was Ella. Bad feet, though. Never really got over that injury after the glass slipper smashed. Still, she sued the Fairy Godmother and made a pretty penny on the settlement.'

As my pen raced across the page, Goldilocks lifted a spoonful of soup to her lips and tasted it.

'Too hot,' she said, replacing the spoon in its bowl. 'I'll give it another minute. Funny things, spoons, ain't they? You know that story about the one that ran away with the dish?'

Again, I nodded.

'Well, that's baloney. Turns out they got mixed up with the wrong people and were, how can I put it, "made to disappear". Of course those were different times, tough days. Tougher for us girls. Tangle with the wrong people and you'd end up broke like Old Mother Hubbard or living in a big shoe as a single mom with ten kids. I mean to say, a *shoe*, for God's sake! Talk about taking away a person's dignity.'

I saw how easily I could be side-tracked with these kinds of anecdotes, but I was keen to get to the bottom of her own story.

'Tell me about the bears,' I said. 'What really happened in that house in the woods?'

She was silent for a few moments and at first I thought it was because she was trying to recall events from so many years before. Then I realised she was listening to make sure there was no one outside in the corridor. Satisfied, she spoke again.

'First thing you need to know is that I was always a bit of an outsider. The others, well, they worked for the big boys like Grimm or Andersen, but I was a bit of a free spirit. I liked it that way. I saw what they made those other girls do. Snow White was being forced to share an apartment with seven guys.

They weren't even dwarves, just short men who'd had no luck on the dating scene. And Red Riding Hood was shacked up with a wolf who liked wearing women's nightgowns. It was all too weird for me. So I got myself a cushy little job up at the palace, working in the kitchen. I stayed well clear of the rich and the powerful. Not that you could escape all the crazy stuff. I once had to bake a pie with twenty-four blackbirds inside. Live blackbirds … can you imagine?'

'Must have been difficult to eat,' I said, 'especially if they started singing.'

'You can say that again. Almost as bad as one of those plum pies that Little Jack Horner delivered. You could tell he'd been, well, fingering them, if you know what I mean.'

I gave an involuntary shudder and tried to shake off the image forming in my mind. 'If I could bring you back to the bears?'

'Oh sure, sure. You see, I was also in charge of outside catering. You know, like the Mad Hatter's tea party or the teddy bears' picnic. Those kinds of gigs. And that's how they tricked me, see?'

'Not quite. Who tricked you?'

'The big bosses, or at least their henchmen. The goons working for Andersen, or Grimm, or Carroll. It doesn't really matter which one. They were all as bad as each other. And you couldn't speak out or you'd be "finished in Fairyland", as the saying goes.'

'And when you say they tricked you?'

'They told me there had been a complaint. Said the teddy bears hadn't been happy with my last spread and that I was to go into the woods and see what they had to say. Customer feedback and all that. So off I went, down to those goddamn woods.

'Hang on, let me try this soup again.' She dipped the spoon back into the bowl, brought it to her mouth and slurped, loudly. 'Crap! Now it's too cold.' She let the spoon splash back into the bowl.

'You went to the woods,' I prompted.

'Yeah, I went down to the woods and, surprise, surprise, no sign of no teddy bears. Just two kids crying about some missing breadcrumbs. At least that's what they told me, but that turned out to be a crock. So, call me soft-hearted, but I asked these kids if they needed help and they were all over me saying they were trying to find some cockamamie gingerbread house and could I walk with them for a little while.'

'This would be Hansel and Gretel?'

'Well, it sure wasn't Jack and Jill. *They* were both in the booby-hatch after that accident up on the hill. The docs were saying it was a failed suicide pact. I say they were pushed. Humpty Dumpty style. They cracked up, if you catch my drift.'

I was getting confused. 'Most versions of your story don't feature Hansel and Gretel.' I was trying not to sound sceptical, but my editor had warned me to look out for inconsistencies. He was only going to run this story if it was airtight.

Goldilocks seemed to read my mind. 'Well, most *versions*, as you put it, are written by the very people who did what they did to me. They sanitise things. There's always a cover-up. Anyway, these kids led me through the woods but not to any gingerbread house. Sign above the door says 'Bears' Cottage', and I'm thinking this might be where those teddies hang out when they're not picnicking under the trees. At this point the kids run off laughing like half-wits, so I knock once and the door swings open. Nobody's home, but on the table in front of me are these three bowls.'

'Of porridge?'

'Yeah, porridge. So I figure, maybe this is what the bears were belly-aching about, so I'll give this stuff a taste and see what's what. I take one spoonful and next thing I know I'm waking up in a bed and looking down at me are three of the biggest bears you ever saw. Not teddy bears neither. Grizzlies.'

'You'd been drugged? Awful that they could do that to someone.'

'I wasn't the first and I wasn't the last. Just ask Alice or Sleeping Beauty. *That* girl woke up with some minor royal slobbering all over her. Course they sanitised that story too. Made him out to be some kind of hero.

'Anyway, I was lucky. All I had was three badass bears with a proposition. They gave me the usual soft-soap routine. Said someone as pretty as me shouldn't be hiding herself away in the kitchen. Said I was meant for better things. They told me that certain very important people, extremely high up people, wanted me to work for them and that if I didn't, well, things could get very sticky. And you know, these bears weren't fooling around. They had honey and were prepared to use it.'

'And that's when you jumped out of the window?'

'No, that was all part of the cover-up. They tried to make the whole story sound like I had been trying to rob the place and was fleeing the scene before the cops could come. Victim blaming, they call it nowadays.'

'So what *did* happen?'

'I stood up to them. I got up out of that bed and told them to leave me alone or that I'd go straight out and expose the whole damn lot of them. See, I'd picked up so many stories while working at the palace. I said I knew about the whole Georgie Porgie scandal and about the Pied Piper too. And don't get me started on Rapunzel. We're talking abductions, false imprisonment, missing kids, poisoned apples. Enough to fill a book.'

'Which brings us to your book. What are you calling it?'

'*Goldilocks: The Truth Fairy*. Hardback is out next month and there's a pop-up version for the kids.'

'Nice. But all these events happened decades ago. Why did you wait so long to tell your story?'

She thought about this as she reached again for the bowl of soup.

'I didn't think anyone would believe me. I was up against some powerful men. Born story-tellers. Who was going to believe a poor immigrant girl like me? They wouldn't see past the curls. But now that others have spoken out, I feel the time is right.'

I looked at the scrawls of shorthand in my notes. There was enough there for a front-page splash and maybe a two-page spread inside too. Goldilocks' story seemed credible and everything she had said made sense. Until, that is, she took another sip of the soup that she had already said was too cold.

'Yummy,' she declared. 'That's just right.'

I closed my notebook and thanked her for her time.

THE DAY OF THE DOG

I prefer to sleep late, maybe until half seven or eight, but recently I've been woken by the voices from upstairs. Loud. Louder than they used to be and that's saying something, because I'm now a bit deaf in one ear. I can only understand a few dozen words, of course, but my good ear pricks up when I hear 'food' or 'walkies'. The latter is usually preceded by that phrase 'your turn' which my people are using a lot these days. That's when the voices get louder. If I hear words like 'bath' or 'vet' I'll lie down again and pretend I'm still asleep. I no longer try that trick of sticking my head under a cushion. Took me a long time to figure it out, but I now know they can still see me even if I can't see them. My people are clever that way, I'll say that for them.

When I hear creaking on the stairs I know that one of my people is coming to get me. As a Lhasa apso I'm a natural alert dog. My ancestors used to guard the monasteries in Tibet. If we Lhasas heard an intruder, we'd bark to wake up the bigger dogs and those hounds would handle the rough stuff. It was a good arrangement. In here, though, the shouting makes things easier to know if someone's approaching. If it's the man, I know he won't come for me right away. He'll go into the kitchen and make one of those noisy smelly drinks. But by then I'm all geared up for my morning poop, so I'll give a few short barks to remind him I'm still waiting. He'll shout 'Coming!' but not in a nice way. He has a *tone*, if you know what I mean. Anyway, it will be a good five minutes before he appears. Five minutes might not sound too long to wait, but in dog time that's more than half an hour.

It wasn't always like this. When the small people were in the house things were different. The boy and girl would have me out in the garden while there was still dew on the grass. Those were crazy days. Lots of running and chasing. They must have tossed that tennis ball a million times, but I always ran after it and brought it back for them. Then they'd just toss it away again. Those small people were nuts, but it was fun all the same.

They got bigger, those small people, and then one day they went away. Just like that. There was a commotion in the hall and lots of boxes full of books were being carried out to the car. Then there was hugging and crying. I got lots of cuddles and treats that day. I didn't know why, but I wasn't complaining. Then they went out the front door and didn't take me with them. I waited and waited, but only the big people – the man and the woman – came back. I waited by that door all night and all the next day. That's like two weeks in dog time. I felt such a fool. The house got quiet after that. Apart from the shouting, that is.

There's more shouting after breakfast and then the man or the woman will take me for my walk in the park. These days I like to take that slow and easy. The woman doesn't seem to mind that so much, and she usually meets someone she knows and they stop and talk a while. If it's the man across the street, she'll talk for ages. I'm quite a sociable animal myself and if a neighbour's dog wants to sniff my rear end, I'll allow it, up to a point. But if things get *inappropriate*, I'll do one of my growls and usually the woman will see what's happening and pull us apart.

The man isn't so attentive. Most days he tugs and pulls me along before I've even had a good sniff of the fence posts. Sometimes he spends the whole walk staring at that little black box he carries with him. Sometimes he talks to the box more than he talks to me. In that case I know he's not paying any attention to me, which is bad form, don't you think? Once, when he was talking to the black box, I went and hid under a bush and didn't come out until I heard him calling my name for about a billion times. Serves him right.

Actually, I didn't really hide from him in purpose. Truth is, I took a bit of a funny turn when I was under that bush. I got all dizzy and couldn't walk properly, so I just sat there until it passed. I didn't want another trip to the vet. It gave me a bit of a fright, to be honest with you. Personally, I blame the food mix-ups that have been happening recently. Sometimes, when the man and the woman are doing that shouting thing, they don't notice what they're putting in my bowl. Only last week they opened a can of spicy meat. I could see from the label that it was the wrong stuff. It had a picture of a man in a big hat. My stuff has a picture of happy dogs on the front. But I was hungry, so I ate what they put down to me. Then I let them know they'd made a mistake in my usual way. I coughed it up. That always gets their attention, unless I cough it up in the next room and they don't see it immediately. In that case I'll just try again in a more prominent location. The fireside rug is a good spot.

I have to be careful not to overdo that, though. This week I've been sick about ten times and that's got them talking about the vet again. Looks like I'm going there today.

Otherwise it's not been a bad day. My people have been very affectionate. I've had lots of strokes and cuddles and even the small people put in an appearance. The boy and girl aren't so small any more, of course. I almost didn't recognise them. Oh, I know it's only been three years since they left, but that's like twenty in dog time.

I'm wondering if it's my birthday today, because everyone is being so nice to me. I hear them talking about when I first came to this house as a puppy. Sounds like I was a bit of a tearaway in those days. Did I really eat shoelaces? Can that be true? Then they found some old videos of me chasing the Frisbee at the beach. Honestly, it looked like I could fly in those days. At least the video had everyone laughing again. Even the man and woman were smiling at each other and holding hands. No shouting at all. Just a little bit of crying.

Anyway, something special is definitely happening today. Maybe there's going to be a party for me when I get back from the vet. Hopefully, I'll be feeling better then, because right now I'm not really up for it. I'm feeling pretty sick, to tell the truth. I might feel more lively after a good sleep.

A party might cheer me up. Let me see – this will be my thirteenth birthday. What's that in dog years? Woof. I don't even want to *think* about that.

ROOM FOR ONE MORE ON TOP

A day or two after Pete had the idea for his latest tax wheeze he began to notice the woman with the amazing hair. He first saw her on Monday morning while sitting on the top deck of the bus and then again on Tuesday as he came out of the off-licence on Alexandra Parade. On Wednesday morning she was in the park while he walked his dog and then on Thursday, in the Nisa, she was standing in front of the home-baking shelf, concentrating far too intently on a jar of cake sprinkles. It was definitely the same woman, because her hair-do was unlike anything he'd ever seen before. He wondered if one of the local hairdressers had invented a new style and maybe he was seeing different women with similar hair. But what were the chances that a stylist in Dennistoun would come up with something this good? The woman's hair wasn't just blonde and shiny, it positively glowed, almost as if it was lit from within. You saw the effect more clearly in the dark, but even under the harsh fluorescent strips of the corner shop it looked – what was the word he was looking for? Iridescent. Yes, that was it. Iridescent.

Not that hair had ever been his area of expertise. Pete had started going bald in his twenties and now, ten years later, he had the full pink snooker ball. Combine that with those debt-laden bags under his eyes and he was now rocking the kind of look that had strangers on the bus calling him 'old fella' and offering to give up their seat for him. Early-onset financial decrepitude was how he described his own condition. A series of failed get-rich-quick schemes had left him almost broke and barely able to afford dog food, vet bills and the mortgage payments on his one-bedroom flat in Aberfoyle Street. If not for his bible, his *personal* bible, he would barely have been able to keep his bald head above water. The 'bible' was how Pete described *Accountancy for Losers*, a book he had picked up from the Oxfam shop last year.

The Government tax people were rather good at hiding all those rules that allowed you to get money back from them, but he'd already been able to claim a decent rebate from his various loss-making ventures. Who knew that VHS tapes were not going to make the same kind of comeback he had seen with vinyl discs? And his brainwave of attaching tiny cameras to paper kites had been superseded by the out-of-the-blue trend for powered drones. Still, thanks to *Accountancy for Losers* he'd worked out how to defray all his costs and losses against the payments made when he was actually earning enough money to pay income tax. But it had been three years since he had quit that steady job in the council Housing Department, and he was running out of options. Now he was pursuing a Mr Micawber strategy and hoping that something would turn up.

And it did, or rather, *she* did.

Ludo, his tiny Jack Russell, was the first to detect her presence. He'd gone scampering to the door of the flat a full minute before the bell rang. He was still sniffing and whining when Pete caught up with him. When the bell did ring, he opened the door and there she was: the woman with the glowing hair.

'Good morning, Peter,' she said and then, looking down at his feet, added, 'and a very good morning to you too, Ludo.

You are such a good boy!'

Evidently pleased with the compliment, Ludo turned on his back and allowed the woman to rub his belly. Pete was still trying to work out how this woman knew both of their names, never mind why she was at his door.

'I've seen you before,' he managed to say. 'You were in the Nisa yesterday. I remember your ...'

'My hair? Yes, it's a bit of a giveaway, isn't it? Not much help when I'm trying to be discreet. But I think you're the only one who could have spotted me, so that's fine. Do you mind if I come in for a chat?'

'Well I ... I mean, yes, come in. No, I mean, who are you? What's this about?'

The woman smiled, bent to pick up Ludo and carried him past Pete as she glided into his front room. There was a three-piece suite, but the sofa and armchairs were stacked with piles of VHS tapes, mostly old movies or box sets of TV shows. The woman hovered the way people do when they are not sure where to sit. The difference was that this woman *literally* hovered. Pete took a moment to notice it, but then realised her feet were just a few inches above the carpet, partially hidden by the hem of her flowing white dress.

'You have a lot of old tapes here,' the woman observed. 'Some of my favourites too. *Ben-Hur*, *The Ten Commandments* ... *Monty Python's The Meaning of Life*. Oh, I do love that one. I like the bit where the main film is invaded by the short feature they show at the start. What was that called again?'

'*The Crimson Permanent Assurance*,' said Pete.

'That's right. All those boring insurance guys become pirates. So funny. Of course, you can get that film on DVD now, you know. Blu-ray too. Really good quality. Cheaper to download it, though.'

'Yes,' said Pete, 'so everyone keeps telling me. But let me clear a space.'

He moved two of the stacks to create one big tower of tapes in the corner of the room and gestured for the woman to take a seat on the sofa. He himself perched on the arm of a chair, not wanting to commit himself to a long conversation. The woman sat down, and Ludo went straight to sleep on her lap.

'Let's get down to business,' the woman began. 'I understand you've been planning a new venture, something with a few tax advantages. Would that be correct?'

Pete blanched. So is that what this was about? How could it be? He hadn't discussed his new plans with anyone yet. How had the tax people got wind of it already?

'Are you from the Government?' he asked.

The woman smiled. 'In a way, yes I am,' she said. 'But probably not the government you're thinking about. In fact, I know it's definitely not the government you're thinking about.'

Pete's mind raced through the possibilities. Not our Government? Maybe something overseas? The Cayman Islands?

'No, not the Cayman Islands,' the woman laughed. 'I had better put you out of your misery. You see, I'm God.'

'God?'

'Yes, God. You know, Supreme Being, Lord of all Creation, blah, blah, blah and so on.'

'I don't understand.'

'I know, and I really don't have time to sit here and persuade you, so let me just pop this certainty into your mind. I'm God and that's that.'

And somehow, Pete needed no more convincing. Something in his mind now told him that the woman sitting on his worn sofa was, indeed, God.

'I don't like doing that too often,' said God, 'but it's one of the advantages of being able to tell what people are thinking. Usually I leave them alone with their own thoughts. Free will and all that. But we're in a hurry and I need your help.'

'You need my help? God needs my help?'

'Yes,' she said. 'Now, let's talk about this new venture of yours. Take me through it. Some kind of new religion, wasn't it?'

Pete now felt utterly ashamed of himself. Yes, he had been planning to set up a new religion. He suspected there would be so many tax advantages. Of course he'd need to have a proper read of his bible again, but now, sitting here with God, he wondered if the whole thing might sound a bit blasphemous. Would he be risking the wrath of the Almighty right here in his own living room? Should he shut the windows in case of thunderbolts?

'No thunderbolts,' said God, reading his mind again. 'But what were you planning to call this new religion of yours?'

Pete got off the arm of the chair and found a dog-eared exercise book on the sideboard. He leafed through it looking for the list he had made in his bed the previous night.

'I hadn't quite decided,' he explained, 'but here are some possibles: Peter's People, Passport to Beyond, Religion 2.0, The Newly Chosen—'

'That's the one!' said God, and her sudden exclamation startled Ludo so much that he opened one eye for five seconds before going back to sleep. 'I don't need to hear any more. The Newly Chosen. That fits perfectly.'

'How come?'

God settled herself back into the sofa, tickled the dog's ear gently and began her explanation.

'In a nutshell, Heaven's getting too crowded. Too many good people are dying. To some extent, it's always been that way, but now, with famine and pestilence on the loose again, well, it's getting more than a little cosy up there. I mean, we've tried imposing stricter entry requirements and barring certain types of people – litter louts, obviously, and people who talk loudly into their phones on a train. Seems a bit petty, but it's been a popular move with the existing residents.'

'Sounds like a good call,' said Pete.

'But we've still got everyone and their dog demanding entry.'

'There are dogs in Heaven?' asked Pete, glancing at Ludo.

'Of course,' said God.

'And cats too?'

God hesitated and Pete noticed she avoided the question.

'Look, we can discuss all that later, but what I need from you now is your promise that you will set up this new religion. The Newly Chosen. Such a good name.'

'Well, you know it was really only meant as a tax dodge. You sure you're not a bit, er, "wrathy" about that?'

'Render unto Caesar the things that are Caesar's, and unto God the things that are God's. Matthew 22:21.'

'What does that mean?' asked Pete.

'It means pay your taxes, you cheapskate. How do you think they pay for schools and hospitals?'

'Oh.'

'But you've got it all wrong as usual,' God continued, 'because religions per se don't really have many tax breaks. It's only if they set themselves up as official charities, and even then you need to prove that your religion is fulfilling some kind of public need. I think I can count on you not to do that.'

'How come you know so much about tax rules?'

God shrugged.

'I'm all-knowing,' she said. 'Plus, I read a lot. Anyway, what do you say we work together on this plan of yours? It would really help me get a grip on things upstairs. At least it might buy me some time until I can expand the universe a little and make room for New Heaven.'

'New Heaven?'

'It's my big plan. New Heaven. Lots of lovely bijou self-catering chalets. Pods, maybe. You see I really need to start lowering people's expectations. This old-fashioned nonsense about Heaven being a "house with many mansions" – well, it's just not realistic. Economically unfeasible. Besides, those mansions in Heaven are very draughty.'

Pete scratched his head. He was having trouble following God's logic and was hoping she would just pop the explanation straight into his brain like she had done before.

'It's simple really. I'm going to designate your religion as the only *official* religion. The only one that guarantees you entry through the Pearly Gates. It will be like having a triple A pass at a music festival or when Coca-Cola endorses the Olympics and no one is allowed in carrying a can of Pepsi. Your Newly Chosen people – all two of you if you count Ludo here – are being officially approved by Heaven at a corporate level. Now do you understand?'

'I think so.'

'And now you know so,' said God, using her mind cheat again. 'Also, I'm looking forward to having some time to myself. A bit of "me" time, as it were. A chance to relax and do a bit of baking.'

'You bake?'

'Used to. Daily bread and all that. And cupcakes with sprinkles. Love those.'

God gave Ludo one last pat on his head, lifted him off her lap and was making a move to leave when Pete thought he had discovered a flaw in her plan.

'But what if my religion really takes off? What if I attract hundreds and thousands of followers? Won't you be back to square one with all those souls demanding entry to paradise?'

God gave him a look, a mixture of suppressed mirth and pity.

'Don't worry, I won't make that mistake again.'

'Again? You mean you've done this before?'

'Of course. A couple of times. But not recently. Didn't work out the way I had planned, but I've figured out what I did wrong. Those guys had too much charisma. They attracted a lot more followers than I had expected.'

'And you think I won't? I could get something going on social media. I mean, now that I know for certain that God exists, it'll be easier for me to convince others. I might surprise you.'

'Oh, I'll take my chances with that,' she said, giving the chaos of his room a final glance before stepping past the tower of unsold VHS tapes. 'I've been watching you very closely. I've watched all your dreams come crashing to earth, watched you pick yourself up again and then watched more of your schemes go awry. And you know what, Peter?'

'What?'

She smiled. 'It's why I chose you.'

This stung. To think that God, of all people, had picked him precisely because he was expected to fail. It made him more determined than ever to prove her wrong. As he walked her to the door, he couldn't resist one parting shot.

'Here's what I think, God,' he said.

'Tell me.'

'You may be all-seeing and all-knowing, but when it comes to people—'

'Yes?'

'You just don't have enough faith.'

He closed the door behind her and went straight to work.

TEACAKE TALES WITH HECTOR AULD

Hullo, it's your pal Hector Auld here with another of my *Teacake Tales*. This week I want to tell you a story about my wee friend Jessie and about the time she had the whole village up in arms. Even the Kirk Minister was fair angry with her, I can tell you. And yet it all started innocently enough, at the tail end of the tattie-picking holidays. With every dreel in every field howked clean, there was nothing much for us weans to do but fret about going back to our classrooms for the new term and wondering if our big country feet would still fit in those tight leather school shoes. Of course that wasn't going to be a problem for wee Gordy McAlpine, who had managed to hack off three of his toes while mucking about with the farmer's scythe, but he was cheery enough about it and I think he enjoyed having all his pals queue up to have a gawp at his scabs.

In those days there was no television and nothing much on the radio except posh folk talking about Sir Walter Scott all day long. To keep us scamps out of mischief, Mother would organise her distemper-and-tea parties. She brewed up a big pot of strong tea using crushed toadstools and a wee sprinkle of her 'special herbs'. Then she invited all the village weans inside to watch her slap the distemper on the scullery wall. It's no word of a lie to say that our family often had but two farthings to rub together but Mother aye insisted on using the best distemper – the kind with the good lead in it. So we sat there watching her disappear into a cloud of white dust, coughing and choking as she worked the big brush up and down the wall and us scallywags sitting gulping cup after cup of that magic tea. Oh, it was bliss, and when it grew dark in the afternoon, Mother would light some candles so we could drink more tea and watch the paint dry. A rare treat indeed.

Aye, we made our own entertainment in those days and that's how, by sheer fluke, Wee Jessie discovered she had a bit of a talent for hand shadows. It's when you fankle your fingers in front of a candle or a lamp and cast funny shapes on the wall. It was like Jessie's fingers and thumbs were made of elastic and with a few twists and turns she could make an entire menagerie of birds and animals appear on that blank wall in Mother's scullery. There were eagles and lions and snakes and spiders, and as the shapes danced across the room and flew onto the ceiling, she'd tell stories about what was happening. Good stories they were too, and us bairns would sit with our mouths wide open as she told us about big-game hunters tracking tigers in Africa or undersea adventures involving fights with sharks and an octopus. Some of her stories were a wee bit frightening, so Jessie would cross her fingers to make the shadow-shape of a big 'x', and that was the signal for the younger ones to get to their beds. Jessie could then tell the rest of us how the big-game hunter met a grisly end in the tiger's jaws, or how the giant octopus swallowed an entire fishing boat with all hands on board and how the skipper's head floated in with the tide, still wearing his bobble hat.

At first, Jessie would tell her stories indoors, but as weans from the next village got to hear about her shows there wasn't enough space in Mother's kitchen. No matter, because as the nights got darker, we pulled on our scratchy balaclavas and moved the shows out to the open air. Jessie would hang a paraffin lamp on the door of our outside cludgie and make the hand shadows jump about on the side wall of our crofthouse. And because the lamp was that bit further away from the wall, the birds and animals were now gigantic, and the audience – which had grown to about twenty weans and a few older folk too – were absolutely transfixed by Jessie's stories. She'd do all the voices as well, and we'd laugh at how the hunter sounded like the local Laird and how the shark sounded like big Sandy Macpherson, the schoolteacher. Ach but, as you might have guessed, the Scottish weather played havoc with the fun. As the days got colder, the wind got up and it could be hard to hear what Jessie was telling us, even when she was shouting herself hoarse. The final straw came when the paraffin lamp got blown down and smashed on our pile of cut peat. That might have started an inferno had Mother not come running out of the scullery with her big kettle of cold tea and doused the flames.

Now, that should have been the end of the hand shadow shows, but it was the Kirk Minister himself who saved the day. He had heard about Jessie's gifts as a story-teller and came to her with the idea that she could use her talents in the service of the Lord.

'You can do your shows in the Kirk on Thursday nights,' he told her. 'I'll hang a big bedsheet in front of the pews and you can stand at the back in front of my big oil lamp. It's the one I took off my old boat and much brighter than the other one was.'

Well, Jessie was delighted with this plan. It would be much cosier doing her shows inside the Kirk and there would be plenty of room for all the weans and even the grown-ups if they wanted to stop by for a look. But there was a catch, because the Minister had two conditions he insisted that Jessie abide by.

'I have no objection to your adventure stories,' he told her, 'but try not to make them too bloodthirsty. And we must remind everyone that they're in a house of God, so make sure the last story you tell each night is something inspired by the Bible.'

'The Bible?' Jessie asked. 'You mean like yon story of the loaves and fishes, or the Good Samaritan. That kind of thing?'

'Exactly!' the Minister told her. 'Just one Bible story to end the evening, but the rest is up to you.'

Jessie agreed to this rule, and because her hand shadow shows now had the approval of the Minister himself, lots more folk wanted to see them. That first Thursday night, the Kirk pews were almost half full. The next Thursday it was 'standing room only', as they say. That's when the Kirk Treasurer came up with the idea of charging admission so as to control the numbers. Adults paid threepence for a ticket, bairns were charged a halfpenny and the old folk got in for free. The queer thing was that just made more people want to come. Funny how folk value things a bitty more if they have to pay for them. Like I say, queer, eh? So the very next Thursday the Minister had to turn folk away, and the following week it was decided that Jessie would have to do an extra show on a Wednesday night as well. Folk were coming from far and wide, including one or two from the big towns like Glasgow and Edinburgh.

Jessie mostly stuck to the deal she had agreed with the Minister and always ended the night with a Bible story, but she didn't make much effort to tone down the violence in her adventure yarns. The Minister got huffy about that and reminded her that she should cut out some of the blood and guts. That didn't work so well. In the new version of the story about the big-game hunter, there was no grisly end. Instead, the hunter suffered a flesh wound and was rescued by Tarzan before the tiger could pounce. Everyone agreed that Jessie's flexible fingers did a mighty good job of showing Tarzan swinging from vine to vine, but the story's happy ending didn't seem as satisfying as the original. It was the same with the octopus story. I mean, we should all have been glad that the shark bit the octopus just before he wrapped his tentacles around the fishing boat – those poor fishermen made it safely back to their wives, after all – but again, it just all felt like a bit of a let-down.

It was hard to explain, but the happy endings didn't sound like real life. The audience started to vote with their feet and soon there was no need for the extra shows on Wednesday nights, and the Thursday night pews started to look a bit empty.

Jessie, I have to be honest, had been getting a bit of a swollen head about the popularity of her shows, especially after chatting to those big city folk. She started wearing a beret and putting on all sorts of airs and graces. She even began speaking differently, swapping her usual voice for the one she had used to make fun of the Laird. But she changed her tune when audience numbers started to dwindle. She held her tongue for a while, but then blew up at the Minister himself in a way that no one had ever heard the like of.

'It's your fault,' she shouted at him in her new posh tone. 'All these changes you forced me to make. You're ... you're stifling my creativity.'

Now you would have thought that would have been an end to the matter. Giving cheek to a man of the cloth was simply not done in those days, but the Minister was a canny soul and he could see that Jessie had a point. Really, though, it was the Kirk Treasurer who finally persuaded the Minister that Jessie should be given a free hand. He had got used to counting all those halfpennies and threepenny bits and even the Kirk hierarchy – the big bosses in Edinburgh – had been taking a keen interest in how those church coffers had been swelling.

Jessie got a telling off for her 'unwarranted impertinence', but was allowed to go back to doing things her way ... just so long as she still had a Bible story as her finale.

As it turned out, though, Jessie – the new fancy Jessie – had become fed up with sharks and big-game hunters, and now that she had been given more control, she decided to experiment with a few new ideas. She put pieces of coloured glass in front of the big oil lamp to add a kaleidoscope effect to the show. She added music of sorts, blowing through a paper and comb to make a mournful opening theme. There was then a whole sequence where she formed her hand into the shape of a question mark and simply intoned 'Why? Why? Why?' for five whole minutes. The Bible story those nights was all about the resurrection of Lazarus, and you could hear some weans sobbing into their mothers' arms as Jessie's fingers portrayed a zombie-like figure emerging from a tomb. She hadn't even bothered with the 'x' warning, because that kind of thing was 'so bourgeois'. My, these new stories of hers left most of us baffled; but the city folk seemed to like them, and you could hear them muttering things like 'too true' and 'so profound', and that made Jessie's head swell to the size of three turnips.

It won't surprise you to learn that people stopped coming to the shows. The Minister, the Treasurer and even some of the Kirk bosses in Edinburgh all begged her to go back to her old way of doing things, but she wouldn't listen.

'I'm not doing this for the money or to please the crowds,' she told them. 'I'm doing it for the art itself. Next week I'm going to add a wee bit of interpretative dance.'

That's when the Minister decided enough was enough. He lectured Jessie about the sin of pride and about respecting your elders, and so on. Even the Treasurer stuck his oar in and muttered something about Jessie disappearing up her own bahookie. In any case, there were to be no more hand shadow extravaganzas. It was all over. Well, almost, because Jessie sulked for a day or two and then sauntered back to the Minister with both an apology and a proposal.

'It's almost Christmas,' she told him, 'so let me do one last show to end the season. No sharks or tigers or big-game hunters. No weird colours or shapes. No zombies. Just one of the best Bible stories of all. The Nativity. The arrival of the holy infant in hand shadow form. It's never been done before. This will be a world first for our wee village.'

The Minister was a careful man, but not unreasonable, and he thought this might be a fine way for Jessie to bring things to a close and demonstrate her contrition to the whole village. He agreed to her plans for one last show and they shook hands. He noticed how tough and muscular her fingers had become after so many months of contorting them into her cast of characters. Aye, he noticed that, but he didn't notice the sly smile on her face.

A few nights before Christmas, we all packed ourselves onto the pews and Jessie stood at the front, the bedsheet screen behind her, and made an announcement.

'Ladies and gentlemen,' she began, 'and all you weans too. Thank you for coming to this, my final hand shadow show of the year. In fact, my last show ever.'

There were a few murmurs of 'aww' and 'wee shame' at that, but not too many. Folk were keen to get things started. Jessie explained that this would be 'a very special version of the Nativity' and then used an expression that none of us had ever heard before.

'In fact,' she said, 'I'm calling this the Director's Cut.'

Jessie walked back to her big lamp, flexing her fingers, and then, on the screen, came the image of two donkeys trekking

211

through the desert and then the shadow-shape of a pregnant Mary and her husband, Joseph. Jessie provided both the narration and the dialogue, voicing Mary in the style of a Scottish fishwife, telling Joseph, 'Haud your wheest, man, and find us a place tae bide for the night.' In a gruff voice, Jessie's Joseph was portrayed as a loyal and long-suffering spouse who assured Mary that she 'shouldnae fuss yersel, wumman. If there's nae room at the inn, we'll bed doon in yon barn for the nicht.'

In the darkened Kirk, the audience saw the Minister's face illuminated by the glow from the screen and that he was smiling at these characterisations. He was an Edinburgh man himself, but he thought it was a good thing if country people used the old Scots words now and then, as long as it didn't get out of hand. His smiles allowed everyone else to relax and enjoy the show. They watched the screen as Jessie's hands transformed into shepherds and farmyard animals, and then it began to dawn on the grown-ups where the story was going next.

'And now,' Jessie's voice boomed out, 'the miracle of childbirth!'

I won't describe to you what Jessie did with those fingers of hers, nor can I repeat the horrible noises she was making at the same time. It all happened so fast it's a blur in my memory. But I remember the Minister running to the back of the Kirk and how he tried to wrestle Jessie's hand away from the front of the lamp. There was pushing and shoving and the lamp crashed onto the wooden floor, and once again it was my own mother who saved the day. It's just as well she never went anywhere without her big pot of toadstool tea, and a good thing that it was still half full when she ran over to douse the flames.

Ach, I see my time is just about up, so I'd better let you know what became of Wee Jessie. Well, she's no' that wee any more, of course, and I'd say her head is bigger than ever. Five turnips. You might have heard how she moved to America and was making films in yon Hollywood. She made some good ones too. They won an Oscar and everything. You'll mind that one about the pirates and the octopus, and the other one about Tarzan and the tigers. That was a few years ago, mind, and now she's in France making those strange films about drugs and religion. Arthouse films, they call them, but they still leave me scratching my head.

Mind you, that might be because of this itchy balaclava.

Cheerio for now.

I SAW MOMMY KILLING SANTA CLAUS – A NELSON S. PIPSQUEAK STORY

It was Christmas time in New York City. I guess it was Christmas a bunch of other places too, but I figured that us New Yorkers would be lifting the annual prize for hypocrisy. No contest, really, because we always got a head start in *that* race. Thanksgiving had been and gone at the end of November, and in this city that's when they fire the starting gun on the whole Phoney Show. The blocks west of Central Park were still dripping with tangled netting and half-deflated balloons – the sad remnants of the big Macy's parade. Now the jerks who had been too busy to even exchange glances the rest of the year were elbowing their way in and out of stores and panic buying the useless crap they would foist on friends and family. That wasn't one of my problems, a bonus that came with having no family and no friends, not unless you count my buddy Jack and, yeah, I always counted on Jack. Jack was my idea of good company, especially on nights like tonight. Christmas goddam Eve.

So here I was, sitting in my office, sipping Tennessee firewater and watching the snow short-circuit the neon signs outside my window. I was about to light my last cigar. It had been in my desk drawer since I'd quit smoking the year before last. I knew it would stink up the office with tobacco smog, but that would be an improvement. Then the phone rang. Phones do that sometimes, but I was starting to think mine was an exception. I stuffed the cigar in my jacket pocket, grabbed the receiver and barked out my usual spiel.

'Nelson S. Pipsqueak, private investigator. State your business.'

'You know something, Pipsqueak, you really ought to work on that customer-friendly manner of yours.'

I recognised that voice. It was the nasal honk of Lieutenant Dobski, my old boss. Not the smartest guy ever to be allowed out of New Jersey. The joke downtown was that he thought a protection racket was something that was used by a tennis pro.

'What's up, Dobski? You lost the key to the john again? I've got to warn you, I charge fifty bucks a day plus expenses, but for you I'll add ten bucks.'

'Funny guy, Pipsqueak, but for your information things have changed down here at headquarters. See, we *trust* each other now. We don't even *lock* the john.'

'That's good to know, Dobski. I feel all warm inside just thinking about that.'

'Stow it, Pipsqueak. I ain't calling to pass the time of day. We need your ass down here at HQ. A little unfinished business from your cop days has turned up. An old flame, you might say.'

Suddenly I was interested, but I wasn't going to give Dobski the satisfaction of knowing that.

'Hey, it's Christmas Eve, Dobski. I've knocked off for the holiday. Of course, I could be persuaded if you say the magic words. And here's a clue, they're not "hocus-pocus".'

'Okay, Pipsqueak, I ain't got time to argue. Fifty bucks.'

'Sixty.'

'Okay, sixty.'

'Plus expenses.'

'Whatever. Just get moving. Before someone else dies.'

'What are you talking about, Dobski?'

'You heard. And while you're making your way downtown, have a think about that old flame. Cynthia McBain. Yeah, that's right. She's been asking for you.' Dobski hung up.

Cynthia McBain. The name rang more bells than Quasimodo on steroids. I grabbed my gun and my hat and began sifting through memories as I made my way across town. I had crossed paths with Cynthia, when was it? Ten, twelve years ago? I had just made detective and what became known as the Yule Log murders was one of my first big cases. At the start of December, Santas had started showing up dead all across Manhattan. Some had been street Santas – collecting for charities – others had been working in department stores. In all, twelve members of the ho-ho-ho brotherhood had fallen victim to the killer.

There's no such thing as a good murder, but these were particularly nasty. The killer had used some kind of makeshift flamethrower to torch the victims and leave blackened outlines of the bodies emblazoned on the sidewalk. For a while, those scorch marks had become grisly tourist attractions before the Mayor decided that wasn't doing a whole lot of good for New York's image. Entire blocks of sidewalk were removed and donated to the Guggenheim as pieces of art. Critics were divided. 'Macabre,' said the *Times*. 'Better than Warhol's soup cans,' said the *Daily News*. 'Jejune,' said the *New Yorker*.

Two things made us like Cynthia McBain for the killings. First was her reputation as an outspoken hater of Christmas. After getting her sociology doctorate from NYU she had become a media motormouth on the subject, lashing out at the unfettered consumerism and the role foisted on mothers and wives as festive homemakers, unpaid dishwashers and egg nog mules. When she got married and had a kid, she also took aim at Santa Claus himself. She created a stir on a morning television show when she claimed that she would never, ever take her own six-year-old son to sit on the jolly man's knee. In a famously bombastic appearance on *America's Awake*, she told the host, Chandler Madison, that December 25th in the McBain household would just be like any other day. No tree, no tinsel, nothing. Then she crossed the line by claiming that any parent who subjected their own kids to such nonsense was no better than an abuser and that their little darlings would be justified in suing them in years to come. I guess the lawyers applauded that, while the media hacks dubbed her 'Doctor Grinch'.

But it wasn't just her opinions that made Cynthia a murder suspect; there had been deliberate clues left at every crime scene. Beside each crispy stiff was a beautifully wrapped Christmas gift and each turned out to be a child's toy – a doll, a teddy bear, plastic building bricks and so on. What clinched it was the fingerprints found on each of the parcels: all of them belonged to Cynthia McBain. She had no explanation for this and insisted the forensics must be wrong. I had checked with the boys in the lab, but there had been no mistake. It seemed like a slam dunk until the DA said we didn't have a case. Cynthia had an alibi for every one of those murders. She'd been out of town, lecturing in Chicago or Boston or Washington, while her husband stayed home and played homemaker and nursemaid. She walked, the killings stopped and the case went so cold it was filed under B for Birds Eye. But now?

'It's started again,' Dobski told me as I sat in his office. 'Another Santa deep fried over at 77th street. And before you ask, yes, another Christmas gift wrapped and tied in a bow. A toy train. And, yeah, Cynthia's prints are all over it. We hauled her in but she's keeping that big mouth of hers zipped.'

'Has she lawyered up?'

'Not yet, but someone's talking. That pain-in-the-ass reporter Chandler Madison has already called. He's network prime time these days and says he'll run with the story tonight. Film at eleven, you know how it goes.'

'Yeah, I know,' I said. 'But tell me this, Dobski. Why am I here? When was the last time New York's Finest doled out greenbacks to a gumshoe like me? What gives?'

Dobski sighed, and then he laid his cards on the table. There was a joker in that pack.

'She asked to see you. Look, Pipsqueak, you and me ain't bosom buddies, but I got to admit you had a certain flair for interrogation. So maybe you'll get lucky.'

This was the closest Dobski had ever come to a compliment and maybe he was right. Maybe it was more luck than skill, but it was true. So many bad guys over the years taking the Fifth, and then I'd start in on them and suddenly their lips were flapping faster than a shutter on a stormy night and they were spilling more beans than a cowboy with the shakes.

'You lead the way,' I told Dobski, 'and let's see what Doctor Grinch has to say for herself, if anything.'

They had been letting her stew in one of the interview rooms. She was sitting at the metal table, the kind that had hooks for restraints, but she hadn't been cuffed. It was too soon for that. She looked up at me as I walked in. I closed the door behind me and sat facing her. It had been a dozen years since I'd last looked into those cool green eyes, but they hadn't lost any of their sparkle. Her auburn hair was cut a little shorter than I remembered and she still had more curves than a Grand Prix circuit. Sure, she looked good, but she was the kind of woman who couldn't give a rat's ass about what you thought of her appearance. It's what I liked about her. Maybe if things had been different …

'Detective Pipsqueak,' she said, 'It's been too long.'

'It's just plain Mister Pipsqueak these days,' I told her. 'I had a falling out with the NYPD a couple of years back. I quit the force and I quit smoking. Both decisions are adding years to my life.'

Cynthia gave a thin smile. I decided to circle round to the murders by way of some family chitchat. It was my usual technique.

'So, how's married life … and how's that boy of yours?'

'Divorced,' she told me. 'And little Damien is all grown up now. He signed up for the Marines. He likes spending time at the beach. Any beach in any country.'

I pondered that. Anyone in the military might have access to weaponry. Flamethrowers maybe? I didn't push it. I noticed Cynthia hesitating and then, just like Dobski had predicted, I got lucky.

'Those presents at the scene of the murders. I've worked it out. The prints on those toys. They *are* mine.'

I leaned forward and then glanced at the camera in the corner of the room, its red light blinking. All of this was being recorded. No one had read Cynthia her rights, but then I wasn't a cop. Dobski was a smart guy, after all.

'So, you're confessing to murder?'

'No. Not at all. But I did handle those toys, on that TV show. *America's Awake*. The set was all dressed up for Christmas. A tree with presents all around it.'

I sighed and leaned back.

'Forget it, Cynthia. We looked at those tapes. We watched the entire interview. You were sat at the desk the whole time.

You never went near that tree. There's no video of you touching those toys.'

'No, not in the interview. It was before that. They were recording a whatchamacallit, a *promo* for the show. Chandler Madison had me sitting beside him at the tree. He was opening some presents as he talked to the camera, and handing me some of the toys as he told viewers how I disagreed with all the crap about Christmas.'

'I'm not buying this, Cynthia. If he was handling the toys, then his prints would be on them too.'

'But they weren't all toys, Mister Pipsqueak. The first present he opened was a pair of gloves and—'

Suddenly I got it.

'And he put them on!' I finished her sentence. 'So you're saying he framed you because he's the killer.'

'Exactly!'

'But what was his motive?'

'Ratings, Mister Pipsqueak. *America's Awake* was at rock bottom before those murders, and then, somehow, they always seemed to be right on top of the story, the first to break the news of each killing, first with some of the details. Everyone thought Madison had a source. Someone on the case. They even suspected you, as I recall.'

She was right and I was still sore about it. I remembered the whispering campaign and I never really shook off that suspicion. It was one of the reasons I finally quit.

I took a few moments for what she was saying to sink in. Chandler Madison kills *twelve* Santas, the *twelve* days of Christmas. But he thinks ahead. Before he starts on his body barbecues, he invites Santa-hating Cynthia onto the show and makes sure her prints are all over those toys. Then he leaves them as clues.

I looked up at the camera and hoped that Dobski and his flatfoots would be on their way to the network's studios to pick up Madison. A search of his apartment might even turn up the smoking gun – or a hot flamethrower.

'Looks like you might be in the clear, Cynthia,' I told her.

'And you too, Mister Pipsqueak. We really ought to celebrate.'

And we did. Dobski's men snatched Madison just as he was about to host the network's Christmas Eve special. He protested his innocence, but he'd be behind bars until a lawyer could arrange bail – and the Christmas holidays would mean that wasn't going to happen anytime soon.

Cynthia came back to my apartment for a glass or two of the good stuff. I decided I'd finally treat myself to that last cigar, prompting Cynthia to fish an aerosol can of deodorant out of her handbag. I puffed on my illegal Havana and didn't notice her pick up my Zippo lighter.

'I saw this in a movie once,' she said. 'You spray the aerosol and spark the lighter. It creates a mini—'

'—flamethrower,' I said. 'Yeah, I saw that movie too.'

Cynthia smiled and handed me my Zippo.

'Good thing I'm afraid of fire,' she said. 'Now, how about that whisky you promised me?'

In the cleanest glass I could find, I poured her a shot and then topped up my own.

'Merry Christmas,' I said. I hadn't forgotten how she felt about the so-called season of goodwill, but I wanted to see her reaction. She surprised me by leaning close and clinking her glass against mine.

'Merry Christmas, Nelson,' she said.

'You've mellowed,' I said. 'You want to stay for dinner?'

'It's a bit late for dinner,' she said, 'but I'll stay for breakfast.'

'Sounds good,' I said. 'I have eggs and there are eggs to follow.'

'Good thing I like eggs,' she said. 'But I have one condition.'

'Name it.'

'You do the cooking.'

She poured us both another shot of Jack. This was turning out to be a pretty good Christmas after all. So what if I had forgotten to buy the mistletoe? As it turned out, we did okay without it.

JOHNNY SELLOTAPE: AN OBITUARY

**Self-styled pioneer of 'adhesive comedy' achieved success
so late in life he was actually dead**

In any roll-call of Scotland's comedy greats you will hear the likes of Stanley Baxter, Billy Connolly and Kevin Bridges – names which span the evolution of the country's comedy and entertainment scene from the days of variety theatre, through the advent of radio and television and, latterly, to sell-out arena events. Until recently, however, one name was always absent from such lists. Johnny Sellotape, whose death was reported last week, rubbed shoulders with so many of those legendary figures and achieved early notoriety in legal circles because of a court order that specifically forbade the whole shoulder-rubbing thing.

He was born Joseph Selinski – the only child of Roman and Tania Selinski, Hebridean crofters who had changed their own names from Mary and Fergus McGregor after being caught up in the bitter Herring Wars of the late 1930s. After agreeing to blab about their fellow islanders, they entered a witness protection programme, were given new identities and relocated to Glasgow. In 1941, as Nazi bombs rained on Clydebank, Mary gave birth to their son. His arrival into the world went unnoticed for some days, even by Mary, who boasted to neighbours that her new diet seemed to be 'working a treat' until she came across the infant while sweeping the carpet. Later she would blame the noise of the bombs for this oversight.

Young Joseph's lust for fame and fortune developed at an early age, and by the time he hit his teens he fancied himself as a writer of newspaper cartoon strips. He collected dozens of rejections slips for his wide-of-the-mark storyline ideas for Broons and Oor Wullie strips. A plotline presupposing a mishearing of the words 'Broth' and Brothel' led to some unwanted advances for Daphne Broon and a line of men forming along the length of Glebe Street. Similarly, Grandpaw Broon's penchant for confectionery known as Granny Sookers formed the basis of another jaw-dropping story that got no further than the editor's waste-paper bin.

As he entered his twenties, Joseph set his sights on a stage career and, noting the popularity of Glasgow's famous 'Five-Past Eight' variety shows, he auditioned with an act which he described as a new form of silent comedy 'like Charlie Chaplin but without the hat, moustache, cane or funny walk'. When baffled producers told him that meant he would just be walking across the stage like a normal person, he exploded with fury and accused them of 'typical Scottish parochialism'.

Undeterred, Joseph decided to hit back by launching his own variety show. Pawning his mother's dentures, he raised money to lease a run-down theatre in the Gorbals and created the 'Eight Minutes to Five Show'. It was then that he adopted the alias Johnny Sellotape and found a kindred spirit and new partner in an old schoolfriend called Billy, who was to become Billy Bostik. Together they styled themselves as 'adhesive comedians' and with the catchphrase 'it's a bit tacky but it sticks' they headlined their own stage show. While most double-acts of the time had a funnyman playing off feed lines from a straight man, Johnny and

Billy defied that convention in that they were both, for the most part, straight men. The one concession to conventional comedy, however, was the emergency jokes that Johnny had taped to his jacket. When, inevitably, audiences responded with silence, boos or thrown vegetable matter, Johnny would tear one of these jokes from his jacket and relay it aloud in the manner of a man who had only learned to read that morning. Others on the bill included Rosemary Maley – Glasgow's Tallest Abattoir Worker – and the Amazing Mister Flick, who performed with a giant set of tiddlywinks and no safety net. Theatre historians now cite many reasons for the failure of that show, not least a curtain-up time of eight minutes to five which was exactly eight minutes before most of Glasgow's factory and shipyard workers would hear the whistle for the end of their shifts. Little credit is given for the avant-garde ambition of the production.

All was not lost, however, because one man who came to see the double-act was a record producer from London. Lacking in self-confidence after a colleague had turned down the Beatles, the man was determined not to make the same mistake and so put reaction aside and chased any act he felt had absolutely no talent. He signed Johnny and Billy after hearing their song 'Icky Sticky', a simple reworking of a traditional Irish folk tune with the hook chorus: 'We're Icky and we're Sticky and we haven't got a lot / Like a story from Dickens, we're poverty-stricken and now we've lost the plot.' The record failed to dislodge the Fab Four from the number one spot on the hit parade, having entered the chart at ninety-three and then slipped back to oblivion. Vinyl copies of the record did, for a time, become popular among the new pirate radio stations that had been broadcasting at that time. The trendy DJs used them as ashtrays or Frisbees, and few tears were shed when an overenthusiastic throw saw the discs go overboard.

225

The failure of their music career led to cracks in the duo's relationship and, unbeknownst to Johnny, Billy had been negotiating with an agent for some traditional cabaret work in America. When an offer came in for a solo season in Vegas, it presented Billy with a moral dilemma and one that he struggled with for all of five minutes as he stood in the check-in queue at Glasgow airport.

Johnny Sellotape resumed his solo career, but needing cash to pay off debts and to redeem the ticket on the pawned dentures, he took on two roles. By night he worked as a stand-up comedian in pubs and nightclubs, but by day he presented himself as a children's entertainer, doing magic tricks at kiddies' birthday parties and delighting toddlers as he wrestled coloured balloons into the shapes of animals. The long hours took a toll on his mental health and on his concentration. The tabloid press described events at little Sally Campbell's fourth birthday party as 'obscene and depraved', but Johnny always insisted that the condom he had inflated in error was intended to form part of a giraffe's neck. A judge disagreed and he was jailed for thirty days.

Johnny found himself in Glasgow's Barlinnie Prison, then the home of the Special Unit, which offered hardened criminals the chance to find their creative spirit as artists and writers. Johnny saw his chance to do for the killers and gangsters of Glasgow what Johnny Cash had done for their counterparts at San Quentin. He offered to stage a special concert and perform his jokes and songs. The subsequent riot and rooftop protest gave the authorities little choice but to bow to the inmates' demands and get Johnny as far away from them as the rules would allow. He was transferred to a solitary confinement unit in Inverness but released early when prison officers could hear him humming in his cell.

With his reputation now in tatters, Johnny spiralled into a period of despair, and those who saw him during that period remembered that he was drinking heavily and there was reason to suspect other kinds of substance abuse. The white powder around his nostrils was not, in fact, cocaine. It turned out he had been sucking Sherbet Fountains out of a leaky liquorice.

It was the launch of BBC Radio Scotland in the late seventies that brought Johnny back to public attention. Exploiting BBC executives' unfamiliarity with the concept of entertainment, he secured himself a weekly show as a late-night disc jockey and assumed the new persona of Doctor Sticky. Unusually, for its time, the *Doctor Sticky Show* included regular features such as studio acrobatics and a face-pulling competition. When executives dared to question the value of such things on a non-visual medium, Johnny told them that they were out of touch and that this was what 'the kids were into'.

Radio fame led to the occasional guest spot on BBC television and it was one such appearance on the quiz show *SuperScot* that brought about another downfall. The show's regular format involved contestants being asked various undemanding questions about Scottish history, geography and shortbread recipes, but at Christmas, a celebrity version was scheduled and Johnny – sporting a punk hairstyle and his trademark Doctor Sticky sunglasses – took his place on the panel alongside stars of Scottish panto and out-of-work politicians. While the others saw the show as the opportunity for some festive fun, Johnny decided that he would confound expectations by winning the game and so, after watching dozens of taped recordings of the show, he developed a strategy. He decided he would give the same answer for every question and that answer would always be 'Mary, Queen of Scots'. No matter the question, he would buzz first and say 'Mary, Queen of Scots'.

Within minutes he was ten points in the lead, but producers were appalled that he had found this obvious loophole in the format and demanded that he leave the set. He refused and had to be strong-armed out of the studio by uniformed security guards. The BBC's top bosses were furious and exacted revenge by cancelling his radio show. They made the mistake of allowing him one final appearance on air so he could say goodbye to his listeners. With characteristic dignity, Johnny used this opportunity to plead his case with the audience and tearfully beg for the bosses to rethink his sacking. Sobbing, he promised to introduce new features such as puppets on the piano, but it was to no avail.

Once again, he was out of a job. A half-hearted attempt to reinvent himself as a novelist ensued when his manuscript for a romantic comedy – *Tango at the Sticky Toffee Café* – did the rounds of agents and publishers. The kindest rejection letters offered advice that Johnny might try his hand at the then thriving genre of 'Tartan Noir' crime thrillers and rework his heart-warming romance to include the surprise appearance of a serial killer. The result was *Death by Chocolate*, but it fared no better among what he regarded, bitterly, as the closed shop of publishers and literary agents.

The era of alternative comedy arrived. While many of his contemporaries were enraged at being sidelined from mainstream television, Johnny saw an opportunity. He enrolled at an elite university summer school and insisted his part-time, mature student status entitled him to an audition for their annual revue. Fearing accusations of age or class discrimination, the committee gave him his moment on the stage and were favourably impressed. The students praised Johnny for his 'ironic satire' on the traditional mother-in-law joke. An absence of punchlines combined with a backstory of misery was exactly right for the times, and soon he was headlining sell-out shows at the Edinburgh Fringe with his own 'Twilight Revue'. He won critical acclaim and there was talk of arena events at the Hydro in Glasgow and the O2 in London. A Netflix special was mentioned and then came lucrative sponsorship deals. Among them was a five-figure contract with a Scottish bakery that had developed a new kind of biscuit marketed at denture wearers. A secret ingredient prevented the biscuit turning to mush in the mouth, and the advertising slogan 'That's wan thing you won't have on your plate' became Johnny's new catchphrase.

Then, just as it seemed Johnny Sellotape's time had come, it was all over. The Brittle Biscuit company continues to deny responsibility, but questions remain about the indigestibility of their product. While these matters remain under investigation the conspiracy theories abound. The comedy world is rife with jealousy and bitterness, and some have pointed the finger at fellow comedians. Others say the newspaper articles exposed Johnny's original family name and that Herring War vendettas can carry on down through the generations. These outlandish notions deny the obvious, that Johnny Sellotape died in a manner familiar to many who dare step into the spotlight to seek the attention of the crowd and garner the approbation of the masses.

Put simply, he choked.

Johnny Sellotape, comedian (1941–2020)

THE BACK ROOM

Can I tell you about these dreams I've been having? No, stop glancing at your watch – I know it's late and you have to be going soon, but just hang on, have another glass of wine, because, I get it, I *know* that other people's dreams are the dullest things to hear about. Even if I said that you, yes *you*, were in this particular dream, you'd only be a tad more interested. But hear me out because I do know a thing or two about dreams. I studied psychology for four years, remember – got my degree and everything – and the whole subject fascinates me. Always has. I mean, have you ever wondered why you dream? Why any of us dream? If you believe in Darwin, believe in evolution, then there has to be some reason for it. We know why we have arms and legs and fingers and thumbs, but what's the point of dreaming? We go to sleep to rest and recharge ourselves for the day ahead, but then these stupid little stories pop into our minds. Stories about falling off buildings or walking about the street in your pyjamas or about having all your teeth fall out. Oh, you've had that one? Yes, lots of people have. So many daft dreams, surreal. But not like the ones I'm going to tell you about. These dreams, well, they turned me upside down and inside out. Honestly. Look, there's the waiter. Another Malbec? Argentinian? Large one? Great.

So it was just over a year ago. Last July. I wasn't in a good place. Very unhappy. Miserable, to tell you the truth. Working in life insurance was not how I'd imagined my career after university. Absolutely hated my job and hated my boss even more, and I was having the same dream over and over again. Every night. I was in the office and it was the worst dream possible because all that was happening was the same thing that would be happening in the real world. You're laughing, I know, it's crazy. I was getting on with my work. I was sending emails, replying to emails, booking rooms for meetings, going to those meetings and talking about those emails at the meetings. In the dream I decided I was going to quit. I was going to march into Hargreaves's office and tell him exactly what he could do with his never-ending requests for reports and presentations. His unachievable deadlines. I was going to tell him to stuff it. I was going to quit, walk out of that depressing office building forever. But here's the thing, *that* never happened, because the dream always stopped just before I got to his corner office. I'd wake up and, well, it was exhausting because I'd wake up every morning feeling like I'd done a full day at the office and then I'd actually have to get up, get dressed and go to the office. It's like I was doing an extra shift every day but for no extra pay.

I tell you, this had been going on for weeks, months even, and then one day it all stopped. I mean the dream just stopped half-way through. It stopped, but I didn't wake up. It was like going to see a movie in the days before digital and the film snapped. So one minute I'm walking across the office, heading for the photocopier and all around me are the desks and computers and phones buzzing and reports being printed out of the big laser printer, and then suddenly, nothing. Like I say, as if the film snapped, but instead of an empty white screen, it's all dark and there's no sound at all. Yet I knew I was still asleep.

Sort of. So I reach out my arms, trying to feel my way forward, and my hands touch this thick material. It was like a black curtain or something. Rough like an old coal sack, not velvety, not silky. Scratchy. I start feeling my way along this curtain, trying to find some kind of a gap, and as I'm moving along, I can hear voices. Quiet at first, but then louder. Then I find the edge of the curtain and I pull it to one side and step through.

I was expecting to be back in the office, but instead I'm in a long grey corridor. It was like that weird hotel in Edinburgh we stayed in once. That night we went to Lisa's party. Do you know the one I mean? All curves and no edges. Anyway, it was a bit like that but not so clean and modern. The walls are grey with patches of dampness and flickering fluorescent lighting. Pretty grim. So I keep walking and I come to a fork where the corridor branches left and right. And there's a signpost. No, it's almost like a big totem pole with carvings all the way up. But it also has these wooden pointers like you get at the seaside. You know, the ones that tell you how far you are from Land's End or John O'Groats or Moscow? Only there are no names on those pointers, just more carvings. Images of, oh, I dunno, frogs and kites and trees.

On the right side of the pole there's a pointer with images of trumpets and love hearts. Don't ask me why, but I decide to go that way. That takes me to a wooden door. It has frosted glass panels and behind the glass I can make out shapes, people, people's heads, and the voices are louder here. I can hear snatches of actual conversation. Some of the voices sound familiar, but I can't quite place them, and that makes me curious, so I open the door and ... No, look, I'm getting to the point, I promise. I open the door and there's this old-fashioned café. Wooden floors and tables with red gingham tablecloths. Bit like the old theatre café bar we used to go to in our student days. Remember

232

it? Except it was also like one of those nostalgia bars you get everywhere now, with all the old posters on the wall, adverts for chocolate you can't buy any more or seaside holiday destinations in Scotland. Foreign posters too. Prague, Vienna, Warsaw. There are objects mounted on the walls too; an old brass euphonium, pretty bashed up, and a manual typewriter. And there are these people sitting at the tables, some in pairs, some alone, and when I walk in, they all look up at me and their conversations stop. And I'm looking at these people, men, women, children and, like the voices, the faces are all vaguely familiar too. I don't recognise anyone outright, but they all resemble people I know or might have known. As I'm looking around, I see this one couple, a man and a woman, both elderly. The woman has a kindly face, but the man is very stern. The woman waves to me and invites me to sit with them. At first it doesn't look like there's a spare chair, but one appears as I draw closer. That's the kind of nonsense that happens in dreams. I sit down.

'Where am I?' I ask them.

The woman opens her mouth to answer, but the man speaks first. 'You shouldn't be here,' he says. 'This is all quite wrong.'

'Shush,' says the woman. 'He probably has more right to be here than anyone. Besides, it's about time we met face to face, don't you think? Now we can ask him some questions.'

'Don't ask him anything,' says the man. 'We're on strike, remember. We're not speaking to management and we're not talking to him.'

Well, I had no idea what these two were talking about, but the woman seemed, you know, *chastised*, and she said nothing else. I kept looking at their faces, from one to the other. Then there were the clothes they were wearing. An odd mixture of styles and fashions. It was like they'd all gone to a jumble sale and picked out different coats and skirts and cardigans. One man was even wearing flares, flared trousers. And there was a girl in hot pants. I mean, when did you last see anyone wearing hot pants?

No, look, I know that doesn't matter and I am getting to the interesting part. Please, just stay a while longer. It's been so long since we last had a catch-up. What's it been – five years? Six? Too long. But I need to tell you about the rest of the dream. You see, no one in the café was talking to me, so I was looking around at the stuff on the walls when I heard a noise behind me, a creaking noise, a door opening. I turned to see a man standing in the doorway of a back office. He was bald, with glasses, a tie loose around his neck, shirt sleeves rolled up.

'Oh,' he says, 'it's you. I was wondering if you would show up.'

'Who are you?' I ask.

'I'm Max. I'm one of the directors,' says the man. 'There used to be more of us, but the rest of them quit. So it's just me.'

Well, this sort of made sense to me in the dream, because, as I said, I was reminded of the theatre bar. So I point to the people sitting at the tables.

'Who are they?' I ask Max. 'They look familiar somehow.'

'They should be,' says Max. 'They're your actors. Or at least, they used to be. They're on strike.'

'I don't understand.'

'It's simple, really,' he says. 'You fall asleep at night, yes? And there are these little plays that go on in your head, yes? So, I direct them and the company out there perform the various parts. They're a very versatile bunch. You see that couple near the door of the café? The two you were talking to? They play your parents a lot of the time, but they can also do your work colleagues, old schoolteachers, next-door neighbours. Their faces are quite malleable. Of course, some in our wee company are more gifted than others. You see that tall chap standing by the fire exit? He only ever plays the manager of Woolworths who caught you shoplifting when you were fourteen. Books, wasn't it? But you haven't dreamt about that for a long while, so he's pretty fed up.'

That's when I realised. It was why I thought I had recognised all these people. I *had* seen them before, but only in dreams. Not recent dreams, but the ones I used to have before I started dreaming about work night after night. Why had things changed?

'Now my dreams are so dull. Always about work, always about being in the office. Do I blame you for that?'

'Nope. That's your fault. You see, we can only work with the material you give us. Frankly, we've exhausted all those memories about your childhood, trips to the seaside and your time in the school orchestra. We've worn out a lot of the props, as you can see. The fact of the matter is, your dreams are reflections of your everyday life, and at the moment your everyday life is just boring and repetitive. That's why the actors are refusing to perform. They took a vote. There's just no job satisfaction in it. You don't go anywhere; you don't have adventures. You don't like to think about your past and you certainly don't think about your future. You're just stuck. There's not even a love interest any more.'

It was the 'any more' that intrigued me, so Max points to a woman sitting by the window.

'Well, she has played your girlfriends over the years. Both of them. Though playing Paula was a bit of a challenge, because she was really a pen-pal more than anything, wasn't she?'

He was right about Paula. All those letters. I stopped writing to her when she got engaged. I can take a hint. But I didn't want to talk about that. I wanted to know how I could stop having those dull dreams about the office.

Max was pretty blunt. 'You need to get off your backside and do something with your life. You keep talking about quitting your job, so do it.'

'And then what?'

'Then use your freedom, do some travelling, meet new people, take risks, fall in love. Give us something to work with, *please.*'

It was really hard to say no to that, because when I turn back to the people in the café, the actors, they all have that expectant look on their faces. The children are the worst. Big sorrowful eyes.

'Okay,' I tell him, 'I'll start first thing tomorrow. Now, is this where I wake up?'

'What's your hurry?' says Max. 'Stick around for a bit. Meet some of your actors. Tell them a bit about yourself. It will help them nail your characters.'

And that's what I do. A bit of mingling, a bit of glad-handing. I spend a lot of time talking to the couple who played Mum and Dad. I tell the woman she's got Mum pretty much down to a tee, but the man's version of Dad was coming off a little bit too grumpy and aggressive. I also have a good chat with the woman at the window. I give her some advice about accents and how people's voices change when they move to different places. I talk about my tragic love life and that makes her laugh. By the time I leave the bar, these people are slapping me on the back and wishing me all the best for the next day.

Anyway, I make it back down the corridor, past the signpost, back to the curtain and then I'm awake in my bed wondering what the heck has just happened. Of course, I knew it was a dream, but I also knew what I had to do next.

I went to work, asked Hargreaves's secretary if I could have five minutes and then I told him I was leaving. I was pretty polite about it, to be honest, no point burning all my bridges, but that was that. I quit that day, went to the bank, changed a pile of cash into Euros and spent the next three months travelling across Europe. I went to all the places that you and I used to talk about when we were students. Paris, Rome, Athens. Prague was my favourite, I think. It's got that whole Franz Kafka thing going on plus the Cold War vibe, and that made for some amazing dreams. It was like I was in a crazy spy adventure. I was being chased by villains, dodging assassins on the Charles Bridge and having romantic encounters with a mysterious femme fatale. We'd go to the Smetana Hall and drink in the American Bar in the basement. What an atmosphere!

Yes, there was always that same woman in the story. Sure, she changed her clothes and her voice, but I knew who she was. In fact, once or twice I went backstage to speak to the actors afterwards. You know, I found the curtain, took the right corridor at the signpost and went into the café bar. The mood there had become totally different. Everyone was so excited, competitive even, vying with each other for the best roles. Even the tall man who only ever played the Woolworths manager had upped his game. He was getting bit parts as a bodyguard or chauffeur in some of my racier dreams. Max was happy too. He told me he was now the envy of other directors and was loving being in charge of these big-budget productions.

But then he told me a few home truths. 'These romances you dream about,' he said, 'they're no substitute for the real thing. And our colleague at the window, your femme fatale, you know who that really is, don't you?'

Of course I knew. I had always known.

'Then make it real,' said Max. 'Go and make it real.'

I told him that wasn't possible. I told him I'd blown my chance years ago. That the woman I loved had walked out of my life because, frankly, I wasn't having a life. I was stuck, paralysed, afraid to take chances.

'But that's not who you are now,' Max said. 'You're unstuck. Go and find her.'

'I'm afraid to,' I said. 'If she rejects me again, I'll be back where I was. I might as well go crawling back to Hargreaves and beg for my job back.'

Max thought about this and then he tapped a finger on the side of his nose and told me what I should do.

'Tomorrow night we'll take a rest. No big dramas, no big car chases, nothing like that. But tomorrow, when you dream, come through the curtain again and when you get to the signpost, follow the pointer to the left. Walk that way for a change.'

'What will I find?' I asked, but he was keeping schtum.

'You'll see,' he said, smiling.

So, the next night, bed early for me, off to sleep immediately and there I am at the signpost. I follow the pointer on the left and come to a gold-framed door with smoked glass. I push it open and suddenly I'm in one of those yuppie wine bars we used to joke about back in the day. Everyone wearing jackets with the sleeves rolled up. You remember *Miami Vice*? Yes, that's it.

'Max told me you might pop in,' says a bartender. Naturally, he's mixing cocktails and looking like a body double for Tom Cruise.

'What is this place?' I ask. The bartender points to a green neon sign that's glowing above a gantry of similar green bottles. One word is illuminated: 'Dreams'.

'Different kind of dreams,' says the bartender. 'Not the kind of dreams you have at the end of the day. These are the dreams you have about the next day and the day after that. Dreams about your future.'

'You mean fantasies?' I ask.

'And possibilities,' he says. 'But we're all just jobbing actors in here too, waiting for our next big gig. So why don't you have a chat with that young woman on the high stool. You tell her your dreams and she'll tell you if they can come true.'

'I don't get it,' I said.

'Think of Darwin,' says the bartender. 'Why have we evolved the ability to dream? It's because we're social creatures. Dreams allow us to imagine things that might happen to us, to try them out without risk. In a dream, it doesn't matter if you fall flat on your face. Rejections don't count here. But it's all good practice before you have to test yourself in the real world. Now, go and speak to that woman, tell her you're sorry about what happened in the past. See what happens.'

And so, to cut to the chase, that's why I'm here, Pennie. It's why I've come all the way to New York. It's why I called you up and asked you to join me for a drink. You see, in the dream, it didn't work. Dream Pennie rejected me. She told me there had been too much water under the bridge. She actually said that. Awful dialogue. But you know what? It *was* worth the risk. And I think it's worth the risk in reality. So look, here's the waiter again. Another Malbec? Just a small one? Great. So, that's enough about me. How about you? Had any good dreams lately? You have? Well, tell me about them. I'm all ears.

EPILOGUE

My leg was getting worse by the day, but I was loath to make an appointment at the medical centre because the lockdown had begun. I imagined local doctors were being deluged with calls about the coronavirus. I didn't want to waste anyone's time, but after three days in pain I could barely walk, so I made the call and described my symptoms.

'What kind of car do you have?'

It wasn't the question I was expecting a doctor to ask me, but I told him about our Renault Clio and wondered if he was about to reveal that certain French cars were notorious for driver leg injuries. That wasn't it at all. He was adhering to the new social distancing rules and limiting the number of patients coming through the reception area.

'Drive round to the surgery in half an hour,' said the doc. 'I'll come out to the car park and let you in the back door.'

It all felt very cloak and dagger, but it was just as well I had gone to see him. The cause of my sore leg turned out to be a blood clot – a deep vein thrombosis. It was a lagging consequence of my cancer surgery and I was put on blood thinners for three months. The pain eased within two weeks and I was soon back on my new e-bike and taking full advantage of the Government-permitted hour of personal exercise.

The lockdown also meant there was no longer an excuse to put off those tasks I'd promised to tackle whenever time allowed, and now there was plenty of that. So, into the attic I went to retrieve the old black bag that I'd taken from my parents' house in Craigend just before the clearance crew arrived to gut the place. It was a large vinyl handbag and it contained a jumble of old black and white family photographs dating back to the 1930s. There were photographs of Mum taken before she was married, and one particularly striking picture showed her posing among a group of office workers, with senior managers in the forefront wearing stiff double-breasted suits. When was this taken? Who were these other people? The staff at the film repair depot? Of course, it was too late to ask.

I began sorting the pictures into different categories and realised that almost a hundred of the photographs in the black bag were taken during Dad's war years in the Polish Navy and on board his destroyer, the *Piorun*. There were posed pictures of the ship's crew on parade and of the officers on the bridge, but the best were those many candid shots of Dad himself, a young man in his early twenties, standing smoking a pipe or enjoying some rye bread and vodka. I spent a week or so scanning them into my computer and retouching them to eliminate the obvious tears and scratches. It was odd looking at the images in such magnified detail that I spotted a missing button on Dad's jacket or fancy watch on his wrist. It made me feel very close to him again. As with Mum, I wished I had sat with him during his lifetime and asked him to tell me more about each photograph. I also wanted to tell him about how proud I was of the part he had played in the war and, though it had taken me too long to reach this point, the pride I now felt in my Polish heritage.

I was sorry the planned trip to Krakow had been cancelled, but I also had the odd feeling that another kind of trip had been postponed too. Thinking back, I realised I had done a good job tying up loose ends before I'd gone into hospital. I sorted things out, legally and financially. I suppose, somewhere in my mind, I had faced up to the possibility that something might go wrong during my surgery. It was as if I'd been preparing for a one-way journey, but somehow there had been a glitch and I'd come back after all. That, plus the so-called 'new normal' of the Covid world, gave me the eerie feeling that I didn't really belong here. I guess lots of people were feeling the same way for different reasons.

As the lockdown continued we all got used to rare and disinfected shopping trips, multiple parcel deliveries and frequent video calls with family and friends. One such was instigated by an old school pal from Easterhouse. Paul Curran, now an internationally acclaimed opera director based in San Francisco, invited me to a Zoom video conversation with former pupils from St Leonard's. I decided to take part, but not without a little hesitation. Speaking was still difficult for me, and a conscious effort to enunciate words left my tongue feeling ragged and nipping like someone had sprinkled my mouth with pepper. Nevertheless, I thought it best not to avoid these kinds of small challenges; I'd already gone ahead with an hour-long question and answer session at the Portsoy Book Festival and had belted out a few bars of a Sinatra classic to demonstrate how I was using singing as part of my speech therapy. I'd taken part in a BBC Radio Scotland interview about my diagnosis and treatment, shocking the audience by revealing that I'd lost my taste for chocolate. Sure, my new stitched-together tongue was a nuisance at times, but Mr Shekar had promised some remedial reduction surgery which would, hopefully, improve my diction and pronunciation. In the meantime I spoke like I had two toffees in my mouth and half a bag of wine gums.

Those old schoolmates were scattered far and wide across and beyond Scotland, and it turned out I was one of the few who had been back to our old neighbourhood in the recent past. After leaving the BBC, I'd joined the board of the Platform arts organisation and would attend meetings in Easterhouse every three months. On the Zoom call I broke the news that all our old Catholic schools had been demolished and a bright new Lochend Community School now catered for kids of all denominations. 'They wear smart black uniforms with ties and blazers,' I said. 'A far cry from when we turned up wearing nylon anoraks, woolly jumpers and denim jeans.' I described how the old three-storey council flats had been redeveloped into modern two-storey blocks with security entry. I told them about the new retail park, the college and the multiplex cinema, and how the original population of fifty thousand was now half that number. Many of the old streets had been bulldozed completely, while others had been reborn as rows of semi-detached private houses with, as Mum used to say, 'their own back and front doors'.

As the call ended I had flashes of my old life like snapshots in that old black bag: Mum standing in that tiny kitchenette night after night, cooking meals for a brood of eight; Dad marking their wedding anniversary with a piece of jewellery, a brooch hidden in the second layer of a box of Black Magic chocolates; my brothers playing Beatles records in their smoke-filled bedrooms, the walls decorated with pictures of Elvis; a trip to Glasgow Zoo – not a patch on its rival in Edinburgh, with caged animals that seemed to know it; Danny's little sister, who mistook the manufacturer's logo for the name of her plastic doll and called it Palitoy; my brother Brian letting me sit on his knee and steer his milk float all the way up to my school, and another brother, Michael, taking me to school on the back of his Vespa scooter – in both cases, provoking the envy and admiration of classmates.

And then me and my sister Rose in those old bunk beds and Mum coming in to tuck us in for the night and tell us to get to sleep and have good dreams. That wonderful feeling of being warm, safe, secure and loved.

The best of memories and the happiest of thoughts.

JEFF'S TWILIGHT GUIDE TO SCOTLAND

Both the 'memory' and 'make-believe' stories in this book feature actual places across Scotland. The following alphabetical list gives me the chance to tell you a little bit more about each one and why I'd suggest you visit them. Of course, it's not the definitive guide to my favourite places in Scotland, because my self-imposed rule is that I could only list places that I've mentioned in the book or have some tangential connection with the writing of it. Okay, I've cheated once or twice, but it's my book so I'm allowed. I was going to make it a simple list of pubs, but that seemed a tad irresponsible, and, as I head toward those twilight years, I suppose I had better start thinking about growing up. To that end, I've mentioned a few tearooms too.

ABERFELDY

In 'You're in the Book, Mum' I talk about my love of public libraries and how many of the new ones are contained within a modern community hub or campus. The one I had in mind was in Aberfeldy, where book-lovers can also enjoy a dip in the swimming pool after reading a steamy novel. A shout-out to the librarians there, including the ever enthusiastic Karen, who invited me to give a talk and didn't bargain on me donning a straw hat and striped jacket to perform in the guise of Johnny Sellotape. Karen even laughed at my terrible jokes. Aberfeldy is worth visiting for so many reasons, not least the proximity of the Highland Chocolatier and the restored cinema.

ALLOA

One of my childhood haunts, as it were, when visiting my slightly spooky Auntie Jean and Uncle Jimmy. This is where Jimmy visited a spiritual healer so that the demons giving him a bad back could be removed by the careful placement of invisible eggs. More fondly, I think of Alloa as the place where we bought our first puppy, Rascal. He was a fluffy Lhasa apso remembered for his complete ambivalence when it came to chasing balls. Alloa, Sauchie and the whole of Clackmannanshire are must-go destinations for Scottish history buffs.

ARBROATH

As I said in 'The Summer Hut', Arbroath was a late discovery for me. As children we only ever went there when it was raining, and we sat in the car while Dad went in search of a place to buy smoked haddock. As a grown-up I discovered the Riverside Park and the amazing cliff-side walk to a tiny, secluded beach. On one occasion, having made the seven-mile return trek to that beach, I discovered my car keys were no longer in my pocket. I walked back again to look for them, but to no avail. Later, having half hobbled and half limped back into town, I discovered I had dropped them when leaving the car and some kind person had handed them into the police station. A great place for walking, but you can have too much of a good thing. Tasty fish and chips from any of the harbour cafés.

AUCHTERARDER

Between Auchterarder and Perth lies the road where, over the years, Dad cajoled various cars and vans up what we called 'the big hill'. It's still big, that hill, but they cut through it to make the new dual carriageway so it's not as steep as it used to be, and a breeze for modern cars. From Auchterarder it's a hop, skip and a jump to the famous Gleneagles Hotel. They do a nice lunch there and don't seem to care if you don't look posh. Of course, I wouldn't go there dressed in a manky boiler suit or anything, but you know what I mean.

AYR

The destination for numerous school trips, like the one I describe in 'Where Seagulls Dare'. I was in Ayr as recently as August 2020 and the place was teeming with families, and the sight of busy beaches and queues at ice cream shops brought me right back to my childhood. Ayr is also the place where, in an amusement arcade, I played my first and last game of bingo. I was ten years old, sitting alongside a half-dozen local women perched on plastic stools. As the numbers were called, we closed the tiny plastic covers on our fixed consoles. Within minutes I had a winning line but was too shy to shout 'House!' The woman beside me called for me and I went home with a charming purple table lamp and a vivid memory of the seething resentment of the other players. A wee shout-out to the lovely folk at Ayr Writers' Club who have invited me to blether about radio once or twice.

BAILLIESTON

At ten years old, walking to Baillieston from Easterhouse felt like a journey to another world. It was a world of well-established shops and terraced houses with vast gardens and sheds that no one seemed to worry about being broken in to. It was also where Mum's other sister, Georgina, lived. Auntie Gina would visit us from time to time and would always bring us a bag of Rainbow Drops – those multicoloured puffs of sugared rice. Mum always got anxious when Gina visited, and there would be hushed conversations in the kitchenette that ended with Mum fetching her purse and giving Gina whatever cash she could spare. Baillieston was also the place where our music teacher, Mrs Kerr, would take a few select members of the school orchestra and treat us to a plate of pancakes. It's now more famous for the monstrous motorway interchange – Scotland's own spaghetti junction.

BROUGHTY FERRY

Mentioned in 'The Summer Hut' as the place we bought our holiday rock before returning home to Glasgow. The seafront Broughty Castle now houses a museum and tells the history of the town in the centuries before it was incorporated into the city of Dundee. There are cafés and coffee shops aplenty. One of the best features of the town is the long promenade which stretches along the coast almost to the outskirts of Barnhill and Monifieth.

CAMBUSLANG

In 'When I Grow Up' I describe going to Cambuslang when Dad took me on a tour of the Clydebridge steelworks. It's also right in the transmission area for a great wee radio station called Camglen, which also serves Rutherglen. If you take a cycle trip from Glasgow city centre and follow the route alongside the Clyde, you pass through Glasgow Green, past the Athletes' Village built for the 2014 Commonwealth Games and under the big motorway bridge, and you arrive in Cambuslang with a sense of achievement. On the way back, take a detour over the new footbridge at Dalmarnock, hang a left and find the Cuningar Loop forest park. It's amazing that such a place exists in the middle of the city.

CARNOUSTIE

I can't look back on my idyllic childhood summers without thinking of the many times we visited Carnoustie. It's changed a lot over the years – so many more houses, for one thing – and the new beach promenade offers a wonderful seafront walk in any weather. You might associate Carnoustie with golf tournaments, but I always remember the Gala Weeks and the talent shows in the Beach Hall. That hall is now a modern leisure centre with an open-air café to boot.

CLYDEBANK

Across from the old town hall – now a museum – there's a memorial to the crew of the *Piorun*, which was stationed there during the Blitz. The *Piorun* was a destroyer in the Polish Navy and Dad served on it after he was released from a Siberian labour camp. It had docked at Clydebank for repairs and used its guns to blast the Luftwaffe bombers overhead. Clydebank is also home to my former employer Radio Clyde and their big studio complex, complete with indoor swimming pool. We were banned from using the pool during our night-shift tea breaks because there was no one else in the building who could save us if we got into trouble. I can now reveal we all ignored that rule.

CRAIGEND

We moved to Craigend in the cold winter of 1973 and thought nothing of living under the gigantic concrete water towers that dominated the skyline. Many years later, the city council decided to paint them white and light them up at night. You can see them from miles away. I'm not saying they rival the Eiffel Tower or anything, but they are worth a look close up. And I once told my son that Buzz Lightyear used them as his HQ when he was in Scotland. Being so high above sea level, Craigend also has its own microclimate. When winter snowfalls begin to thaw and drain across the rest of Glasgow, you can be sure the pavements in Craigend will still be caked with ice until about July.

DENNISTOUN

In 'Room for One More on Top', our tax-avoiding hero lives in Aberfoyle Street. It's where my sister lived when she got married and moved out of our family home in Craigend. I associate the area with pints of Fürstenberg in the Lea Rig pub and tasty Indian takeaways from the long-demolished Jasmine. I still think Alexandra Parade wins the award for best street name in Scotland – and Alexandra Park is a gorgeous place to walk a dog or push a pram. But I miss the old Parade cinema. Celino's pizzeria is the place to go for some good nosh.

DORES

My editor is wary of locating fictional stories in real places, so in 'The Tartan Traveller' I describe an unnamed village pub on the south side of Loch Ness. So, I'm not saying I was thinking of the Dores Inn, but if you are looking for a place to spot Nessie, then the beach at Dores is for you. It may not have the classy visitor centre you'll find at Urquhart Castle on the north side of the loch, but just behind the beach at Dores you can follow the path through the forest until you come to the Aldourie Estate and Aldourie Castle. It's like something from a Disney movie. The road to Inverness to Dores can get a bit fast and busy, but there's a new cycle route that takes you safely across acres of rolling farmland.

DUNDEE

I've never understood why people in Glasgow and Edinburgh subject Dundee to such mockery. I always felt like it was the wee brother being bullied by the big boys and maybe that's why I, as the youngest sibling of eight, have always been keen to defend it. The redevelopment of the city's waterfront has been nothing short of spectacular and has, just about, reconnected it with the city centre after so many decades of architectural blunders and monstrosities. Everyone's been raving about the new V&A museum, but I'd point you to Discovery Point or even suggest you take a walk across to Fife on the Tay Road Bridge.

EAST HAVEN

A wee hidden gem on the Angus coastline. In 'The Summer Hut' I mention Monifieth and Carnoustie, but go a little further north and you reach East Haven. You snake your way through a few streets, cross over the railway bridge and there is this little beach that not everyone knows about. Plus … free public toilets!

EASTERHOUSE

The early chapters of this book are mostly set in Easterhouse, and while I've described its slow decline during the 1970s, I also talk about its resurgence in recent years. Indicative of that is The Bridge complex, which houses the Platform Arts Centre and a swimming pool. I think Platform is one of the underplayed success stories of Glasgow's cultural life. It has a truly international outlook when inviting visiting performers, which it combines with supporting scores of local community artists and initiatives.

EDINBURGH

We Glaswegians are brainwashed at an early age and taught to dislike Edinburgh because, well, 'they think they're better than us'. So, don't tell anyone, but I love Edinburgh. In fact, I love any big city that feels small enough to walk around. I feel the same way about Prague, Boston and Seattle. Edinburgh is home to the Storytelling Centre, where the tale of Dad's welding examination ('The Day I Didn't Die') got its first outing, and also comedy clubs like The Stand, where my alias, Johnny Sellotape, is yet to be invited.

FIFE

I have a confession to make. My sense of geography didn't kick in until halfway through my teenage years, so before that, when I looked across the Tay from Barry beach, I thought I was looking north towards Aberdeen. Worse still, I thought the glow of lights from St Andrews was actually 'the northern lights of old Aberdeen', as in the song. Then one summer Dad took us across the Tay Road Bridge to Fife and the world started to make sense. So, yes, go to St Andrews, a beautiful university town, but also seek out what else Fife has to offer, especially the towns in the East Neuk. My own favourite is Kingsbarns and the amazing beach there.

GLASGOW

In 'Boy about Town' I describe my off-the-rails period as a school truant and how I got to know the city just by walking around it day after day. Favourite places in the city would include the People's Palace Museum and its winter gardens on Glasgow Green. It's dedicated to the social history of the city and I'm fascinated by the minutiae of people's lives, such as the brand of soap flakes they used or the gadgets used to pull teeth. It's the kind of place where you find yourself exclaiming, 'Oh, my grandparents used to have one of those!' I'd also recommend the vast Mitchell Library, perched just above the chasm that was cut through the city to accommodate the M8 motorway. Glasgow planners probably spent far too many years knocking down buildings to make way for road traffic, so it's good to see the investment that's now going into creating special cycle lanes in the middle of town, and there's an abundance of bike-hire stations dotted the length and breadth of the city.

HAMILTON

Hamilton gets a mention in 'The Shock of the Bunny' as one of the tour-date venues when I accompanied my sister to Neil Reid concerts. In my memory, it took ages to get there and back by bus, but I recently went to Hamilton on the train from Glasgow city centre and it took no time at all. Strathclyde Country Park is nearby, but so too is the beautiful Chatelherault Park. I prefer the latter, but for a daft reason. Once, when larking about with friends in Strathclyde Park, our school priest emerged, mysteriously, from some bushes and we all had to engage in some polite small-talk. Ever since then, I've associated Strathclyde Park with that strange moment.

INVERNESS

I've now lived in Inverness – albeit not continuously – for more than half of my life and I'm still in love with it. It was a great place to bring up a family, and now that Anne and I are heading into the twilight years, I don't think we'll ever leave. If you're just visiting, let me recommend a walk alongside the Ness, past the Cathedral and down towards the Ness Islands. It's lovely in summer, but magical in winter when the snow falls and the iron footbridges and Victorian lampposts make it look like a scene from Narnia. In the past thirty years I've watched Inverness grow from a big town to a small city (if that makes sense), but I don't think it's lost any of its charm or beauty. At Eden Court you'll find one of the best theatres in Scotland, and a drive or (bracing) bike ride across the Kessock Bridge will take you to North Kessock. Enjoy breakfast or lunch at the White Cottage tearoom and then you have all the delights of the Black Isle ahead of you. The beach at Rosemarkie has a community-run tearoom with a good stock of second-hand books for sale. That's my idea of a wild day out. Back in Inverness in the evening? No better place for a pint and good food than the multi-award-winning MacGregor's Bar on Academy Street, owned and run by my friends Jo and Bruce. They deserve a mention because they were the first to visit me when I got out of hospital and presented me with a fine bottle of Malbec. See, if you buy me booze you might get a mention in my next book.

LINLITHGOW

Another gem of a town, rich with history, and benefiting from the existence of the Far from the Madding Crowd bookshop, which hosts literary lunches and evening events. It was at one such event that I read aloud an early version of 'Take Me to the Orphanage'. It was the night before Halloween, so I regaled the audience with the story of the knife coming though the bedroom door while my sister and I cowered in our bunk beds. It went down well enough and convinced me (and my lovely publishers Lyn and Laura) that there might be a book in such tales and memories.

LOCHWINNOCH

I'm coming around to the belief that Lochwinnoch is the cultural centre of Scotland. So many writers, artists and performers seem to have moved there. In safer, happier times, it is home to an annual arts festival and attracts an exciting array of talent. It's also home to Lunicorn Press whose directors have regular meetings in the dog-friendly Brown Bull pub. Just outside the town is the Loch House restaurant, with a terrace to the rear offering panoramic views across either Renfrewshire or Ayrshire, depending which way you point your head.

MONIFIETH

A few weeks before my son left home for university, I took him on a boys-only road trip and we ended up on Monifieth beach trying to light a camp fire. I suppose I was trying to recreate the moment with my dad that I describe in the final pages of 'The Summer Hut'. Alas, I couldn't persuade our fire to light, and even spraying the sun-bleached driftwood with 3-In-One oil only gave us a few moments of warming flames amid the suffocating fumes. Defeated but not dispirited, we retired to the Vault pub for a few pints and then back to the Panmure Hotel where, I think, we were the only guests. That hotel has now been converted to luxury flats. On a more recent visit I noticed the dunes – once swept away by a fierce storm – had been restored to the beach and the place was heaving with holidaymakers and campers. I was also going to recommend the smart Bookhouse bookshop on the High Street, but as this book went to press it was on the move to Broughty Ferry. Worth a good walk for a good book.

MOTHERWELL

Home of the aforementioned Neil Reid from 'The Shock of the Bunny' and another of those Scottish towns that is unfairly maligned by people who have never visited the place. Mind you, the people who live there are often just as scathing about it, but that may be because they don't want other people visiting, discovering it's a great place to live and inflating the house prices.

PERTH

Back in the day, before they built the Friarton Bridge, a trip from Glasgow to Dundee meant you had no choice but to drive through Perth and usually get caught up in a traffic jam. As we headed to our summer hut, Perth became our stopping-off point where we'd get the chance to stretch our legs and Mum would head for the local Coopers Fine Fare store to get bread and milk. I didn't really get to know Perth until my career led to regular weekly commutes from Inverness to Glasgow. Sometimes I'd miss the train connection at Perth and use the time to explore the surrounding streets and the odd pub. Once or twice, bad weather forced an overnight stay in the Station Hotel. Not unpleasant, but its long corridors did always remind me of the Overlook Hotel that featured in the movie version of *The Shining*.

PORTSOY

Any journey along the Moray coast is worthwhile, but only if you come off the main Aberdeen road and actually visit those coastal towns. I love the cosy wee inn at Garmouth and I've taken pictures of palm trees at Hopeman that have convinced people I'm in the Caribbean. I have a real soft spot for Portsoy, though, because, just a few weeks after leaving hospital, I was due to speak at the Portsoy Book Festival. Well, my mouth wasn't really up to reading extracts from my book, so I asked some radio chums to record a few pieces and I played these on the day. The event went well and the festival organisers were so encouraging that it gave me a much-needed confidence boost. I don't know if and when book festivals will get back up and running, but here's hoping the Portsoy festival has continued success.

PRESTWICK

Its airport is famous as the only place in Britain visited by Elvis Presley, but Prestwick is a genteel little town – more tea and scones than rock and roll – and was home to a pen pal of mine called Alison. We exchanged about three letters a week at one point and, if nothing else, it taught me how easy it is to write thousands of words in one sitting when properly motivated. Once, for a laugh, I decided to pay my pal a surprise visit and cycled the forty miles from Glasgow on my sister's three-speed Raleigh. When I arrived Alison wasn't even at home and by the time I biked it back to Glasgow, a rare Scottish heatwave had set in. I was in bed for a week afterwards with dehydration. All subsequent visits to Prestwick were by train.

RENFREW

While I'm in the gratitude groove, let me raise a glass to the unknown editor who decided to publish my first ever story in the *Renfrew Line* magazine – a tiny publication produced by Renfrew District Libraries back in the early 1980s. The thrill of seeing my story in print was just as exciting as the first time I saw one of my books in a bookshop window. Renfrew is also the birthplace of my wife, Anne, and the Piccolo Mondo restaurant was a favourite of her parents and the place we went to celebrate our engagement.

STIRLING

Again, back to my Auntie Jean and Uncle Jimmy and their *in situ* history lessons. Of course they couldn't resist throwing in ghost stories at every opportunity, so when we got to Stirling Castle, it wasn't good enough for us just to admire the splendid view across Stirlingshire and the Forth Valley. They had to tell us about the Green Lady who haunted the castle dungeons. Many years later, when working for Radio Clyde, I produced a short feature about that ghost, and the castle warden told me the appearance of the Green Lady was always accompanied by the smell of roast beef. That wee story won me an award at the New York Radio Festival. Thank you, Jean and Jimmy. And you too, Green Lady.

TULLIBODY

While doing some memory-jogging research for this book, I went back to Tullibody and the street where my auntie and uncle lived looked exactly as I remembered. There was that magnificent view beyond the primary school and out towards the Ochil Hills, and standing in the garden and looking left, there was the Wallace Monument. It takes about twenty minutes to climb all 246 steps to the top, but they used to give you a certificate of achievement if you managed it. One thing I didn't remember about Tullibody, though, was the ruined church at the top of the hill. I wandered around for half an hour and looked at names on the gravestones. I was struck by the many Polish names there. That's indicative of the changing nature of Scotland's population and the new generations of Poles who have come here in recent decades.

ALSO AVAILABLE BY JEFF ZYCINSKI

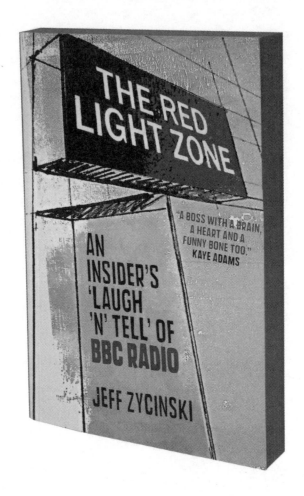

ISBN: 978-0-9929264-6-5